FAVORED OUTINGS

of the Huron Valley SIERRA

by members of the Huron Valley Group

Editorial Committee

Bob Cornish
Charlotte Lawrence
Vince Smith

SARAH JENNINGS PRESS
Ann Arbor, Michigan

Library of Congress Cataloging in Publication Data

Favored Outings of the Huron Valley Sierra.

Includes bibliographies
1. Outdoor recreation - Michigan - Ann Arbor region - Guide books.
2. Ann Arbor region (Michigan) - Description and travel - Guide books.

I. Cornish, Bob, date. II. Lawrence, Charlotte, date.
III. Smith, Vince, date. IV. Sierra Club, Huron Valley Group.

GV191.42.M5F38 1987 917.74'35 86-27256
ISBN 0-931781-03-5

Printed in the United States of America

Acknowledgements

Many individuals contributed to this book by relating their outings experiences. They are recognized, in random order, following.

Bob Cornish	Linda Wotring	Norm Roller
Pat Bauer	Vince Smith	Julie Griess
Charlotte Lawrence	Jim Ballard	Lisa Lava-Kellar
Ned Sharples	Ken Langton	Ralph Powell
Connie Hertz	Dave Diephuis	Janet Olszewksi

Jack Woodward acted as organizer and writing supervisor. All art work and maps, unless acknowledged otherwise on the spot, are by him. Cover design is by Mary Meade.

Disclaimer All contributors acted as individuals. Although their expertise is related to their membership in the Sierra Club, neither the Sierra Club nor its Huron Valley Group (Washtenaw, Lenawee, and Monroe Counties of Michigan) participated in the preparation of the book, nor are these organizations responsible for its contents.

Preface

This book is unlike any other outings guide. You'll see. And if you are one of the readers for whom the book is intended, you will appreciate its uniqueness.

The uniqueness comes, first of all, from the mixed coverage of several different kinds of outings - hiking, backpacking, skiing, canoeing, biking are all treated, and in a deliberately randomized order. A second element of uniqueness is the absence of concentration on a particular geographic region. To be sure, the densest coverage is of the environs of Ann Arbor, focus of the Sierra Club's Huron Valley Group, and the more distant realms of Michigan get only slightly less attention. But "distant outings" (in Ontario, for example) are also reported. A third element - perhaps the most important of all - is the personal reportage; all of the outings described here have been experienced by members of the Huron Valley Group, and the distilling of these experiences is the essence of every chapter. The coverage is therefore not extensive, for only the favored and reported outings of a small group of people are treated.

The title tells it: *Favored Outings*. These are outings enjoyed by members of the Sierra Club's Huron Valley Group, an eclectic group whose members typically savor outings of several kinds. One weekend's backpacker may be next weekend's canoeist, and on to skiing (most often crosscountry) in the winter. Those places and doings which they favor are well worth the knowing about, because these people are not only eclectic in their outdoor activies, but are experts as well.

The people who contributed to this book live in Ann Arbor, or in communities close by, and yes, the outings favored tend to be concentrated in that part of Michigan - within an hour's drive of Ann Arbor, say. Such, at least, is the rule used here for the meaning of "southeastern Michigan." But adventuresome people can move far in a day; the radius of a day's driving, taken to be 12 hours one way, is used as the geographical scope of this book. That barely includes the Porcupine Mountains within Michigan, but does include a sizeable chunk of the mountain pleasures of Appalachia, as well as a big segment of Ontario. "Distant Outings," though few in number, occur over an area of close to one million square miles.

We hope that many diverse readers will find this book useful. However, the principal target is the person who is greatly interested in outings of one or more kinds, but is unfamiliar with what southeastern Michigan and the wider territories just outlined may offer. Things favored by the Sierra Club people are almost certain to be things worth trying, so that reader finds here the experts' menu of outings to try until she/he also becomes an expert and (perhaps) may favor places and activities not listed. As aides to wider knowledge, we begin with chapters that broadly discuss the varied activities for which Michigan is a good place, with emphasis on more specialized sources of information and more specialized organizations. For example, a birdwatcher newly arrived in Michigan should immediately gain some for-starters insight from what is written in the appropriate chapter, but will also learn how to contact the local Audubon Society. And in appendices we give lists of information sources and organizations. For example, an appendix lists all of the Michigan canoe liveries that belong to the state-wide livery trade group.

Now about the maps we provide. Every outings description is illustrated by at least one map whose principal purpose is just that -- illustration. But our illustrator has attempted to make them field useful. That is, you can run one of our pages through a copying machine (it's okay, it's okay, we'll surely never catch you at it!) and put the copy in your pocket as an adequate sole map for your outing. This adequacy we do intend, but warn you that most of the maps do not include the detail found on a U S Geological Survey topographic map, or on a Michigan county map. Sources such as the latter two are listed in every case, and a careful outer will at least look at them before leaving for the outdoors.

The outdoors! Yes, the Great Outdoors. You should enjoy it.

For the Sarah Jennings Press
Jack Woodward

Contents

1

Outings as We See Them

Hiking

Start in Ann Arbor. Several of the city's parks offer hikes of the "nature trail" kind, i.e. well marked pathways, usually with signs and a wood-chip paving on which a stroller can spend a half-hour to an hour. Dolph Park (which has a chapter in this book) and Bird Hills Park on the west side of Ann Arbor, and Gallup Park on the southeast, offer this kind of hiking experience.

Longer urban hikes can be put together through several parks and attractive connecting links. For the most prominent example, one can follow the Huron River from the Dixboro Road crossing at the extreme eastern edge of Gallup Park to the North Main Street bridge at the upstream end of Argo Pond. The route follows pathways in Gallup Park and along the river edge of the Nichols Arboretum, past the University Hospital, then across the Maiden Lane bridge (a short interlude on city streets) to the Riverview Park riverside pathway that begins at the northern end of the bridge, then along the north bank of the river to and through Argo Park to the end. Distance, one way, is approximately five miles.

The Nichols Arboretum, abutting the western extremity of Gallup Park, offers alternatives to the route just outlined. One alternative is to turn up hill at a point where an Arboretum path is obviously intersecting the road along the river's edge, follow it up to Geddes Avenue, and from there return to Gallup Park by walking downhill along Geddes.

Footloose in Washtenaw (reference 3) supplies additional details, maps, and descriptions of other excursions in Ann Arbor.

Beyond the city limits, but no more than a half-hour's drive beyond, lie several protected areas that offer trails that can occupy a hiker from several hours to a whole day. Stinchfield Woods (a University preserve), Waterloo Recreational Area (state), and Pinckney Recreational Area (state) command chapters in this book. Maps and details are laid out for you. Also, *Footloose in Washtenaw* covers these areas and several others.

The longest loop trail in the Pinckney Recreational Area, known as the Potawatomi Trail, is 17 miles long. When carrying all the stuff of backpacking, many hikers regard 17 miles as far too many for a single day, so here is a place for backpacking and "camping out." On the other hand, many hikers, carrying only a bit of lunch and a water bottle, walk the trail in eight hours or less. The Potawatomi Trail also has a link to the trails of Waterloo, greatly expanding the length of hikes possible from a single parking spot.

And if you would venture into the greater expanses of Michigan? The Upper Peninsula and the northern half of the Lower Peninsula offer many possibilities. To learn of the greatest number in the shortest time you should consult *Michigan Hiking Opportunities* (reference 2), a book that describes and maps 63 trails. (Many are suitable for crosscountry skiing as well as hiking.) A sampling of these hikes is given in this book, and we'll present the big picture right here. Hiking opportunities indeed abound, though Michigan is not wild enough, nor rugged enough, to offer the long trips that demand the expedient of the back pack. In fact, there is no spot in Michigan (excluding islands) so far from a decent road that it cannot be visited via a day hike. If you do *want* to backpack for the pleasures of primitive camping, then there is certainly room enough to practice that art. The Lower Peninsula offers the High Country Pathway in the Pigeon River Country State Forest, the Jordan River Pathway, and the Shore-to Shore Hiking-Riding Trail across the northern tip of the peninsula. The North Country Trail, which will eventually traverse the lower peninsula from Ohio to the Straits of Mackinac, is under construction at publication time.

Nordhouse Dunes (a national forest recreational area) and Ludington State Park, lying adjacent to each other just north of Ludington, offer combined areas and distances that are suitable for short backpacks. We have a chapter.

Beaver Island and South Manitou Island, both in Lake Michigan, and reachable by commercial ferries, are sometimes used by Sierra hikers for backpacking.

In the Upper Peninsula, with its vast areas of lightly-inhabited territory, backpacking becomes more feasible, and closer to being a real necessity, although the assertion of the preceding paragraph that no spot is beyond the reach of automobile plus day hike is valid throughout the upper as well as the lower peninsula. The best opportunity for an extensive hike is provided by the North Country Trail, trail whose UP segment runs through the length of the peninsula, hard by the Lake Superior shore. See our chapter on long trails in Michigan.

The Lake Superior littoral of the Upper Peninsula offers numerous points of access for day hikes to the Lake, or for short backpacking expeditions. Although day hiking can easily get you to the beach and back, the pleasures of camping in the wild woods just back of the beach seem to justify overnight expeditions. Our chapter on the Two Hearted River area covers just such a possibility. The Pictured Rocks National Lakeshore, just east of Munising, also offers roadheads from which a few miles of hiking brings a visitor to the beach. However, within the Seashore, camping is allowed only in designated campgrounds, perhaps dampening the fun for the more primitive spirits among us.

The Porcupine Mountains (Porcupine Mountains Wilderness State Park) are unique in that, yes, they do constitute a wilderness area, except for an access road, and a few cabins. Bears lend authenticity. Trails are organized into 16 segments, ranging from one to 16 miles in length. Given the rugged terrain (real mountains!), the unspoiled streams (with waterfalls), and the attractiveness of the Lake Superior shore, extensive visits via backpacking seem well justified. See our chapter.

Isle Royale, far, far away in northwestern Lake Superior, lies well beyond the one-day-drive-from-Ann-Arbor limit set for this book, but deserves a mention because it is, after all, in Michigan. Backpacking the length of the island, forty-some miles, seems to be the thing for the hiker to do there, but so many enthusiasts have done it that the Sierra Club has become concerned about overuse, and since about 1980 has refused to conduct any of its national outings on the island. As a handy source of information on the island, see reference 2.

Beyond anything that you may read in guidebooks lie the individually discovered hikes. A study of county maps (reference 1), especially in the northerly parts of the state, shows uncountable miles of poor roads that make decent hiking trails (though you may have to step aside for an occasional four-wheel driver, or -- ugh! -- trailbikes), and that in many places offer loops of length suitable for a good day hike, or even a backpack. Whether the hike is actually "good" will be difficult to decide from mere map study, so you will have to risk a day of exploration. Odds seem favorable, however; three of the outings described later (Two Hearted River, Charlevoix Pastoral, and Jordan River) were discovered by map study, and all have been enjoyed many times by the respondent who reported them.

And beyond Michigan? A big sweep of country lies within our one-day limit, including a long stretch of the Appalachian Trail, and the innumerable lesser-known trails lacing the eastern mountains. This book has chapters on two backpacking trips to the mountains. And then there's Ontario, with its stretches of wild country much more extensive than Michigan's. Algonquin, Lake Superior, and Pukaskwa Parks all offer trails suitable for day hiking or backpacking, and are given chapters here. One of the most favored distant outings of the Huron Valley Sierra is a three-day, two-night backpack along the Georgian Bay shore of the Bruce Peninsula, following the Bruce Trail south from Tobemory. See our chapter.

No, not elves, just Sierras
on the march

Canoeing

If you like whitewater thrills, then you're a long way from home. In the neighborhood of Ann Arbor, only the rocky remains of a mill dam at Delhi Metropolitan Park (between Ann Arbor and Dexter) produce a short stretch of churning water that frightens - properly so - the novice paddler. Farther, much farther, like 200 miles northwest, the Pine River slopes with moderate swiftness toward Lake Michigan, and requires at least moderate skill to navigate safely. Otherwise, within the Lower Peninsula you will find many attractive rivers that demand competence in negotiating tight bends, and in avoiding the downed trees and and overhanging branches (thick with spiders!) that often lurk just around those bends, but they can be tackled with only the most minimal life-threatening danger by anyone with the strength and skill to maneuver the canoe in flat water. Oh, you may get wet, and your camera too, but some people seem to think that falling in or turning over is fun. Their shrieks as they get their rented craft jammed sideways against a log lying across a current always seem to have a note of joy. Mixed with the bad words, of course.

A sampling of canoe excursions is included among our chapters, but it is truly only a small sample. Detailed guidebooks that cover Michigan are to be found in local (e.g. Ann Arbor) bookstores and outings stores. Two are listed here as references 18 and 19. The latter, in particular, should be helpful since it is devoted exclusively to Michigan rivers. Another source is our listing in Appendix 2 of Michigan canoe liveries. It is a virtual catalog of canoeing rivers, and the liveries can be called for information on their areas.

If you live in the Ann Arbor neighborhood, then the Huron River is an obvious choice for a starter in canoeing. The stretch of the river from Kent Lake in Oakland County (about 20 miles by road from Ann Arbor) to Ann Arbor gives 35 to 40 miles of pastoral river with numerous put-in and take-out points, several dams to carry, and only one or two hazards. See its chapter, later on.

The Ann Arbor Parks and Recreation Department operates canoe liveries at Gallup Park in southeastern Ann Arbor, and Argo Park in the northeast. Both of these locations can be the starting points for flatwater trips of several miles on the associated ponds (impoundments of the Huron River). Livery vehicles shuttle canoes between the two liveries, so that a trip between them via a mile or two of river is possible, and popular. The livery vehicles also deliver canoes upstream to Hudson Mills MetroPark (see map with our chapter on Huron River canoeing).

CanoeSport, a retailer of canoes in Ann Arbor, is a source of information on several rivers that are within an hour's drive of that city. Our chapters on the Portage, Kalamazoo, Grand, and Shiawassee Rivers are condensed versions of detailed data sheets that are available at CanoeSport. The store also organizes canoe outings on nearby waters, free and without any sales connection (the proprietor likes canoeing too much to spoil your day with commercials), and pubishes a *gratis* newsletter that tells of them.

A canoe on the roof of the car is a common sight as the weekenders roar north on I-75, but canoe liveries service nearly all of the canoeable rivers at reasonable rates. See Appendix 2.

A pox on portage

Bicycling

Neither Ann Arbor nor Michigan are hog-heaven places for the bicylist, but they do have their unique appeals, and are surely better for happy biking than many other cities and states.

Ann Arbor has its web of designated bike routes, much of them off-road, so that any point in the city can be reached by bike without the need to ride on major auto routes. Being a college town gives it advantage in a perverse way: it has its horde of youthful cyclists that serve as shock troops to condition motorists to presence in the streets of unpredictable two-wheelers. Stop at a stop sign? Not them. For a traffic light? Well, maybe slow down a bit, maybe even glance left and right before passing guilelessly beneath the red. The native motorists curse, but at intersections just will *not* proceed in front of a bicycle because they are rightly afraid that the bicycle will suddenly dart to its destruction in front of *them.* The stodgy adult riders - the more conservative professors, for instance - benefit from the conditioned caution of these motorists. But, oh beware of the stranger just come to town! Some innocent from Milan or Monroe may assume that STOP means stop for all vehicles (it *does*), and... well, rough contact with front bumper or gritty asphalt pavement could ruin your whole day.

Beyond the town? Roads beckon. Huron River Drive, leading westward, is a favorite. Following the river, its hills are minimal. Being "scenic," its speed limit is 35. Being popular, it draws enough two-wheeled traffic to dampen the motorist. These things sum to a good road for bicycles. Ann Arbor - Dexter Road, and Scio Church Road plus Parker Road, are acceptable alternative routes to and from Dexter, having only moderate traffic, and also often enough bike traffic to give the motorists a caution. See our chapter on the "bike-a-thon" route through Dexter.

But Dexter is just a beginning.

Biking out of Ann Arbor is generally best in the 180-degree arc from south through west to north, or alternatively said, to the west of U S 23. The bike-a-thon chapter just mentioned speaks of routes almost due west, and another bicycling chapter describes a southwesterly voyage to Blissfield. Other possibilities abound, for lightly motored roads grid the flat country of the southern Lower Peninsula in numbers and milage almost uncountable. Study of the Washtenaw County map (reference 1) will show you the prospects in the area close to Ann Arbor. *Bike Rides in Wastenaw County* (reference 7), which is the county map with added markings to show recommended bike routes, can be an additional help ("can be" rather than "is" because opinions do differ on which roads are best for the bicycle).

Beyond the Ann Arbor neighborhood? That grid of roads leads on and on. *Cycling Maps of Michigan,* a complete set of county maps with notation of roads recommended for bikes, covers the entire state, and with their aid you can lay out a feasible route to anywhere in the state. (No, you can't pedal on the Mackinac Bridge, but there is supposed to be a bus that will carry you and your wheels across.) You can get there - most anywhere - from here, given the time and the stamina.

If you prefer organized bicycle touring - and it has obvious appeal on several points - you will find bicycling clubs throughout Michigan. In Ann Arbor the club of general popularity is the Ann Arbor Bicycle Touring Society. Its mainstay and best-known activity is a Saturday morning breakfast ride to Dexter. (The joys of an early-morning ride to Dexter make you forget those growing hunger pangs until you can lay them to rest at the Dexter bakery.) But its other activities are many, and suited to a wide range of riding capabilities. And further, it provides entre to rides staged other organizations throughout Michigan - and beyond.

As a more specific introductionto the Touring Society, there is reproduced on the following page selected material from the Club's April/May 1986 Ride Calendar. It will obviously be far out of date by the time you read it, but if *too* much time hasn't passed, it will give you a fair idea of what goes on. Names and phone numbers many not still be current, but during riding season, at least, the "Events" pages of the Ann Arbor *Observer* will show you the month's activities, and names and phone numbers of the leaders.

Excerpts from
Ann Arbor Bicycle Touring Society
RIDE CALENDAR
April and May, 1986

Classification: "A" — relatively fast, 15-18 mph, able to ride 100 mi. in 7 hrs.
"B" — moderate, 12-15 mph, stops as needed, ride 65 mi. in 5 hrs.
"C" — leisurely, 8-10 mph, frequent stops, excellent for inexperienced riders.
"D" — 5-8 mph, for the slow but determined

Regular Weekday Rides (condensed list)

SATURDAY BREAKFAST. "A/B" 40-100 mi., "C" 25-29 mi.
8:30 a.m. Old Amtrak, destination Dexter and beyond. Sign up at Amtrak or Dexter. This is a very popular ride. A and B riders have been experimenting with alternate routes and departure times to help reduce the congestion at Amtrak, which seems to be working. The ride leader will depart with the "C" riders and new members shortly after 8:30 a.m. The last "C" riders should arrive at the park in Dexter before 10:00 a.m. Most riders should have at least half an hour for socializing before departing on their selected ride. All the rides will depart Dexter between 10:00 a.m. and 10:30 a.m. If you have questions ask anyone in a green AABTS jersey. In spite of the congestion, this is the best ride to get to know other members and to sample the delights of the Dexter bakery. **All riders are urged to observe the rules of the road—no more than two abreast; always remain on the right hand side of the road.**

SATURDAY & SUNDAY LONG RIDE "A" 100-130 mi.
8:30 a.m. on Saturday & 9:00 a.m. on Sunday Old Amtrak or with the regular Sunday ride. Whenever possible extra miles will be added to the regular A/B routes. Emphasis will be to use smooth roads with low traffic density. All riders should be self sufficient and all questions should be directed to the ride leader.
Ride Leader: John Hansen (487-5451)

SATURDAY AFTERNOON "I HATE CROWDS" ALTERNATIVE. "B" 30-50 mi. April Only
1:00 p.m. Scarlett Intermediate School parking lot. For those who work or would like to get weekend chores done in the morning and those who hope for afternoon sunshine.
Ride Supervisors: Judy and Manfred Schmidt (971-5763)

SATURDAY AFTERNOON RIDE "B" 20+ Starts May 3
1:30 p.m. Old Amtrak
Ride Supervisors: Elliot Warner (995-1985) and Steu White (996-2974)

MONDAY "WEEKEND RECOVERY" RIDE "B" 20-40 mi. Starts May 5
6:30 p.m. Dicken School, 2135 Runnymede.
Ride Supervisors: Steve and Diana Lansky (663-0347)

MONDAY EVENING FAR EAST FRINGE TRAINING RIDE "B+/A-" 25-40 mi. Starts May 1
6:30 p.m. Great Scott parking lot. Sheldon and Ann Arbor Road in Canton. Friendly group workouts starting with (LSD) long steady distance on to pace lines and later fartlek intervals. Goal of a 30 mile time trial in less than 90 minutes before DALMAC.
Ride Supervisors: **Bob Staron (455-5363) Doug Krupa (469-8619) and Bill Erickson (453-7485)**

SCHEDULED RIDES AND EVENTS (condensed list)

Below are Club sponsored and Invitational rides for April and May. Invitational rides *(in italic)* these rides are organized and sponsored by groups other than AABTS. However in order to be listed here and count for club mileage one of the AABTS members must act as the coordinator and supply the required information.

Reservations must be made ahead for: Pinckney Brunch and Hathaway House rides.

April 6 Sunday — **YPSI-OLD TOWN BREAKFAST RIDE "C" 30 mi.**
9:00 a.m. Old Amtrak. Don't miss your chance to ride the first Sunday ride of the year
Ride Supervisor: Steu White (996-2974)

April 6 Sunday — **CLINTON MACON RIDE "B" 55 miles**
9:00 a.m. Old Amtrak
Ride Supervisor: Ron Tabb (663-4378)

April 13 Sunday — **PINCKNEY BRUNCH RIDE "A/B" 70 mi. "B/C" 40 mi.**
9:00 a.m. Old Amtrak. This is a repeat from last year which everyone enjoyed. Reservations required
Ride Supervisors: "A/B" John Downey (668-8757) and "B/C" Jim Fisher (761-3738)

April 20 Sunday — **BROOKLYN-MANCHESTER "A/B" 80 mi**
9:00 a.m. Old Amtrak. Enjoy a ride through Sharon Hollow and a visit to Brooklyn, a lovely little town with a famous bakery restaurant.
Ride Supervisor Mike Sanders (663-3724)

Birdwatching

The Huron Valley Sierra does not often conduct outings for the purpose of birdwatching, since a vigorous local branch of the Audubon Society (Washtenaw Audubon Society) has this phase of the outdoor experience so well in hand. That group publishes a newsletter, meets monthly for an educational and/or entertaining meeting, and runs frequent field trips. See the "Events" pages of the Ann Arbor *Observer*. The local branch has an information phone by which you can get current news on activities. The office of the state chapter is in Kalamazoo; its phone is listed in our information appendix.

The Washtenaw Audubon publishes a handy booklet, *A Guide to Bird Finding in Washtenaw County and Surrounding Areas* (reference 14), which lists 38 prime birding areas in Ann Arbor and southeastern lower Michigan, in southwestern Ontario, and in outstate Michigan. Details are given on location and travel, and on expected sightings. If a serious birder, you will surely want to obtain a copy; here, to give you an introductory idea, we abstract a sampling by borrowing freely from the Audubon booklet.

ANN ARBOR AND NEARBY

Huron River Barton Pond and Geddes Pond (Gallup Park), at opposite ends of the river's course through Ann Arbor, are broad sheets of water, and hence are the homes of a variety of waterfowl, both permanent residents and migrators. Ducks and gulls abound throughout the year, large numbers of Canada geese spend the cold season, blue herons and an occasional egret wade the shallow edges during the warm season, and red-tailed hawks and sometimes as osprey eye the water from the bordering trees.

Arboretum The Nichols Arboretum, a large tract of wooded and open land sloping down to the river from Geddes Avenue, is the largest area of obvious bird habitat within urban Ann Arbor. The *Guide* recommends it for warblers in the spring, and cedar waxwings and finches in the winter. Dickeybirds have been reported.

Botanical Gardens The University's Matthaei Botanical Gardens, located about a mile beyond the eastern edge of Ann Arbor on Dixboro Road, provide the habitat for a wide variety of common bird species. The *Guide* also notes woodcock evident in the fields during their spring courting season, and yellow-billed cuckoos during the summer.

Waterloo State Recreation Area This is an area of wetlands, lakes, old fields, and steep wooded hills straddling the Washtenaw-Jackson County line. (We have a chapter on hiking in Waterloo.) The *Guide* details a tour of many turnings and diversions that we do not reproduce here. The area's attractions are sedge wrens, sora, rails, marsh wrens, cranes, grasshopper sparrows, and bobwhites.

Haehnle Sanctuary This is an Audubon Sanctuary in Jackson County north of I-94. Exit I-94 at Race Road (east of Jackson), go north to Seymour Road, then west on Seymour about two miles to an inconspicuous entrance on the right. The principal attraction is a large marsh that is favored by sandhill cranes, especially during the fall migrating season (late October, early November), when the transient flock numbers in the hundreds. The cranes also pass through in March, when they often can be seen feeding in nearby cornfield stubble.

SOUTHWESTERN ONTARIO

Point Pelee National Park Even among the general population (those who probably don't know vireo from vertigo), Point Pelee is renowned as a place of birds, and as a place for the observation thereof. Fame makes for problems of crowding among the watchers, so much so that the *Guide* advises visiting on weekdays, especially during migratory seasons.

Point Pelee is prominent on the most rudimentary maps - it's a finger of land thrust into Lake Erie from that larger peninsula of Ontario that lies south of Lake St Clair. This feature, plus its extensive wild and wet habitat, seems to explain it attractions to migrating flocks. Land birds as well as waterfowl rest in the park before/after crossing Lake Erie. The *Guide* reports that as many as 120 species can sometimes be seen there in a single day. And not just birds - the swarms of monarch butterflies that breed in Mexico and Central America also funnel through Point Pelee.

Jack Miner's Sanctuary You pass close to this on your

way to and from Point Pelee. The attraction is the thousands of migratory geese that stop over to feast on the liberal grain rations dispensed by the proprietors.

OUTER MICHIGAN

Shiawassee National Wildlife Refuge The Refuge is an area of 20,000 acres just south of Saginaw. See the Saginaw county map (reference 1). Its principal attraction is migrating waterfowl.

Seney National Wildlife Refuge The Refuge is an area of about 95,000 acres in the eastern Upper Peninsula's Schoolcraft County. It also features migratory waterfowl, but also has breeding populations of yellow rails, Le Conte's sparrows, bald eagles, and sandhill cranes.

Dead Stream Swamp Dead Steam is a tributary of the Muskegon River lying in Roscommon and Missaukee Counties. The swamp is wild and wet, and is favored by wildlife of many kinds (bears!) because human access is quite difficult. A canoe is best, put into the Dead Stream Flooding (look at the Roscommon County map (reference 1)) just to the west of Houghton Lake's North Bay, then paddled upstream through the Muskegon River to the Stream, then on as far as you dare go. Ospreys and bald eagles nest in sight of the water.

Whitefish Point In far Chippawa County, Whitefish Bay widens into Lake Superior at Whitefish Point. The land in the immediate vicinity of the Point is a Michigan Audubon Society sanctuary. It is best known as a stopping point for migrating hawks and owls. The best time to see the migrators is in April, which, unfortunately, is still winter in the Upper Peninsula.

Crosscountry Skiing

It's better to mount one ski than curse the darkness. The darkness of a cold northern winter, fortunately lightened - say some - by layers of snow. Or to make a mother of necessity when the creatures who cannot endure down parkas and mittens and long underwear have flown far south, or burrowed beneath it all until April. When snow may catch them one more time. And it should be two skiis, of course.

Typically those who have hiked or canoed or biked during the warm months turn to crosscountry skiing as soon as the first few centimeters of snow have covered the surface, and if enthused enough to travel to the northern reaches of Michigan, keep at it into daffodil time in Ann Arbor.

Skiing is scarcely an urban sport, but to a limited extent is quite easily enjoyed within the limits of Ann Arbor. Huron Hills golf course (a public course of the Ann Arbor Parks and Recreation Department), which adjoins Gallup Park, becomes a ski park while snow-covered, and offers equipment rental. The University of Michigan Outdoor Recreation Center (764-6429 for information), and the Washtenaw County Parks and Recreation Commission also offer rentals and areas.

Outside of town, the general picture is that many hiking trails become skiing trails once November's fallen leaves are sufficiently covered by December's snow. Stinchfield Woods (see our chapter), for example, seems to be a favorite for a half-day weekend expedition. The trails of the Pinckney and Waterloo Recreation Areas (also the subjects of chapters here) serve in similar fashion. Burroughs Farms, a commercial recreation area on the outskirts of Brighton, and Mayberry State Park (see our chapter) are skiing areas that offer equipment rental.

The concept of hiking trails becoming ski trails is also generally true throughout Michigan. For instance, most of the 63 trails described in *Michigan Hiking Opportunities* (reference 2) are also designated as cross country ski trails, and its text and maps note steepness of slopes, degrees of difficulty, and other information pertinent to skiing. In this book you will find six chapters on skiing spots scattered throughout the Lower Peninsula. All of them are also described in *Michigan Hiking Opportunities* (though without the personal flavor we give you).

Skiers flock together, of course. The local Sierra Club (Huron Valley Group) usually devotes its winter outings program to cross country skiing. More particularly devoted to the sport are the Ann Arbor Skii Club and the Washtenaw Ski Touring Society. Both have information hot lines; 761-3419 and 662-SKIS, respectively.

If the "real" skiing is your sport, i.e. zooming down a hill, being lifted to the top, zooming down the hill, *ad continuum,* then Michigan has that also, though it is of necessity limited to areas where "mountains" can be found. The nearest one to Ann Arbor is Mount Brighton, a modest emminence on the outskirts of Brighton, about 20 miles north of Ann Arbor. This is the site of instruction offered annually by the Ann Arbor *News.* For information, watch its pages as the weather cools toward the appropriate season.

Similar skiers' mountains are scattered throughout the state, but the largest concentration, and apparently that of greatest appeal, is found in the northwestern lower peninsula, roughly north of Traverse City and west of I-75. These are typically private commercial enterprises, and hence advertise heavily. The travel sections of the Detroit newspapers therefore comprise a good source of initial information about them.

Ann Arbor Area Outings

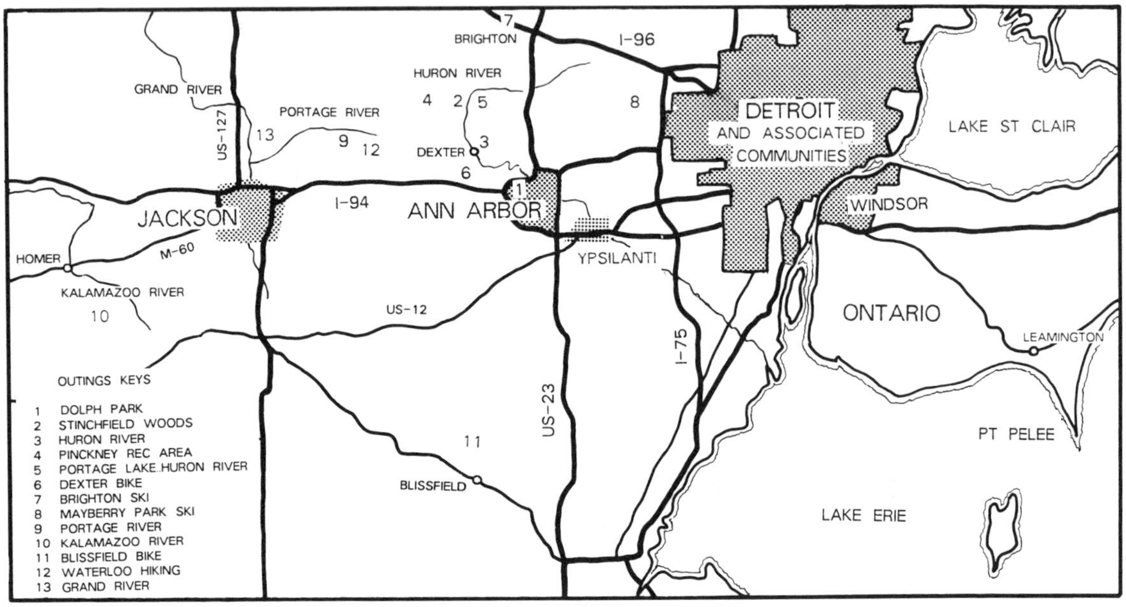

Ann Arbor Outings

"Ann Arbor outings" are those that can be found within an hour's drive of the city. We describe thirteen such outings in the chapters of this section; they encompass hiking, skiing, bicycling, and canoeing, all within this limited menu. There are many other possible outings in all of these categories, many more than a guidebook such as this can attempt to describe. However, it's easy to find out about them, given the number of readily obtained sources of information. The prime purpose of this introduction is is to give you a lead to those sources. (For addresses of publication sources to be mentioned here, see Appendix 1.)

If city parks interest you, Ann Arbor has over 100 individual facilities, most of which are parks (a few are golf courses, a few are cemetaries, etc). A map, entitled *Public Park and Recreation Land,* shows their locations, and can be obtained from the Ann Arbor Parks and Recreation Department. This map also shows University recreational property such as the Nichols Arboretum and the Matthei Botanical Gardens.

City canoe liveries are at Argo Pond (Longshore Park) and at Geddes Pond (Gallup Park).

The Washtenaw County Parks and Recreation Commission operates several parks in the County, and a map showing them can be obtained from its offices.

The Huron-Clinton Metropolitan Authority operates a number of parks along the Huron River. Two, Delhi Metropark and Dexter-Huron Metropark, lie between Ann Arbor and Dexter. A third, Hudson Mills Metropark, lies two or three miles upstream from Dexter, and a fourth, Kensington Metropark, is farther away - it's along I-96 east of Brighton - but still is within easy one-hour range of Ann Arbor. The first three of these parks are mainly of the picnic-volleyball-frisbee variety, and so is the fourth, but it is also big enough for hiking trails that you can cover in an hour or two. The Authority will send you a map that shows all of its park locations, and which contains large-scale maps of the parks themselves.

The Huron-Clinton Metropark Authority also publishes a canoeing guide to the Huron River.

A bicycle route map of the Ann Arbor-Ypsilanti urban area and Washtenaw County can be obtained from the Ann Arbor City Transportation Department. The Department of Natural Resources Bicycling Maps of Michigan also include a cycling map of Washtenaw County.

The Department of Natural Resources publication *Michigan Hiking Opportunities* shows hiking trails in several nearby recreational areas, such as the Pinckney and Waterloo areas.

A guidebook you should surely have is *Footloose in Washtenaw,* great for Ann Arbor's walkers-hikers, published by the Ann Arbor Ecology Center.

The map shows the locations of the outings described here.

Hiking or Skiing in Stinchfield Woods

General

Stinchfield Woods is a forested tract of about 770 acres covering a ridge known as Peach Mountain. The eastern end of the ridge is the site of the transmitter for WUOM, the University of Michigan radio station. Toward the western end, roughly a mile-and-a-half away, is the University's radio telescope, and between them lie several buildings that once housed the University's optical telescopes (now in Chile). The area is otherwise a laboratory and demonstration area for the Univerity's School of Natural Resources, and as such is heavily wooded, both with natural growth and with blocks of "tree farm."

The woods are laced with several miles of trails, making it a favorite with hikers and cross-country skiers. Its unique mix of natural and cultivated forest areas, its freedom from motored intruders, and a spectacular (well, spectacular by midwest flatland standards) view eastward from the heights around the WUOM tower are points much in its favor.

Maps

Washtenaw County map (reference 1), and U S Geological Survey Pinckney 7.5' quadrangle. There is also an informal map distributed by the School of Natural Resources that shows the trails. That map, tidied up a bit, appears in *Footloose in Washtenaw* (reference 3). The map printed here is adapted from the last, with a few contours from the USGS added so you can see the extent of Peach Mountain.

Other references

Footloose in Washtenaw has a few words, omitted here, about the trees and about the rabbits and woodchucks you might see. Its map also shows the tree types, and for the plantations, the dates of planting. *A Guide to Stinchfield Woods*, published by the School of Natural Resources, gives more details about the forest.

Travel from Ann Arbor

Stinchfield Woods is about 16 miles from downtown Ann Arbor. Among several feasible routes, US-23 to North Territorial Road, North Territorial Road to a parking spot (described in the next section) just west of the crossing of Dexter-Pinckney Road is likely to be the fastest.

Details

The most important detail is likely to be the nettling one of where to park. There is no designated parking area for visitors. One approach is simply to park on the roadside near one of the trailheads shown on the map, but... but our respondents report getting parking tickets for not being completely clear of traffic, blocking access to the radio telescope gate, etc. The best solution, at least on Sundays, is to park in the lot of the Territorial Professional Building on North Territorial Road, 0.2 mile west of Dexter-Pinckney Road. (Whether the building occupants object to use of their lot during business hours is not known.) From this lot, which lies on the south side of N Territorial, cross to a dirt road - probably closed to vehicles by a gate - that leads straight northward to a gravel pit. The road and the pit appear on our map, though the parking lot does not. Skirt the northern edge of the pit on a narrow trail (dashed line on our map) to reach the trail network within Stinchfield Woods.

In winter, when parking is most in demand because of the popularity of the area for skiing, several local residents along North Territorial Road allow parking on their property for a nominal price.

The "major trails" shown by the map here are actually narrow dirt roads, apparently used in forest management. There are numerous "minor trails," i.e. narrow footpaths. Only the one just mentioned in connection with the gravel pit are shown on the map. None of the trails of any kind are marked, so that care to avoid getting lost is advisable. Even a compass might be a good idea for the first-time explorer.

One of our respondents remarks "great x-c ski area," but as a warning to novices adds that some of the hills are quite steep. Use caution the first time around.

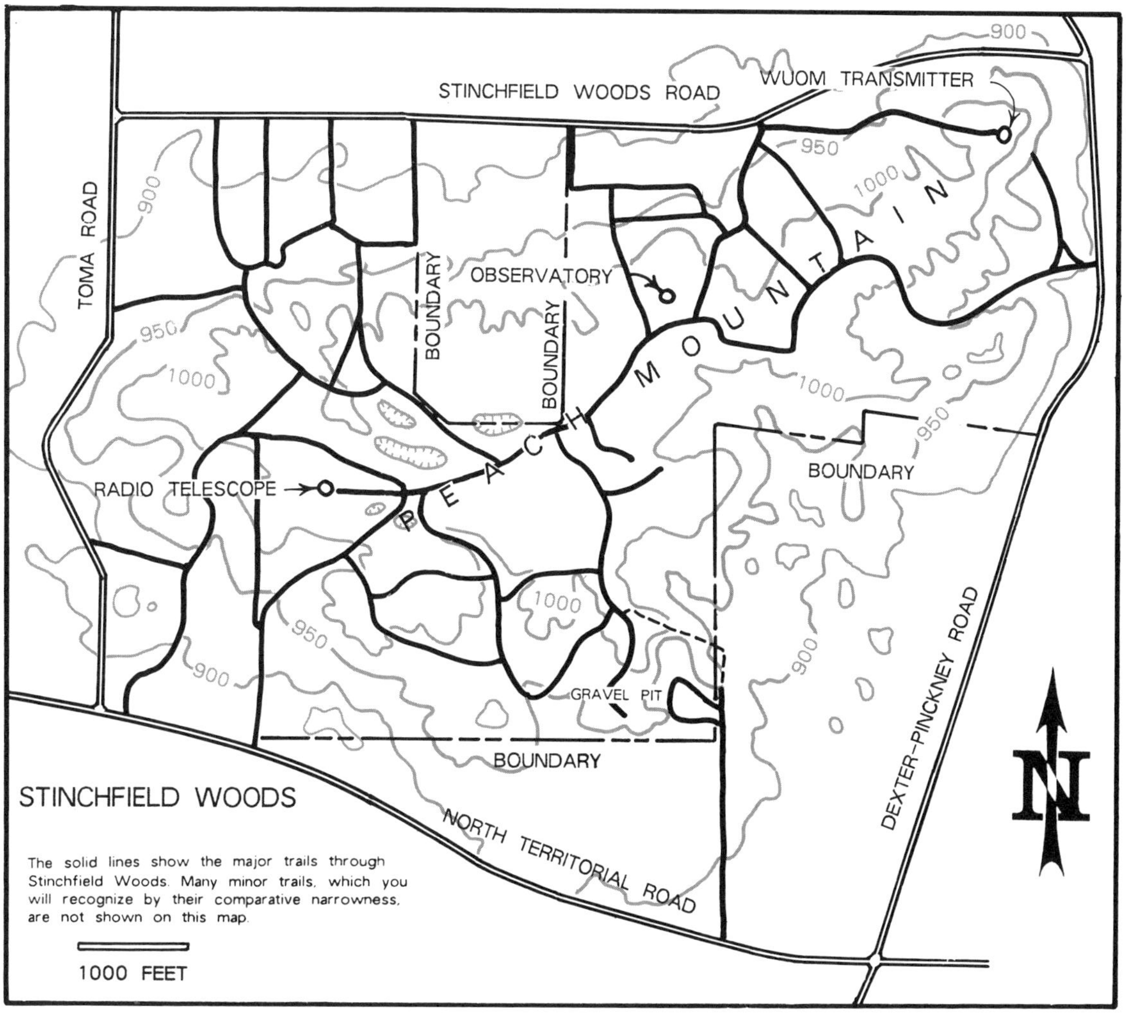

An Ann Arbor Natural Area
Dolph Park

General

Dolph is one of the 100-plus Ann Arbor parks. Unlike most of the others, however, it's not a place for frisbee flinging, but is 44 acres of varied land and water, best suited for wildlife preservation and environmental education. Its major feature consists of two lakes - First Sister Lake and Second Sister Lake - a pond, and wetlands. A well-maintained pathway leads from the parking lot at the entrance on Wagner Road into a loop through the high ground between the two lakes. It features several overlooks from which the lakes and wetlands can be viewed.

Lakewood Woods lies close to the southeast corner of the park, and may make for an interesting bonus excursion. The Woods can be reached by a path from Sunnywood Drive. See map.

Maps

Footloose in Washtenaw (reference 3) has a map of the park. Ann Arbor Parks and Recreation publishes a one-page brochure, *Dolph Park Nature Area,* that has a map showing the several types of dominant vegetation. The map printed here is adapted from the Parks and Recreation map, but omits some of the details.

Other references

The two references mentioned in the preceding section should be quite sufficient. A copy of the brochure is posted on a bulletin board at the park entrance, or can be obtained at the Parks and Recreation office at City Hall.

Details

Of interest are the types of plant and animal life that are likely to be encountered by the visitor, and the human activity that since the settlement of Ann Arbor has strongly influenced the conditions of the two lakes and the development of the park's natural communities. Since the Parks Department brochure that tells you of these things is so easily obtained (or viewed at the park entrance), we'll omit the story here in favor of that source.

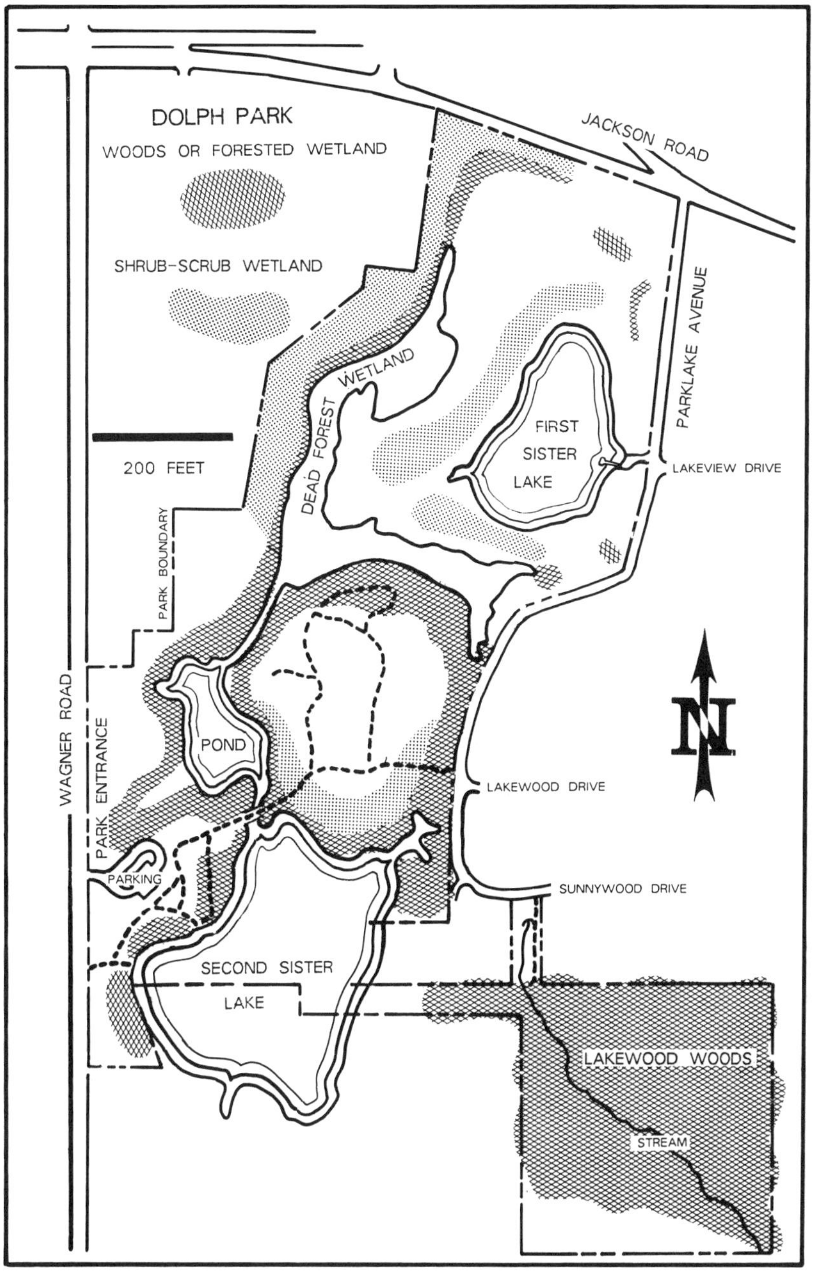

Canoe Trips on the Huron River

General

The Huron River rises in a group of lakes just west of Pontiac, flows soutwestward under I-96 and US-23 to a point roughly five miles north of Dexter, then southward to Dexter, then southeastward through Ann Arbor and Ypsilanti to Lake Erie. Here we shall speak only of the stretch between Kent Lake, which begins about three miles downstream from the point where the river first becomes decently canoeable, and Ann Arbor. As the river flows, the distance is 35 to 40 miles.

The water does not sparkle with pristine clarity, but since the river is nowhere closely bordered by agricultural land, the water is not murky enough to offend the eye. Whatever its less observable faults may be, the Huron serves as a source of Ann Arbor's municipal water - after treatment of course. The scene is otherwise quite pleasant also. Although dwellings crowd the banks in a few spots, the banks are undeveloped for the most part, and are bordered by woodland and wetland. On the whole, a not-bad river in the aesthetic sense.

Thrills, hazards, and difficulties are largely absent. Several dams require carrying, and shallow spots are a nuisance in a few places during the drier seasons. The scattered stone remnants of a mill dam at Hudson Mills Metropolitan Park churn the water enough to frighten an occasional novice, but are of scarce a magnitude to be a danger at anyone. The similar dam remnants at Delhi Metropolitan Park - the locally renowned "Delhi Rapids" - are another matter. They are generally rated as hazardous to all but experts. The prudent of all levels of skill pull ashore and walk the banks to study the tumbling water. And usually decide to carry around.

One of our chapters describes an interesting flat-water trip upward from Portage Lake, which is connected to the river by two artificial cuts. A dam just downstream of the westernmost cut dampens the current upstream for several miles, so that upstream paddling is scarcely more laborious than downstream. You will note from the map that Portage Lake is the lowest of a chain through which the river flows, which makes for a varied interest, but also for exposure to wind, and for possible traffic problems with motorboats and sailboats.

Maps

Washtenaw and Livingston County maps (reference 1) are handy for the road part of a canoeing expedition. For the river itself, a set of four maps covering the entire distance from source to Lake Erie, is distributed *gratis* by Huron-Clinton Metropolitan Authority. See appendices for address.

Other references

Canoeing Michigan Rivers (reference 19) has a chapter on the Huron.

Details

The Huron-Clinton maps are replete with the details. They show launching sites, distances in river miles and estimated paddling time between prominent points, possible hazards, nearby roads, and the locations of canoe rental businesses. A short text gives a few hints that don't seem to fit on the maps. And some goody advice, such as a stern parental warning against "frivolity."

In addition to access sites marked on the HCMA maps, it may be feasible to launch and take out at bridge crossings. One that is not noted, but is popular, is at the US-23 crossing. An exit within sight of the river gives access to Whitmore Lake Road, running parallel to the big road just a few yards to the west, and there is room to park several cars just off the W L Road shoulder within a few steps of its bridge. Except during high water intervals, the current in this stretch of the river is gentle enough to allow upstream paddling with reasonable effort.

Ann Arbor Parks and Recreation Department rents canoes at both Gallup Park and Argo Park, and will deliver them upstream to Delhi, Dexter, and Hudson Mills Metro Parks. Several commercial canoe liveries also serve the river; see the

Yellow Pages of the Ann Arbor telephone directory.

One of our respondents recommends the Huron for tubing as well as canoeing. Good tube trips are said to be from Hudson Mills to Dexter, and from Zeeb Road to Delhi Metropolitan Park.

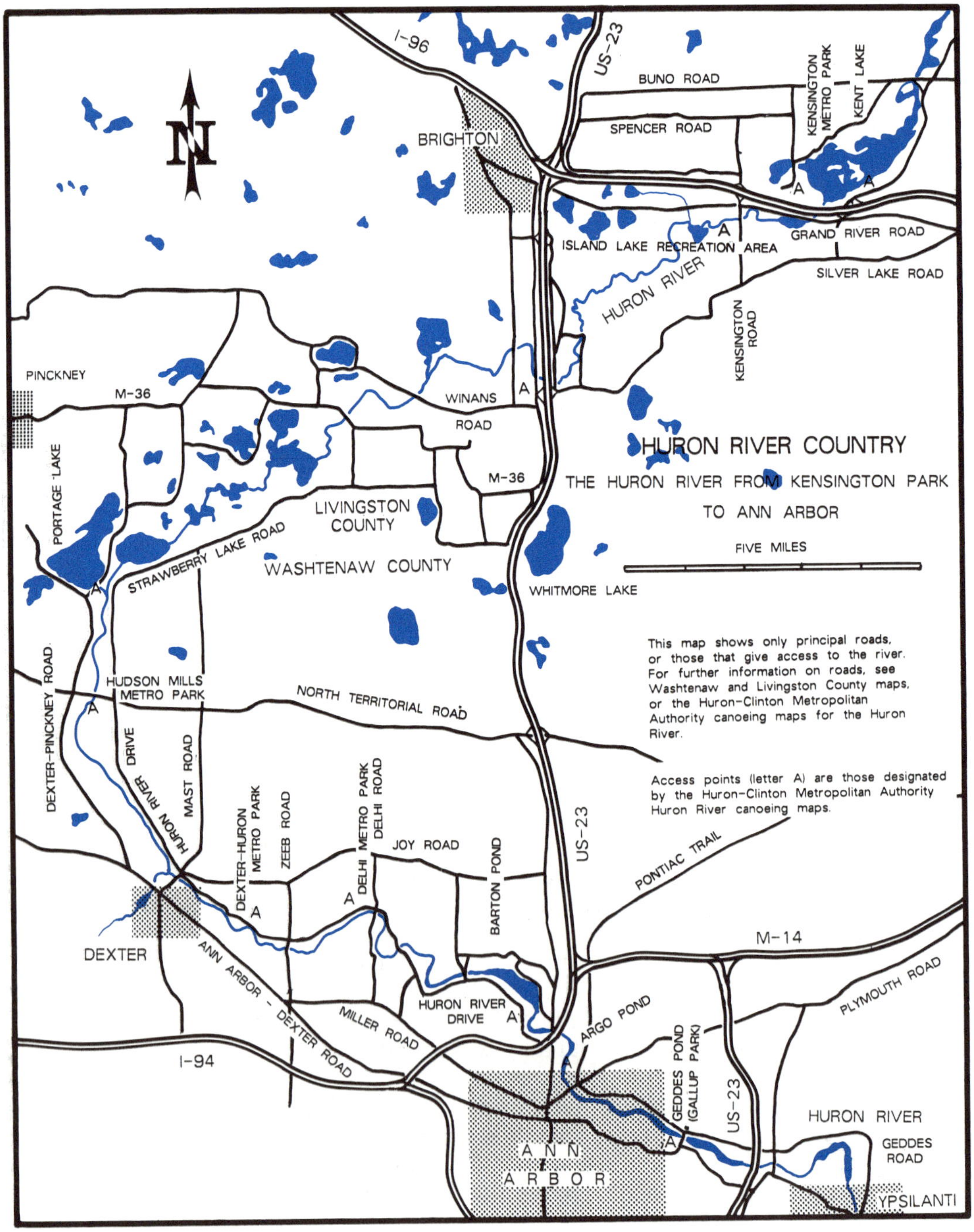

Hiking the Trails of the Pinckney Recreation Area

General

The Pinckney Recreation Area is 15 square miles of rough country, sprinkled with lakes, sinkholes, and glacial hilliness. It is almost completely wooded, although much of it is former pasture or cropland, and therefore will not be mature forest until well into the twenty-first century. Three trails, the Potawatomi of 17 miles, the Crooked Lake of 4.6 miles, and the Silver Lake of 2.2 miles, traverse the area, and together are generally agreed to form the premier hiking ground of Washtenaw County.

At publication time, a trail linking the Potawatomi Trail with the trails of the Waterloo Recreation Area has just been completed. By linking two systems of trails, it makes feasible several days of backpacking within an hour's drive of Ann Arbor.

Maps

Washtenaw and Livingston County maps (reference 1), U S Geological Survey Pinckney and Gregory 7.5' quadrangles, a trail map by the Boy Scouts of America, Wolverine Council (Ann Arbor), and a map of the recreation area published by Michigan State Parks. The last can be gotten from area headquarters on Silver Hill Road (Pinckney Recreation Area, 8555 Silver Hill Road, Route 1, Pinckney MI, 48169, 313-426-4913). The map printed here is compiled from all of these sources. A rather sketchy map also appears in *Footloose in Washtenaw* (reference 3).

Other references

Footloose in Washtenaw (reference 3) contains a brief description of the Pinckney Recreation Area and its trails.

Travel from Ann Arbor

North on US-23, west on North Territorial Road, north on Dexter Town Hall Road (reached about 2.5 miles after crossing the Huron River on North Territorial), left after about a mile onto Silver Hill Road to the Silver Lake parking area within 1/2 mile. Distance from central Ann Arbor is about 19 miles.

Details

All three trails originate at the Silver Lake parking area. Cars entering must have the annual state park sticker displayed, or must pay the daily parking fee. Be warned that Silver Lake is popular for things (swimming, picnicing, frisbee throwing, etc) other than hiking, and hence on a hot weekend afternoon you may find the parking lot full. A prominent sign facing the parking lot points to the starting point for the trails.

Camping along the trails is not allowed, save in several designated spots.Two primitive campgrounds are indicated by the tent symbol on the map. A developed state campground is located at Bruin Lake, found by turning east onto Kaiser Road at Unadilla (see Livingston County map). This campground is not convenient to any of the trails, however, and is not recommended as a hike-in camping place.

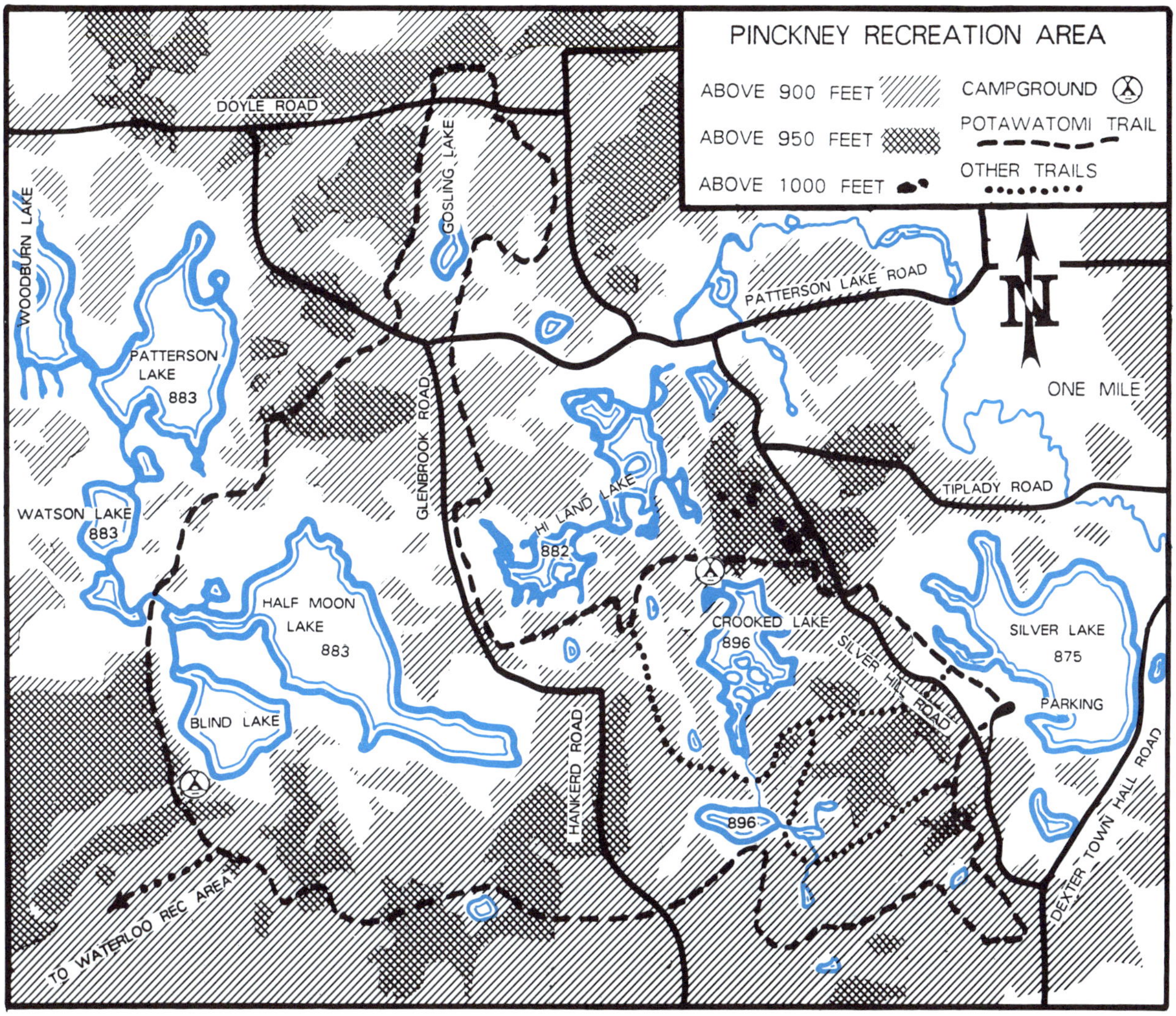
PINCKNEY RECREATION AREA
ABOVE 900 FEET
ABOVE 950 FEET
ABOVE 1000 FEET
CAMPGROUND
POTAWATOMI TRAIL
OTHER TRAILS
N
ONE MILE
DOYLE ROAD
GOSLING LAKE
WOODBURN LAKE
PATTERSON LAKE ROAD
PATTERSON LAKE
883
GLENBROOK ROAD
TIPLADY ROAD
WATSON LAKE
883
HI LAND LAKE
882
HALF MOON LAKE
883
CROOKED LAKE
896
SILVER HILL ROAD
SILVER LAKE
875
PARKING
BLIND LAKE
HANKERD ROAD
896
DEXTER TOWN HALL ROAD
TO WATERLOO REC AREA

A Flatwater Roundtrip Canoe Voyage from Portage Lake

General

The Huron River flows westward for about 10 miles from its crossing of US-23 north of Ann Arbor before turning southward toward Dexter. The westward stretch encompasses a series of small lakes through which the river flows until it reaches a dam in the vicinity of Portage Lake. From the dam upstream through Base Line Lake, the current is virtually nil, and it is weak in the succeeding connecting links all the way to Strawberry Lake, approximately five miles above the dam. This part of the Huron River therefore is well suited for an afternoon's round trip, a trip that doesn't require spotting of cars nor arrangements for a livery pickup. The shores of the lakes are lined with summer cottages, but the river links are mostly wooded. Not quite the wilderness, but a pleasant pastoral scene to enjoy.

Maps

Washtenaw and Livingston county maps (reference 1), and map 2 of the Huron River Canoeing Guide published by the Huron-Clinton Metropolitan Authority. The map here is adapted from the latter.

Other references

The Canoeing Guide listed just above provides a few additional tidbits of information. It is distributed free by the Authority, 3050 Penobscot Building, Detroit 48226, 313-961-5865.

Travel from Ann Arbor

The usual starting point is a Department of Natural Resources launching site at Portage Lake. To reach it, take US-23 north to North Territorial Road, North Territorial west to Dexter-Pinckney Road, Dexter-Pinkney north to McGregor Road, McGregor east (right) to the launching site. Approximately 18 miles from downtown Ann Arbor.

Details

The usual canoeing hazards are absent -- no swift water, no sharp bends, no blockage of the river by downed trees. To be sure, there are a few shallows in the river links, and you *can* get spiders in your hair by running into overhanging limbs, but troubles of the conventional sort are minor. On the other hand, in the lakes you may encounter both motorboats and sailboats. The sailboats often move fast, and have the right-of-way over powered craft, including muscle powered. Motorboats likewise move faster, often much faster than canoes, and even if not legally vested with right-of-way, may act like it. Don't trust 'em.

If the lakes are big enough for sailboats, they are windy and wavy enough on occasion to cause trouble for canoes. Flotation devices ("lifejackets" or buoyant cushions) are essential, and you may meet a sheriff's boat that's interested in checking that you haven't forgotten.

The launching site on McGregor Road is shown on the map. Be warned, however, that the parking lot there is often full on really good boating days. Get there early.

There is a canoe livery at Portage Lake (Pinckney address). See yellow pages of the Ann Arbor telephone directory.

Huron River from Portage Lake

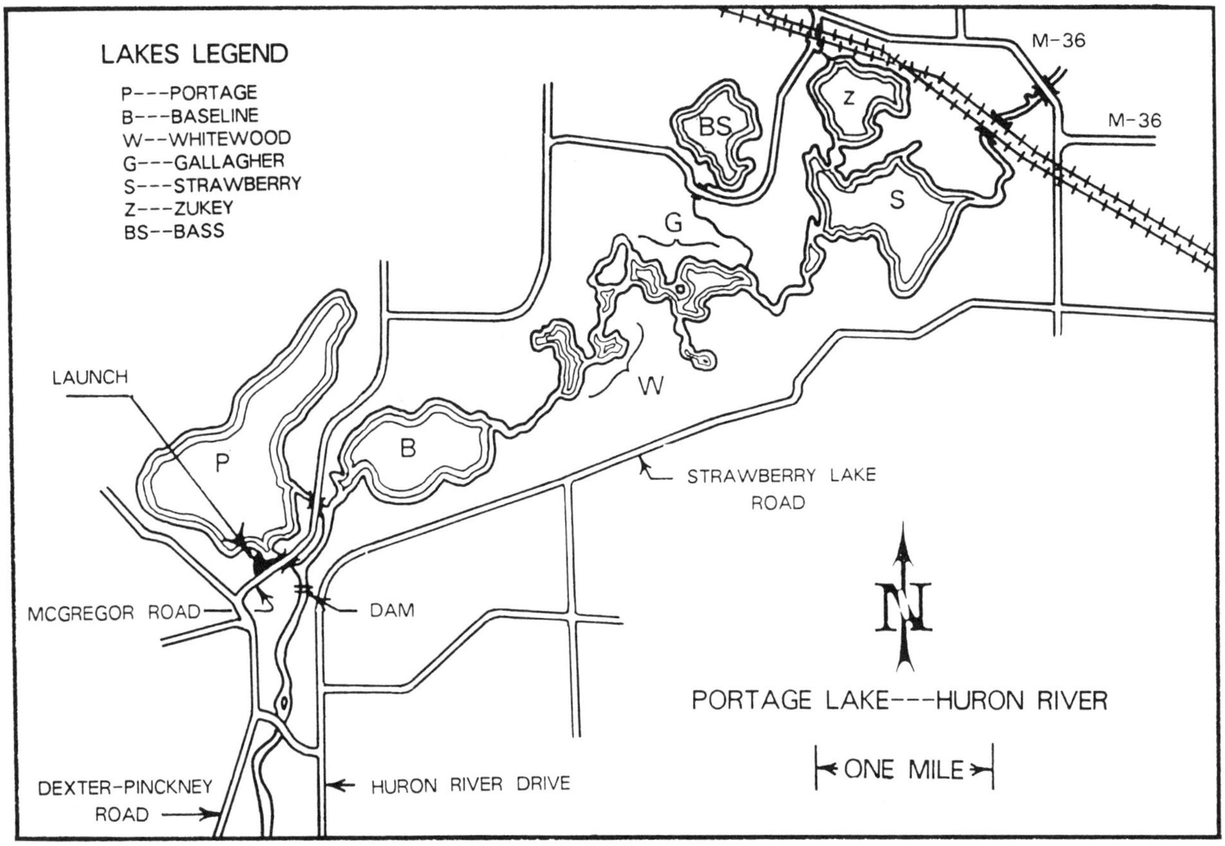

By Bicycle to Dexter with Return via Scio Church Road

General

To the west of Ann Arbor lie many objectives that can be reached by bicycle via lightly traveled roads. The trip described here is a 28-mile circuit that is one of those chosen by the Ann Arbor Ecology Center for its annual (usually in May) "Bike-a-thon." The route follows the Huron River to Dexter for roughly a third of its distance, turns southward for almost another third, then heads due east into the southwestern corner of Ann Arbor. The riverside leg is attractive, and has the appeal of minimal hilliness and a 35-mph speed limit, but the two return legs are more typical of the many routes you can explore in the 180-degree arc west of Ann Arbor. In particular, you will be passing through attractive farm country. From several spots the eye sweep over wide stretches of that country - and the hills that you climb for that privelege require only minor exertion.

Bike Rides in Washtenaw County (reference 7) describes 10 rides in Washtenaw County by means of an individual map of each route. The ride described here coincides in its main features with ride 5 in that group.

Maps

Washtenaw County map (reference 1), the Washtenaw County map from *Cycling Maps of Michigan* (reference 5), and map 5 from *Bike Rides in Washtenaw County* (reference 7).

Details

The Bike-a-thon trip begins and ends at the Farmers' Market in downtown Ann Arbor; the resultant round trip is 28 miles. The preferred direction is counterclockwise, i.e. out to Dexter via Huron River Drive, south from Dexter on Parker Road, with return to Ann Arbor via Scio Church Road. The preference is apparently based on an expectation of winds favoring eastward cycling; Scio Church Road, being on higher ground than Huron River Drive, is more exposed to wind. Since the only significant hills are found along Scio Church Road, a favoring wind is more appreciated there.

The passage through Dexter begins with a left turn onto Mast Road (the first STOP sign you encounter after leaving Ann Arbor), which becomes Central Street after crossing the river. Follow to the middle of town to Dexter's main street (Ann Arbor Street, by name). Go westward on that street to Dexter-Chelsea Road (left, just before the railway underpass). Within about a half-mile from Dexter, you will find Parker Road branching to the left.

Delhi Park and Dexter-Huron Park are possible attractions on the Huron River Drive leg, and just after crossing the river into Dexter you pass the Dexter cider mill on the right. The last is purveyor of cider and doughnuts (for a price, of course) during the autumn months. Some peddlers prefer to stuff up here, then drift back to Ann Arbor via Huron River Drive.

Although Huron River Drive has a 35-mile speed limit, and is a road where most motorists should expect to encounter cyclists, it is also a narrow and winding road that novice cyclists may find scary because of the presence of cars. Caution will never be inappropriate.

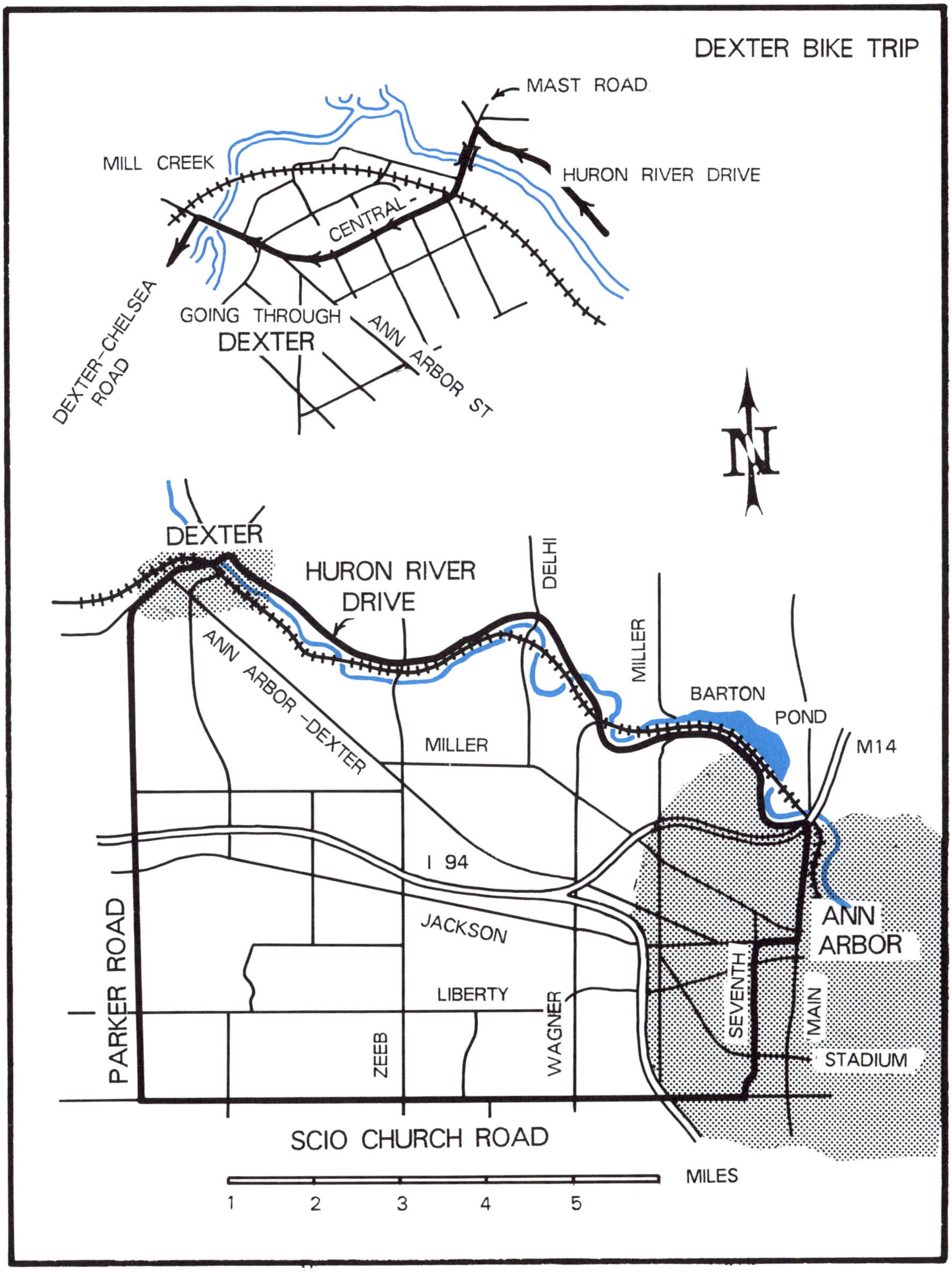
DEXTER BIKE TRIP
MAST ROAD
MILL CREEK
HURON RIVER DRIVE
CENTRAL
GOING THROUGH
DEXTER
ANN ARBOR ST
DEXTER-CHELSEA ROAD
N
DEXTER
HURON RIVER DRIVE
DELHI
MILLER
BARTON
POND
M14
ANN ARBOR -DEXTER
MILLER
I 94
JACKSON
ANN ARBOR
PARKER ROAD
LIBERTY
SEVENTH
MAIN
WAGNER
ZEEB
STADIUM
SCIO CHURCH ROAD
MILES
1
2
3
4
5

Skiing the Brighton Nature Trails

General

The Brighton Recreation Area nature trails - though not designed for the skier - are among the best intermediate level cross country skiing trails in southeastern Michigan. Their excellence comes from both the topography of the area, and the mixture of forest and old-farm vegetation.

The topography shows strong evidence of the Pliestocene Epoch glaciation in Michigan of about 25,000 years ago. Moraines, outwashes, and kettle holes dot the area to the challenge and delight of the skier. Unlike the experiences on typical golf course trails, the skier finds it necessary to "read" the terrain and trail in order to develop the proper skiing rythm. When reading properly, the skier feels the rythm developing until "synch" with the trail is achieved. Short uphills demand proper technique to avoid slipping, but only a few hills require the herringbone, unless the trail is icy or hard packed. Counterclockwise travel around the trails provides the best downhill runs.

The open fields are abandoned farms. Property lines are still evident in places where they were marked by stone fences. Most of the forest is oak-hickory, and is largely second growth. However, several stretches of trail pass by groves of large trees on the order of 80 feet tall. The abundance of edges where forest, field, and wetland meet makes the area attractive to wildlife. Deer are often seen.

There are two trails. The shorter, length 2 miles, is called the KAHCHIN TRAIL (pronounced *kaw-chin*, Chippewa Indian for "short"). The longer, length 5 miles, is called the PENOSHA (*payn-o-shaw*, meaning "long"). The longer should require an hour to and hour-and-a-half by a good intermediate skier. The shorter trail is a good warm-up loop, or an extra run for the enthusiastic finisher of the longer.

Maps

Livingston County map (reference 1). U S Geological Survey Brighton 7.5' quadrangle. A trail map is available from Department of Natural Resources Area Headquarters located on Chilson Road, phone 313- 229-6566. The map printed here is adapted from *Michigan Hiking Opportunities* (reference 2).

Other references

None.

Travel from Ann Arbor

North on U S 23 to the M-36 exit. Go west (left) on M-36 for about 5 miles to Chilson Road. Follow Chilson Road north (right) for 4.5 miles to Bishop Lake Road. Turn east (right) and in about 2 miles look for the parking lot, which is called "Bishop Lake Lot."

Details

The comments here are numbered to match the numbers on the trail map (and on the map here), and are intended to warn the skier of spots of difficult terrain.

1. Very short, steep hill leading down to Teahen Road. Unless snow is deep enough to limit speed, walking down is preferred because of the proximity to the trail of a fence and trees.

2. Walk the road up the hill to where Teahen Road turns north, this because the trail is difficult to find where it parallels the road. At the bend, the trail goes south (right) from the bend.

3. Several long, steep hills that are fun to whiz down. They are not difficult, but it's possible to build up high speed if the snow is packed.

4. A sharply descending hairpin turn to the right presents the only real challenge on the trail. However, unless the snow is hard packed, a stem christy or telemark will get you through. Otherwise, snowplow like crazy!

5. Remove skis, cross road, climb steps, then back to the skis.

The trail provides a useful rating of one's skiing ability. A good intermediate skier should be able to complete the trail, falling no more than once (at point 4), in under 1 1/2 hours.

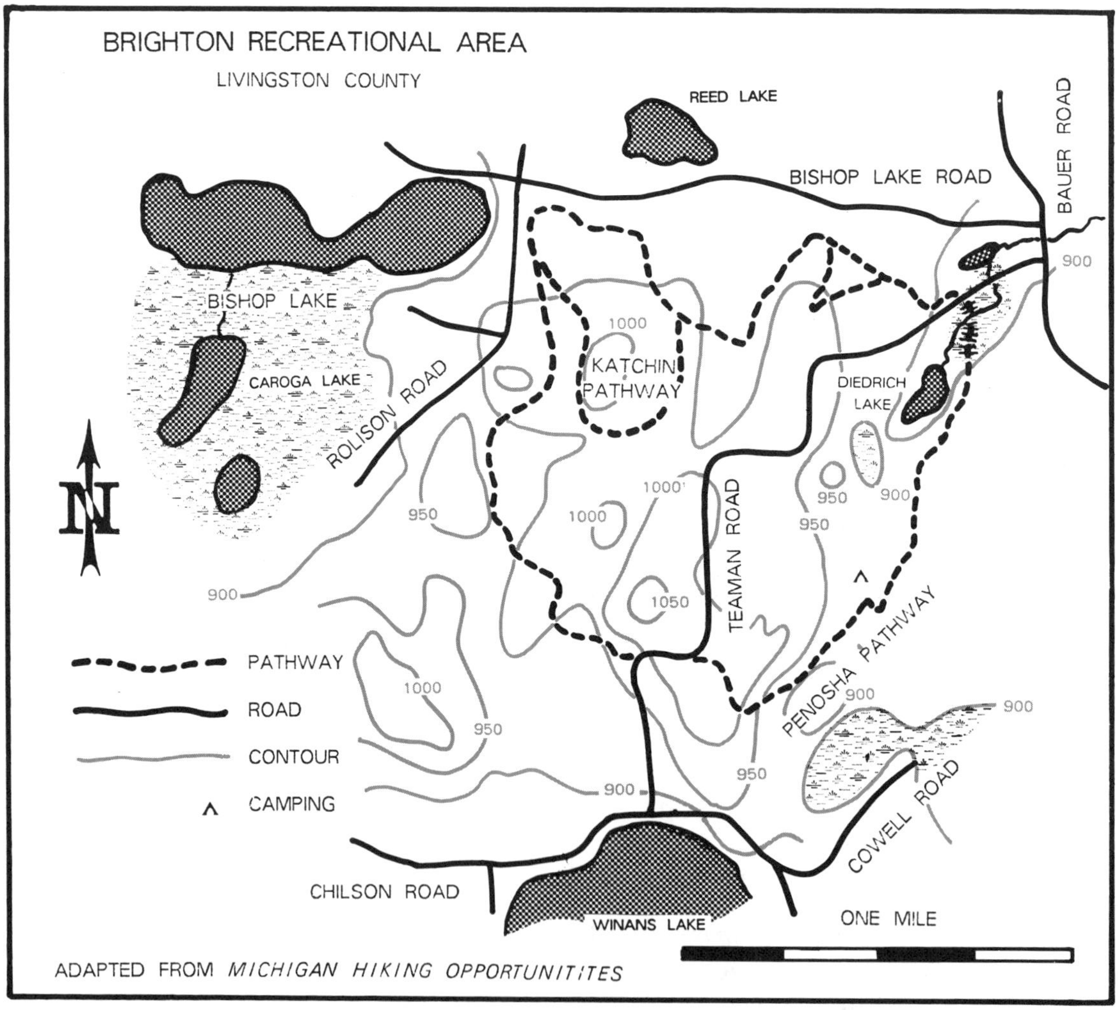

Skiing Groomed Trails at Maybury State Park

General

Finding a place to cross-country ski in well-groomed tracks is not easy in Michigan. What passes for grooming is usually just the packing of the trail by by a snowmobile, or one may encounter the combined tracks of earlier skiers. Tracks made in these ways have several deficiencies, including poor definition, improper radiusing, variable width, and so on. However, at Maybury State Park the concessionaire does a good job of setting and maintaining tracks, making it easy for anyone from the Ann Arbor area to enjoy the pleasures of cross-country skiing in tracks with only an hour or so spent in travel to the site.

Track skiing may be unfamiliar to many cross-country skiers who took up the sport as a way to maintain contact with nature in the winter, and to get away from crowds. To some degree track skiing is the antithesis of these objectives since it tends to concentrate skiers. This negative aspect notwithstanding, track skiing is an excellent way to improve one's technique, and it has charms of its own. One of the most appealing of these is the pleasure of free, unbridled gliding at sustained speeds that only very well-conditioned runners would normally attain.

The esthetics of track skiing can be enhanced by a favorable setting, and Maybury shines in this respect. The smallest of MIchigan state parks, it covers 946 acres of picturesque level-to-gently-rolling terrain that is typical of southeastern Michigan farmland. The absence of any great relief makes Maybury an excellent place for beginners to ski.

Maps

Wayne County Map (reference 1). U S Geological Survey

Salem 7.5' quadrangle. Trails are shown by the park map, which you can obtain at the concessionaire's hut adjacent to the parking lot. The map printed here is a condensed version of that map.

Other references

Michigan Cross Country Skiing Atlas (reference 11).

Travel from Ann Arbor

Maybury State Park is in the extreme northwest corner of Wayne County, approximately 18 miles from the center of Ann Arbor. Take Pontiac Trail to its intersection with Eight Mile Road. The park entrance is on Eight Mile about six miles east (to the right) of this intersection. A Michigan State Parks vehicle permit is required for entrance to the park.

Details

Adjacent to the parking lot is a warming hut where a concessionaire rents skis, and where a park map showing the ski trails may be obtained.

The trail network consists of three trails that total nine miles in length. The orange trail follows roads, and runs through hardwood forest, open fields, and skirts shrubby marshes. The first mile is fitted with street lamps that make lighted night skiing a special treat on certain week nights. Call park headquarters for the schedule.

The yellow trail is a true trail, and runs across open fields and through woodlots into the southeastern part of the park. This trail has somewhat sharper turns than the orange, and has small hills.

The most difficult trail is the white trail. Although it is skiable by novices over most of its length, there are a few short, steep uphills and downhills in the southeast corner of the park that may be difficult for the inexperienced skier. Near the center of the park off the white trail is a sledding hill that is open and steep enough for some fun downhilling, and just right for telemarking if the snow isn't too packed. Before starting down the hill, check for other skiers on other trails which cross the bottom of the hill on two sides.

Park headquarters telephone is 313-349-8390.

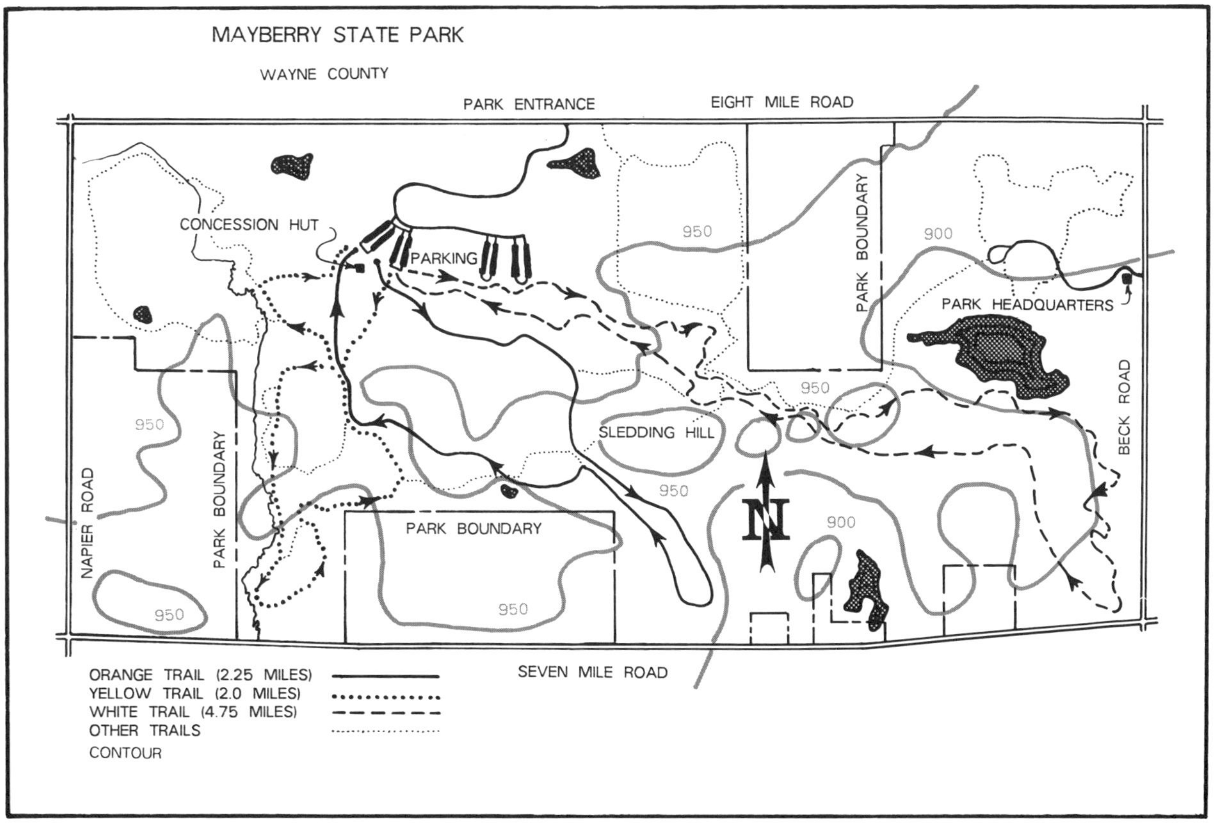

Canoeing the Portage River

General

The Portage River (one of several within 100 miles of Ann Arbor that bear this name) of which we speak rises in western Washtenaw County to flow almost due westward across Jackson County, there to empty into the Grand River about three miles north of Jackson. Driving time from Ann Arbor to the closest launching point is approximately 30 minutes. The river distance from there is on the order of 15 miles, with paddling time three to six hours.

The Portage is a small river, indeed so small for the first few miles from the suggested launching site that you may find it navigable only during spring and early summer. The river also has the interesting (or depressing, you may feel) aesthetic handicap of being straightened for a stretch of several miles to facilitate agricultural drainage. On the other hand, the straightening was done so long ago that the banks have returned to a natural wooded state. As a feature that eases the paddling/steering burden you may even appreciate the straightness.

Maps

Jackson County map (reference 1). The map printed here is a condensed adaptation of that map.

Other references

Canoe Sport of Ann Arbor (313-996-1393) publishes informal give-away data sheets on several southeastern Michigan rivers. The information you read here is condensed from its three Portage River sheets (sections 1, 2, and 3 of the river). Though this information should be adequate for field use, for all possible details you should ask for the Canoe Sport material.

Travel from Ann Arbor

The basic route is I-94 west to Mount Hope Road (Grass Lake exit at about 22 miles from the western edge of Ann Arbor), north on Mount Hope to Reithmiller Road, which crosses the river about two miles east (right) of its intersection with Mount Hope Road. That crossing is the uppermost launching point. Other launching points are noted on our map.

Details

There is no canoe rental service in the Portage River area, nor are there developed areas such as parks or campgrounds along the river.

The first third of the route, from launching at Reithmiller Road bridge to Portage Lake Road, just beyond Little Portage Lake, is clear water over sandy bottom, flowing through marsh and overhanging brush. Sandhill cranes, herons, warblers, and redwings are likely witnesses to river traffic. The current is modest, and there are no hazards save the nuisance hazards of overhanging brush and downed trees (river width on the order of 50 feet). Water may be insufficient for canoeing in dry seasons.

After flowing naturally and pleasantly for about two miles beyond Portage Lake Road, the river is disciplined into an artificially straightened section that extends for six or seven miles, or to within about a mile of the junction with the Grand River. The straightening has been done to facilitate agricultural drainage. Although this act was a blow to the river's charm, the banks are wooded, giving cover to birds and other small wildlife. Water quality begins to decline as runoff from fields joins the stream.

After the straightened stretch is passed, you find the river resumeing a more natural character as it flows through deep woods to its meeting with the larger Grand River. (See chapter on the Grand River.)

The Canoe Sport sheet mentions a short side excursion from the river to the dike that marks the north end of Portage Lake. See our map. The dike provides a good swimming and picnicing site.

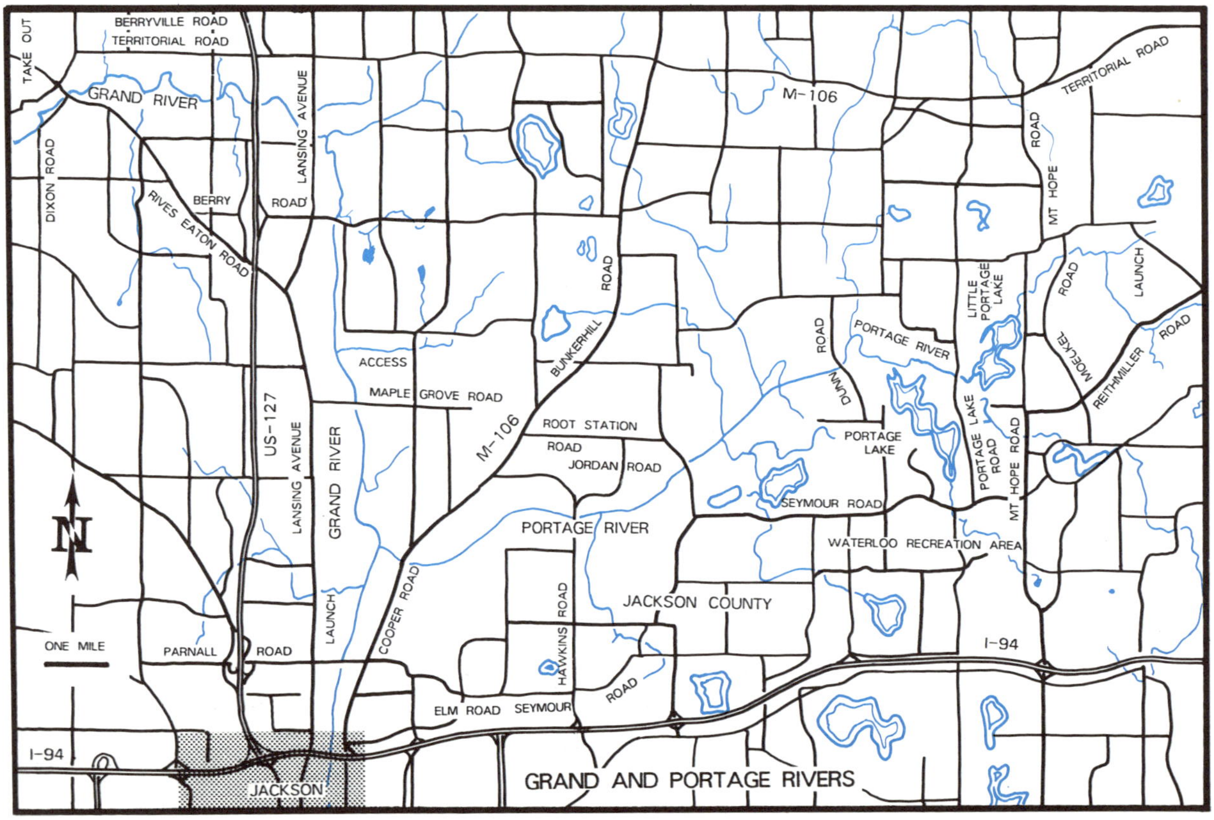

Canoeing on the Grand River in Jackson County

General

The Grand River rises in the northeastern corner of Hillsdale County, then flows northward through Jackson and Jackson County toward Lansing before turning westward toward Lake Michigan. It is canoe navigable over most of this length, a journey of some 200 miles and many days. The section described here is a stretch of 12 - 15 river miles, and three to four hours paddling, beginning on the northern outskirts of Jackson.

From the standpoint of a canoeist, the Grand in this section is wide and deep. It flows steadily with a modest current, and without hazards. Overhanging limbs and occasional downed trees provide obstacles, but obstacles that require carrying are unlikely. For roughly half the trip, the river is almost straight. A respondent describes this part as offering "a shaded avenue through maple, oak, and beech groves, and a secluded, restful ride." A wide variety of birds are reported, including owls.

Water quality appears to be poor. After all, the river has just passed through a city whose streets, and hence storm runoff, are as dirty as any other city's. You weren't going to drink from the river anyhow.

Maps

Jackson County map (reference 1).

Other references

Canoe Sport of Ann Arbor (13-996-1393) publishes informal

give-away data sheets on several southeastern Michigan rivers. The information you read here is condensed from its Grand River sheet. Although the present condensed form should be adequate on its own, for all possible details you should ask for the Canoe Sport material.

Travel from Ann Arbor

Take I-94 west to Jackson, then Elm Road north from I-94 exit 144. At approximately one mile from I-94, Elm Road turns 90 degrees and becomes Parnall Road and crosses the Grand River after another mile. The bridge is the uppermost launching site. Driving time is predicted to be about 45 minutes. Routes to other access sites are shown by our map.

Details

Lyle A Torrant School is located on the west bank of the river near Parnall Road bridge, and offers an alternative beginning point. Permission should be sought. The school's parking lot may be used for parking on weekends, and is advised because the Parnall Road shoulders don't offer safe parking. Another alternative beginning, favored by good river access and good parking, is the state access site at the Maple Grove Road bridge. However, a start there provides about an hour less canoeing.

The recommended take-out site is another state access site just after the second of two railroad trestles. A sign on this trestle indicates the site.

There are no canoe liveries in the Jackson area.

THE GRAND RIVER IS SHOWN ON THE PORTAGE RIVER MAP AT THE END OF THE PRECEDING CHAPTER.

A Bicycle Outing to Blissfield

General

Blissfield is a small town lying about 30 miles south of Ann Arbor. From Saline, which our respondent advises as a starting point, the round trip is about 55 miles over straight, hill-free roads with only light motor vehicle traffic. On Sundays the Hathaway House in Blissfield offers a great Sunday buffet brunch that welcomes damp cyclists, and this can be an objective that gives focus to the trip. Allow time for digestion!

The flat, open farmland between Saline and Blissfield offers little break to the wind, the cyclist's most common bane. However, a southwest wind is the most likely good-weather wind during the warm part of the year, so that the pain is likely to be concentrated in the outbound leg. Coming back with full belly you may love the help such a wind will give you.

Maps

Washtenaw County map, Lenawee County map (both reference 1). *Cycling Maps of Michigan* (reference 5).

Other references

None. However, if you want to alter the route, *Cycling Maps of Michigan* (reference 5) and *Bike Rides in Washtenaw County* (reference 7) may be helpful.

Travel from Ann Arbor

By car, easy; Main Street south becomes Saline Road. If you are going to cycle to Saline, consult *Bike Rides in Washtenaw County* (reference 7).

Details

If you motor to Saline, a good place to leave the car is the parking lot off Ann Arbor - Saline Road just after you cross Michigan Avenue (Saline Main Street, and also US-12).

The road to Blissfield is in fairly good condition (our 1985 report), except for a few rough spots along Britton Highway.

Our respondent advises pushing straight on from Saline to the Hathaway house in Blissfield, with diversions saved for the return. Several may be of interest. A fruit stand in Britton, about one block west on Route 50 from its crossing of Britton Highway, is worth a stop. A model log home, usually open for a visit, is on Ridge Road about a half-mile northeast from its crossing of Britton Highway. And Clinton-Macon Road, which you cross, seems to be the prowling grounds of an unusual number of antique cars.

The Hathaway House is located in Blissfield at 424 W Adrian. Its telephone is 517-486-2141. The part of the House serving the brunch is is called The Stables, quite suitable for the cyclist, and there are also some outdoor tables.

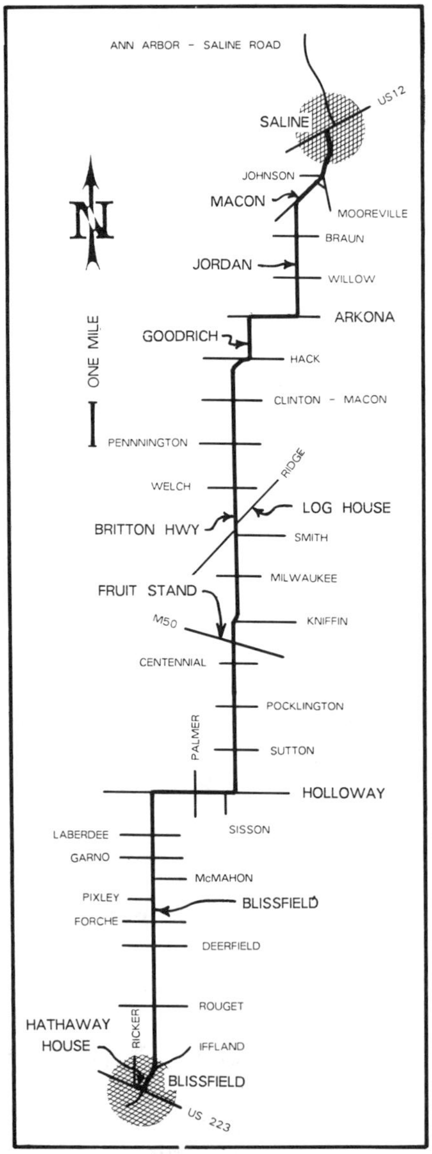

Hiking in the Waterloo Recreation Area

General

The Waterloo Recreation Area lies just west of Chelsea in western Washtenaw County and eastern Jackson County. Its distinguishing feature is a jumble of glacial hills among the relatively flat agricultural land surrounding them, and it is the hills that make the area what it is - land too broken for agriculture, and so left to forests laced with hiking and horseback trails. It is not, however, undiluted by habitations and other human artifices. Roads pass through, and scattered private land supports residences, and in the flatter parts, farms.

The main hiking trail covers a one-way route of about 17 miles east-west through the area. This trail is featured on the first of two maps reproduced here. You may note that it passes over two hills of note, Sackrider Hill and Pond Lily Lookout. Both of these offer wide vistas southward over flatter agricultural country.

The first map also shows the Outdoor Center, which offers exhibits interpreting the local wildlife, and is the origin of several local trails of the "nature trail" variety. (At publication time, the Outdoor Center was closed because of insufficient state support for its operation.)

Backpacking? Well, maybe, though the dayhiking seems to be overwhelm- ingly preferred by local users. Camping is permitted only in a few design-
ated campgrounds. A trail connecting Waterloo with the Pinckney Recreation Area was being opened in 1986, giving a much longer hiking experience, as therefore more incentive for backpacking.

This is a network of horseback trails, shown by the second map, and they are quite usable as hiking trails if you don't mind a certain, well, barnyard flavor. None of the trails have adequate protection against motor vehicles, and in consequence you may be annoyed by trail bikes and those three-
wheel frights. Love thy neighbor!

Maps

Washtenaw and Jackson county maps (reference 1), and U S Geological Survey Stockbridge quadrangle. The first of two maps printed here is adapted from a map published in *Footloose in Washtenaw* (reference 3); the second is based on the U S G S quadrangle, with trail data supplied by a Huron Valley Group respondent.

Other references

Footloose in Washtenaw (reference 3). The phone number of the Waterloo Recreation Area headquarters is 313-475-8307.

Travel from Ann Arbor

West on I-94 is your most likely route. The three exits immediately west of Chelsea (M-52), Kalmbach Road, Clear Lake Road, and Mount Hope Road, lead northward into the Area. Travel time from the center of Ann Arbor is about 30 minutes.

Details

Our principal advice on details is this: the trails are not well marked. Color blazes on trees, which some hikers declare to be the best way to mark a trail, have not been adopted in Waterloo. There is, indeed, a plethora of signs, but they do not distinguish one trail from another, and are at constant hazard from gunshot (yes, there's hunting in season), initials-carving, and assorted vandalism. New trails may be opened, without sanction, especially (so observation indicates) by horseriders taking shortcuts. If you are testing Waterloo for the first time, then it may be best to approach it as an explorer. A map and a compass may be important to your enjoyment.

Crosscountry skiing is possible, but one of our respondents gives the warning "pretty rugged." Trails tend to be narrow, and fallen tree hazzards have been noted.

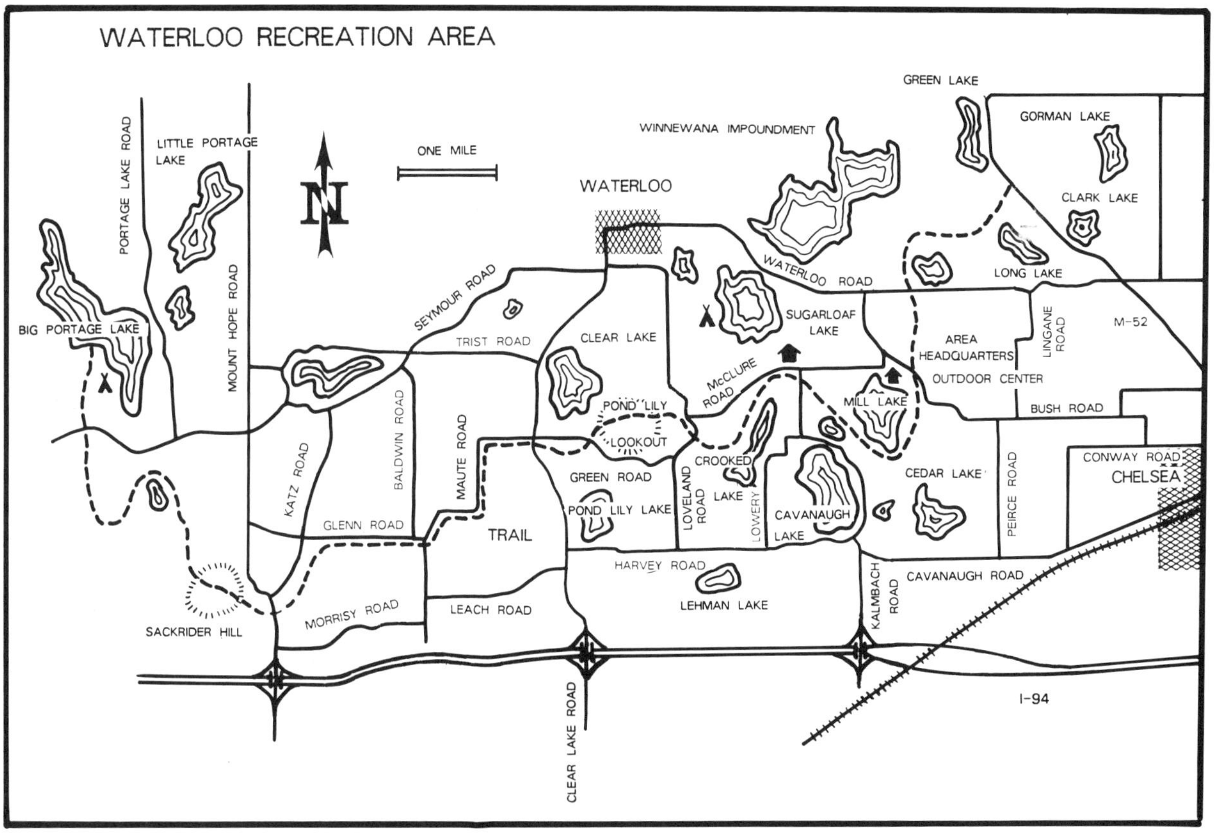

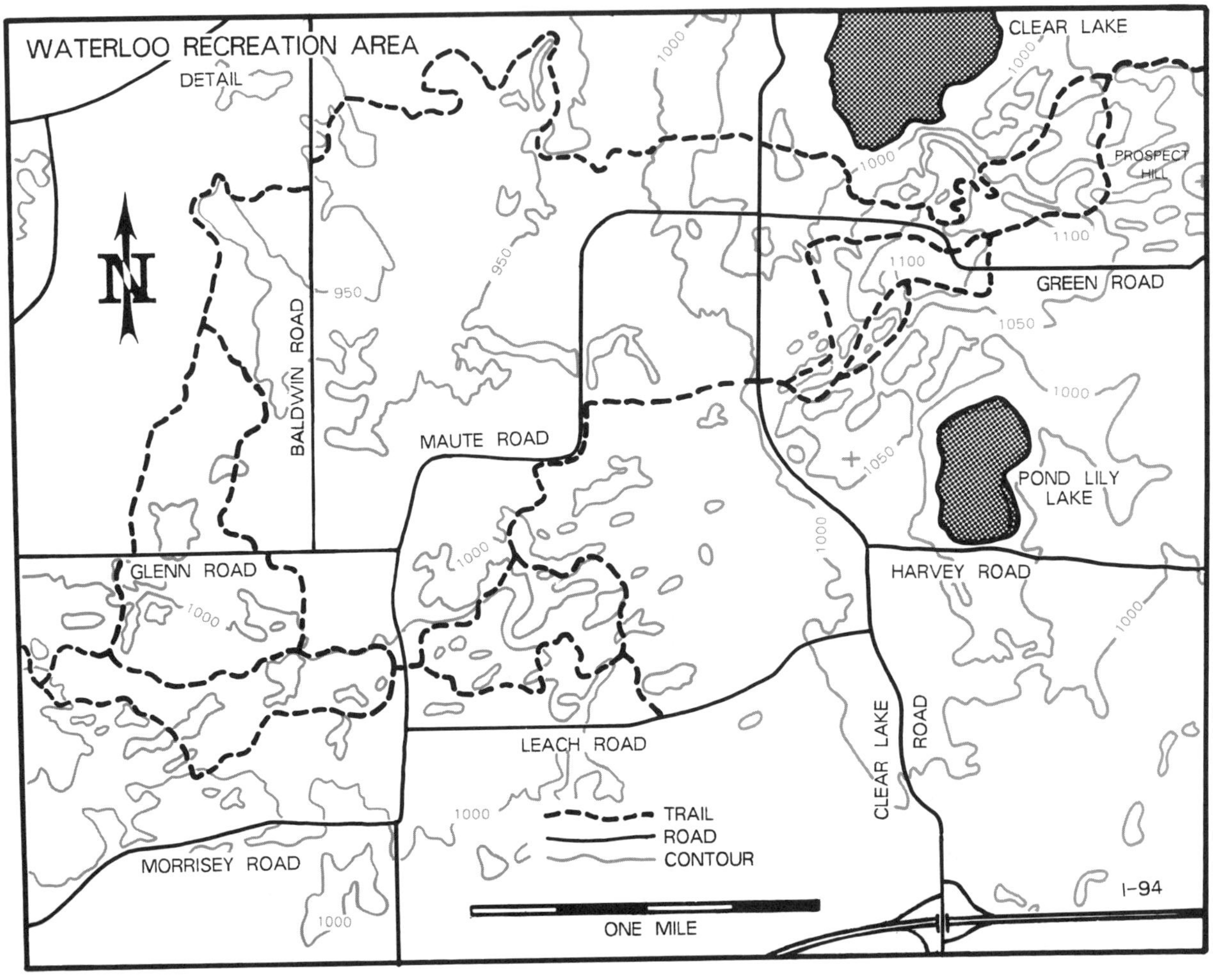
WATERLOO RECREATION AREA
DETAIL
CLEAR LAKE
PROSPECT HILL
BALDWIN ROAD
GREEN ROAD
MAUTE ROAD
POND LILY LAKE
GLENN ROAD
HARVEY ROAD
LEACH ROAD
CLEAR LAKE ROAD
MORRISEY ROAD
TRAIL
ROAD
CONTOUR
ONE MILE
I-94
950
1000
1050
1100

Canoeing the Kalamazoo River

General

The Kalamazoo rises in northern Hillsdale County and flows westward and slightly northward to its meeting with Lake Michigan at Saugatuck. Its total as-the-fish-swims length may be several hundred miles, but here we speak only of a short section of the river in Jackson and Calhoun Counties, not far from the source. The river is shallow, narrow, and twisty, but throughout most of this section the water is clear, the banks are wild, and wildlife is abundant. It extends from the Goose Lake Road bridge in southwestern Jackson County to Homer in southeastern Calhoun County.
River distance is uncertain, but minimum transit time (cruising speed) is about four hours. Driving time from Ann Arbor to either end should be little more than an hour.

The water moves at speeds up to four miles per hour over bottoms of sand, with some gravel. Banks are heavily wooded or brushy, giving the appearance of wilderness, even though roads are close at hand, and frequently cross the river. Agriculture begins to appear in the vicinity of Homer, and there the inevitable runoff begins to cloud the water.

A respondent reports seeing great horned owls, barred owls, yellow warblers, scarlet tanagers, herons, orioles, wood ducks, cedar waxwings, flycatchers, barn swallows, and brown thrashers.

Frequent sharp bends, overhanging limbs, and deadfalls that block the river demand at least moderate skill, and there are liftovers that call for some exertion.

Maps

Jackson and Calhoun County maps (reference 1).

Other references

Canoe Sport of Ann Arbor (313-996-1393) publishes informal give-away data sheets on several southeastern Michigan rivers. The information you read here is condensed from its Kalamazoo River sheets, Upper River, Part 3, and Upper River, Part 4. Although the present condensed form should be adequate on its own, for all possible details you should ask for Canoe Sport's material.

The river is also treated in *Canoeing Michigan Rivers* (reference 19).

Travel from Ann Arbor

The basic route is I-94 west to its exit 136, from there west on M-60 to Wheeler Road (2.7 miles west of Concord), and on Wheeler south to Twin Pines Campground, a possible put-in point. Routes upstream to a launching at Goose Lake Road bridge, or downstream to take-out points at Twenty-Nine Mile Road, or Homer, are shown by our map.

Details

Canoe rental, including shuttle service, is available from Twin Pines Campground & Canoe Livery. Call 517-524-6298.

Canoe Sport data lists several spots where downed trees require carrying or lifting over. These are changeable, of course - a chainsaw working one day, another tree falling the next. However, most of the blowdowns, and the worst, are likely to be encountered downstream of the Twenty-nine Mile Road bridge, which is therefore suggested as an alternative take-out point.

A more permanent potential obstacle is a low (about eight inches) rock dam under the third bridge downstream from Twin Pines Campground. It channels the flow through an easily-run sluice just to the left of the middle bridge support.

The take-out point for this section of the river is at the True Grist Mill in Homer. Reaching it requires passing the mill dam by carrying on the right, or by sliding the boat down a sluice ramp, which you can locate and assess by stopping to scout the the dam.

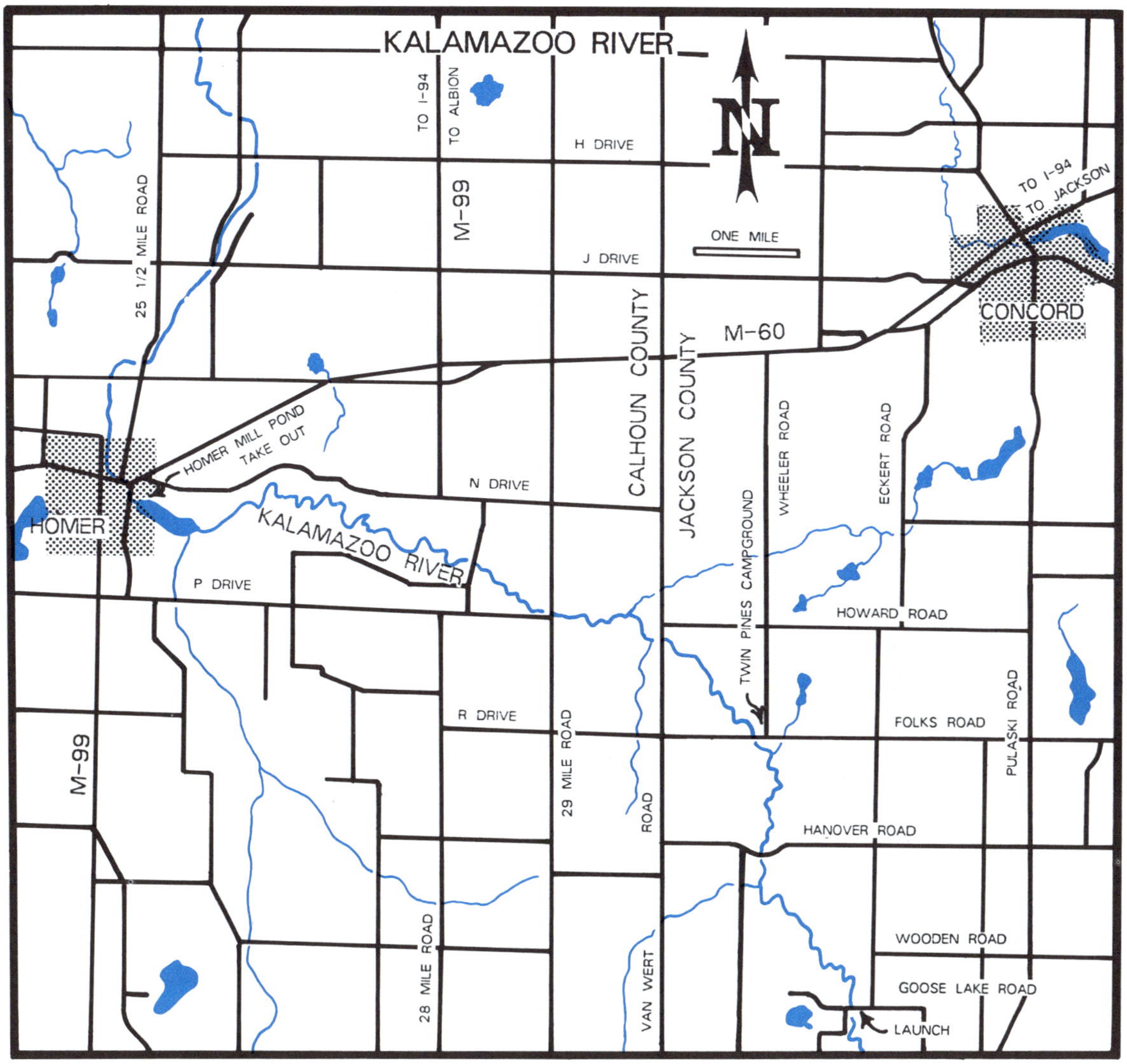

Michigan Outings

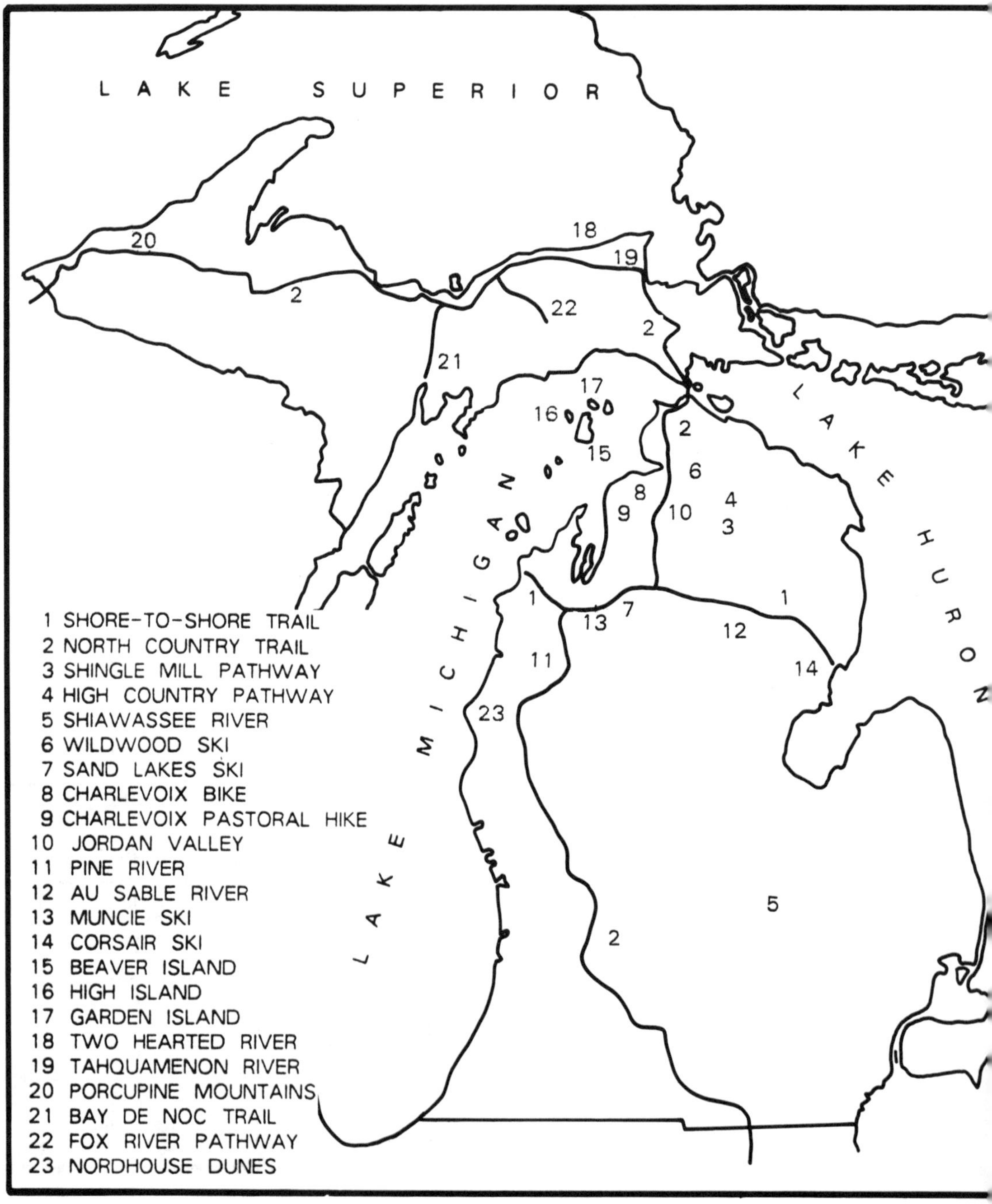

Michigan Outings

This is the heart of the book, and it could be a heart of 10,000 pages if we tried to cover everything of joy to be found over that immense span of country lying between Ann Arbor and Isle Royale. Limited to the recommendations of the connoisseurs assembled of the Sierra Huron Valley Group, it's still a hefty serving of hiking, backpacking, cycling, skiing, canoeing, and like pleasures. Read, and you'll see why the contributors believes you'll love it too.

Long Trails of Michigan

A "long" trail is a trail that... well, definitions are surely arguable, but for our purposes, a long trail is one that takes you from one place to another (i.e. is not a loop), and that requires more than one day to traverse. To really fit the category, it should take *many* days, and should so wear the hikers that they feel terribly proud of themselves at the end, so proud that they will expect recognition - like a shoulder patch - from some sponsoring organization.

The Appalachian Trail, winding along ridge crests (mostly) for 2000 miles from Georgia to Maine, is the American prototype. The Long Trail of Vermont, a branch of the Appalachian Trail that runs the length of Vermont, suggests the generic name we are using here. The Pacific Crest Trail, running from Mexico to Canada, is another prominent example. And likewise is Ontario's Bruce Trail, a trail whose northernmost 20 miles is the setting for a chapter in this book.

Michigan has two named trails that easily fit the long trail definition: the North Country Trail and the Shore-to-Shore Riding/Hiking Trail.

The North Country Trail is intended to run through the northern tier of states from New York (Crown Point) to North Dakota. ("Intended" because it is not complete as this is being written in 1986.) As such, it will be an east-west equivalent of the Appalachian Trail, but unfortunately, after emerging from the Adirondacks in New York it doesn't have the Appalachians to shield it from the multifarious intrusions of the urban Northeast. In consequence, the segment that parallels the south shore of Lake Superior through the Upper Peninsula may be the best part of the trail. A *good* part, at the very least. In 1985, an 80-mile length running from Whitefish Bay past Tahqhamenon Falls to the Lake Superior Shore, then close along the shore to and through the Pictured Rocks, was in service, and more attractive than anything to be walked in places like Ohio, say. Or even in the Lower Peninsula of Michigan.

The Upper Peninsula part is shown in *Michigan Hiking*

Opportunities (reference 2). For addditional information, contact the North Country Trail Association. See our *Information Sources* appendix for address.

The Bay de Noc - Grand Island Trail runs for approximately 36 miles on a north-south axis through Alger and Delta Counties in the Upper Peninsula, from Rapid River at the head of Little Bay de Noc to an intersection with M-94. When the North Country Trail is completed in this neighborhood it will have a short spur south to join the BdN-GI Trail. A map and textual description of the latter are given in *Michigan Hiking Opportunities.*

Another Upper Peninsula Trail that is at least semi-long (as we might also designate the trail just discussed) is the 28-mile Fox River Pathway that follows the Fox River northwestward from Seney in Schoolcraft County toward Lake Superior. The completed North Country Trail will also be joined to this trail at its northern end, and a map and very detailed textual description are given in *Michigan Hiking Opportunities.*

The Riding/Hiking Trail crosses the northern Lower Peninsula on an approximate east-west line from Tawas City on Lake Huron to Empire on Lake Michigan, a trail distance of about 180 miles. Of necessity, it must intersect several major highways, including I-75, as well as lesser roads, but for the most part, stays in the woods following either foot paths or old logging roads. The terrain varies; two broad bands of hill land are crossed, with intervening plain, and plain near the Lakes Huron and Michigan margins. Campgrounds are provided for those who don't like to lie down beside the trail when the sun sets. Most of the campgrounds provide hitching posts for your horses - note that the trail is for riders as well as hikers.

Michigan Hiking Opportunities contains a map that gives the general location of the Riding/Hiking Trail, and shows approximate locations of its campgrounds. However, no textual information is supplied by that book. County maps (reference 1) do not show the trail. The best source of detailed information is Michigan Trail Riders Association. See our *Information Sources* appendix for address.

Hiking enthusiasts with less restrictive definitions than ours might lengthen the list of long trails. The High Country Pathway in the Pigeon River Country State Forest east of Gaylord (see our chapter) is approximately 70 miles in length, and engages the backpacker for a week. However, it is a loop, and so merely brings its users back to their starting point. And the connecting link between the Pinckney Recreation Area and the Waterloo Recreation Area - just completed at publication time - will provide a network of trails that can provide three or four days of steady walking. But again, a truly long hike requires the inclusion of several loops. To each his own fun. And hers.

The outings locations map at the beginning of this section shows approximately the routes of the North Country Trail, Shore-to-Shore Trail, Bay de Noc - Grand Island Trail, and the Fox River Pathway.

Exploring High Island

General

High Island is an uninhabited member of the Beaver group in the northern end of Lake Michigan, lying about five miles west of Beaver Island itself. If you are unfamiliar with that neighborhood, a glance at a Michigan road map, or at the Charlevoix County map (reference 1) will show the location. The island is not served by any form of public transportation; reaching it requires the use of a privately owned boat, and moreover a boat that can safely cross the open waters of Lake Michigan.

The uninhabited status of the island, and the difficulty in reaching it, are large factors in its appeal. Although it once supported a population sufficient to require a post office, and sustained heavy lumbering (a 1915 observation speaks of it as having only "scattered patches of woods") in the early twentieth century, it has been totally owned since 1959 by the state, and is now part of the Beaver Islands Wildlife Research Area. It has returned to a virtual wilderness condition. Dense forests cover the island except for clearings that are the legacy of farming that continued into the 1930s, and a cattle-raising enterprise of the 1950s. Trails remain by which hikers can explore an area that is wild and unlittered, but in which there are intriguing remnants of the departed human population.

The only practicable access point is the halfmoon bay at the island's northeast corner. Here deep water (on the order of 20 to 30 feet) reaches within a few meters of the beach, and the adjacent land provides shelter for an anchored boat. A glance at our map will show that this bay is exposed to easterly and southerly winds, but strong winds from those directions are not common during the boating season. The adjacent shore area was the principal site of past human habitation, and is still open enough for campers to pitch their tents.

The principal point of interest to most visitors is the peak of the dunes that border the western shore of the island. The highest spot, about 225 feet above the level of Lake Michigan permits a

360-degree view that encompasses all of the island and most of the other islands of the Beaver group as well. The dunes are reached by a path that leads leads from the beach through a band of dense woods into a large clearing that extends across the island to the foot of the dunes.

The visible remains of the human population are scant and scattered, but may be of interest to visitors. The most evident remains are those of the most recent occupation, a cattle farm that was in operation for a few years during the mid-1950s. The "state cabins" near the beach (see map), now kept as habitation for visiting wildlife researchers, were the housing for the cattle farmers (apparently it was an "agribusiness" rather than a family farm). Hikers to the dunes will pass abandoned farm machinery, fragments of fences, collapsed ruins of a barn., and even a pole from which obviously hung a windsock such as still seen at small airports. Just behind the beach toward the south end of the bay lie the remains of several dwellings, apparently of older vintage than the cattle business. Remnants of worm fencing can be found near the edges of the clearings.

Another feature of interest is the waterfowl (preponderantly gulls) rookery on the sandy spit that thrusts into the lake from the northeastern corner of the island. A sign asks you to stay clear, and gulls themselves deliver the message to anyone who can't or won't read the sign.

Maps

Charlevoix County map (reference 1), U S Geological Survey Beaver Island 15' quadrangle, NOAA chart 14911, and Map 2058 of the Michigan Department of Natural Resources (dated 1966, and apparently no longer available). All of these maps show roads or trails, but none are accurate in this respect.

The least accurate is the NOAA chart, which shows several double-dashed lines that usually denote "poor dirt road." On-site search has revealed no trace of them in 1986.

The DNR map shows a network of trails that may indeed have existed when the map was made, since some of them can still (1986) be found, but much of the network appears to have disappeared from non-use. This map is reproduced here.

The county map repeats the DNR map trail information.

The USGS topographic map, with the notation "field check 1956" shows a trail network that is similar to the DNR one, but which is less extensive.

The map that was made for this book is a modified version of the DNR map. It shows only those trails whose usability was checked by hikers in 1986.

Other references

None.

Travel from Ann Arbor

You can't get there from here! Not without the proper boat, that is. The closest place that can be reached by public transportation is St James, the settlement on Beaver Island (see our chapter on Beaver Island backpacking). A rented boat or arranged transportation are possibilites. The "Beaver Island Guide," a brochure for the tourist published in St James, lists (1986) the Beaver Haven marina (616-448-2300) as providing "island hopping," and Terry Van Arkle (616-448-2240) and Perry Gatliff (616-448-2311) as providing charter boat service.

Details

If you visit the island, presumably you will land on the beach of the northeastern bay where deep water comes close to shore. The trail to the interior is a sandy path that can be found by walking along the beach while looking carefully. You are unlikely to find a sign or other marker, but the path should be evident. In 1986 a small buoy (plastic bottle) was anchored just off shore from the trail head. The trail takes you to the state cabins at the edge of the woods, follows around the northern corner of the cabins into the woods and on to the main clearing. At that point it becomes indistinct, but in 1986 was evident enough to be followed all the way to the dunes. If not distinct, then a due-west compass course through the clearing will take you to the foot of the dunes.

The only source of water, other than Lake Michigan, is a well that is inside the more northern of the two state cabins.

Wildflowers are spectacular around the first of July. On the other hand, poison ivy is a pervasive threat. Careful!

A unique episode in the history of this island was its ownership by the House of David, a religious order resident in Benton Harbor, Michigan. The House of David began buying island property in 1912 for the purpose of harvesting timber, and soon owned all of the island except for the homes of a few Indian fishing families. After the timber resource was expended, the House of David turned to potato farming, an activity that seems to have been most prominent in the 1930s. After World War II, the House of David declined in numbers and in vigor, and apparently soon abandoned exploitation of the island. In 1952 it sold all of its High Island property to interests who established the cattle-raising operation.

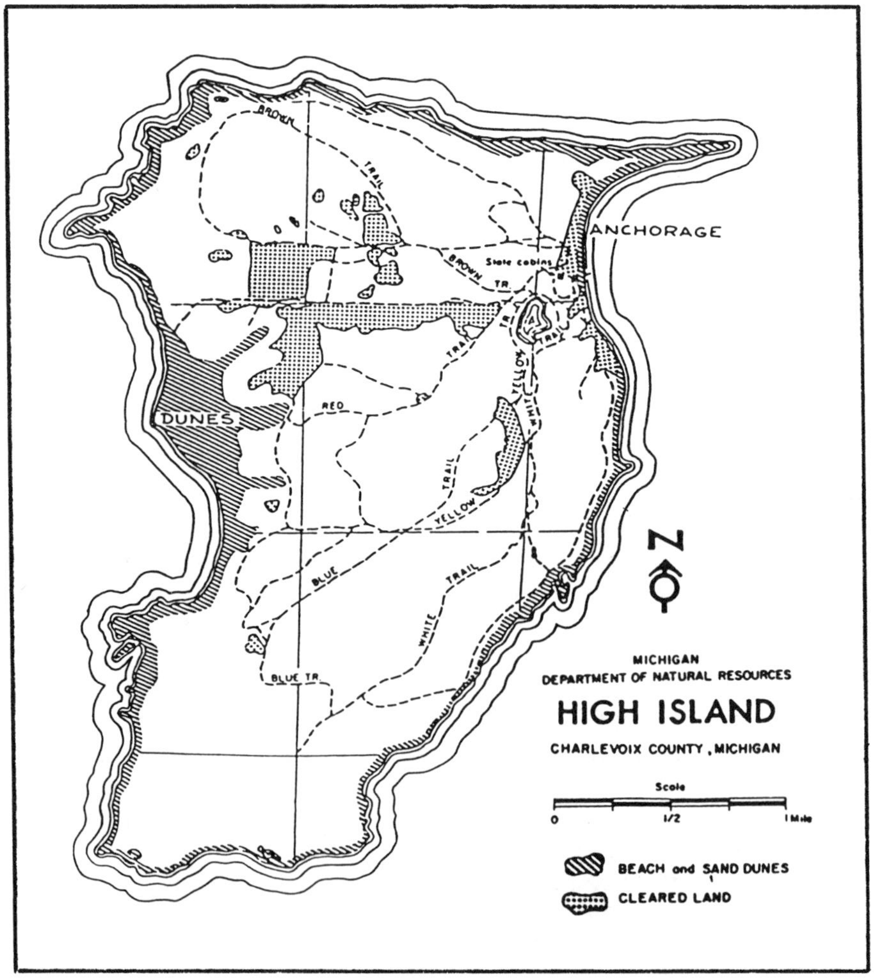

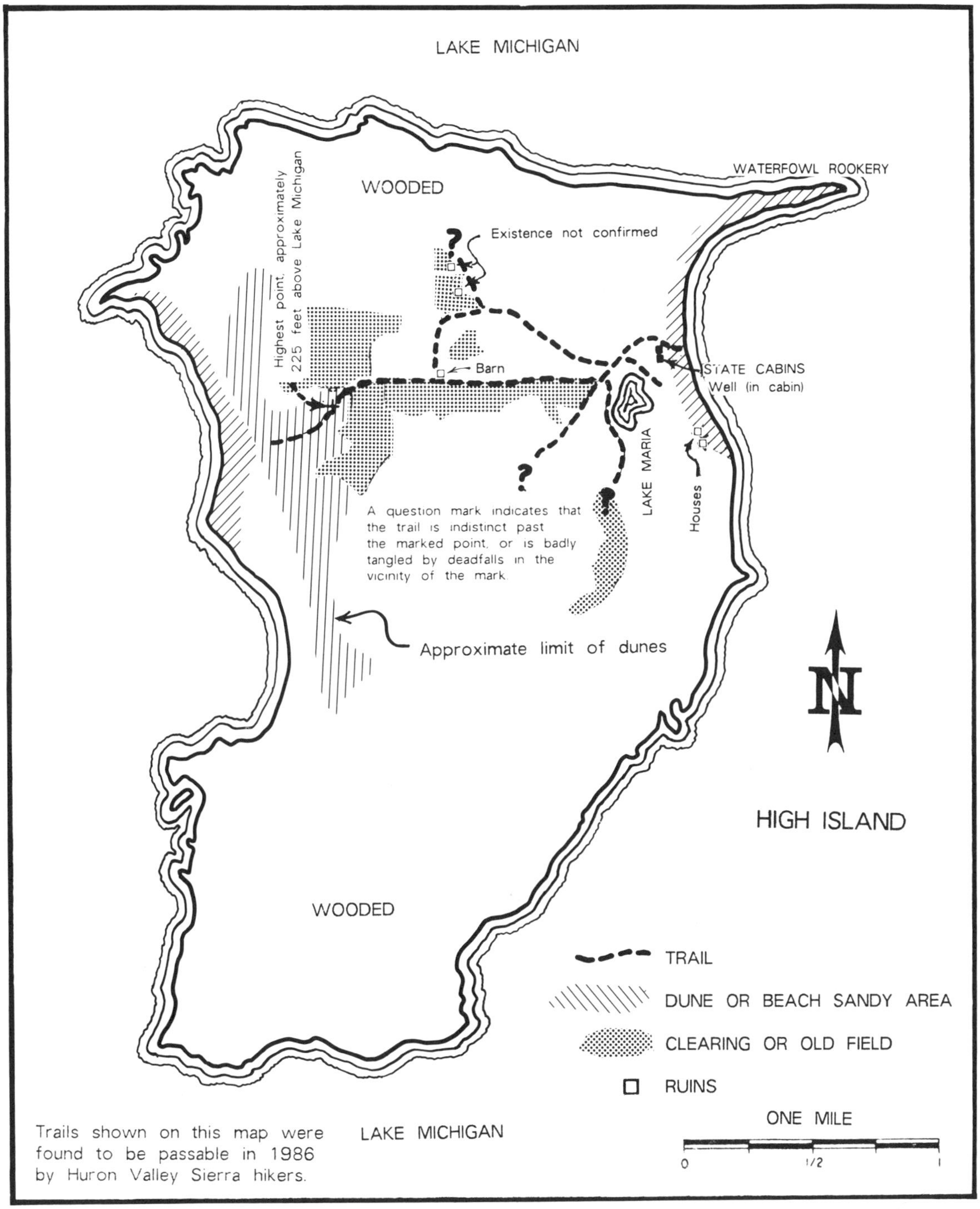
LAKE MICHIGAN
WOODED
Highest point, approximately 225 feet above Lake Michigan
Existence not confirmed
WATERFOWL ROOKERY
Barn
STATE CABINS
Well (in cabin)
LAKE MARIA
Houses
A question mark indicates that the trail is indistinct past the marked point, or is badly tangled by deadfalls in the vicinity of the mark.
Approximate limit of dunes
N
HIGH ISLAND
WOODED
TRAIL
DUNE OR BEACH SANDY AREA
CLEARING OR OLD FIELD
RUINS
ONE MILE
0
1/2
1
Trails shown on this map were found to be passable in 1986 by Huron Valley Sierra hikers.
LAKE MICHIGAN

Exploring Garden Island

General

Garden Island is an uninhabited member of the Beaver group, lying in the northern end of Lake Michigan. It is not served by public transportation, and therefore must be reached by private boat. In these respects it is much like High Island. Garden is somewhat closer to the town of St James on Beaver, and at the closest point to that island is only a little more than a mile away. In fact, one of our respondents reports crossing from St James in a canoe.

Garden is also much like High Island in that it was formerly inhabited by Indians, and then by scattered white families who lived by fishing, farming, and timber harvest. It had sufficient population to support a post office which is still standing, though seemingly standing only because of the support of the densely encroaching vegetation. A respondent who attempted to photograph it reports that it also seems to be guarded by a cordon of snakes. And like High Island, private ownership has disappeared in favor of state ownership, and both islands are now part of the same Beaver Islands Wildlife Research Area.

Trails abound, and although unmarked, are not difficult to follow. (You may find an occasional ribbon gracing a tree along some trails, but their message is not evident.) The presence on the trails of occasional spent shotgun shell indicates that the island has some popularity with hunters, and their use may account for the fairly good condition of the trails.

The island is flat with no significant viewing point like that of High Island. Its major point of interest is an Indian cemetary, which for some years served as the burial place for the native population of all of the Beaver group.

The principal point of entry is the bay (Garden Island Harbor) that faces west on the south side of the island. Unlike High Island, however, the harbor is not fronted by beach, and is quite shallow. Northcutt Bay, facing south almost directly north of St James on Beaver, is another entry point, though also shallow. It does have considerable beach frontage with good camping spots.

Maps

Charlevoix County map (reference 1), U S Geological Survey Garden Island West 7.5 minute quadrangle and Hog Island 15' quadrangle, NOAA chart 14911, and an unnumbered Department of Conservation (now Department of Natural Resources) map.

The NOAA chart is essential for those approaching the island in boats of deep draft, but the "roads" it shows on the island no longer exist. The other maps show essentially the same networks of trails, some of which appear to be the overgrown remnants of those roads. Explorations by our respondents in 1986 confirmed the existence of the trails shown by the maps, although it was difficult to be sure of the accuracy of the matchup between ground and map in some cases.

The map printed here is adapted from the Department of Conservation map.

Other references

None

Travel from Ann Arbor

See the instructions for High Island and for Beaver Island.

Details

There are three feasible points of entry: Northcutt Bay, Indian Cove (a cove branching off Garden Island Harbor), and the extreme eastern end of Garden Island Harbor behind Little Island. These appear on our map, but all are areas of shallow water, so that use of the NOAA chart is essential for a safe approach.

The trailhead at Northcutt Bay is easily found by exploration of the beach. In 1986, at least, no exploration was necessary because a campsite bench was visible at the trailhead from some distance out on the water.

Indian Cove trailhead was obscured in 1986 by the extreme high water of Lake Michigan. Our respondents, landing from an inflatable boat, had to stumble through a mooshy fringe of woods looking for the trail. However, the clearing at Indian Cove shown by the map is visible from the water, and the path through the clearing is easily found. This clearing may be suitable for camping, though no source of potable water is evident. The Indian cemetery is easily reached from the clearing through the guidance of the map printed here.

The trailhead opposite Little Island was formerly marked by a small pier, but high water and decay had destroyed it by 1986. The trail could still be found by close inspection from the water, and reached without wading. A decent camping spot can be found nearby, along the trail south from the state cabin.

Although the map printed here is adapted from and old source, field checks indicate that it still gives a good picture of trails and clearings. However, some cultural features may be overgrown. For example, a 1986 respondent reports reaching the end of Pete Monatou's trail without being able to find any evidence of his farm.

Garden Island

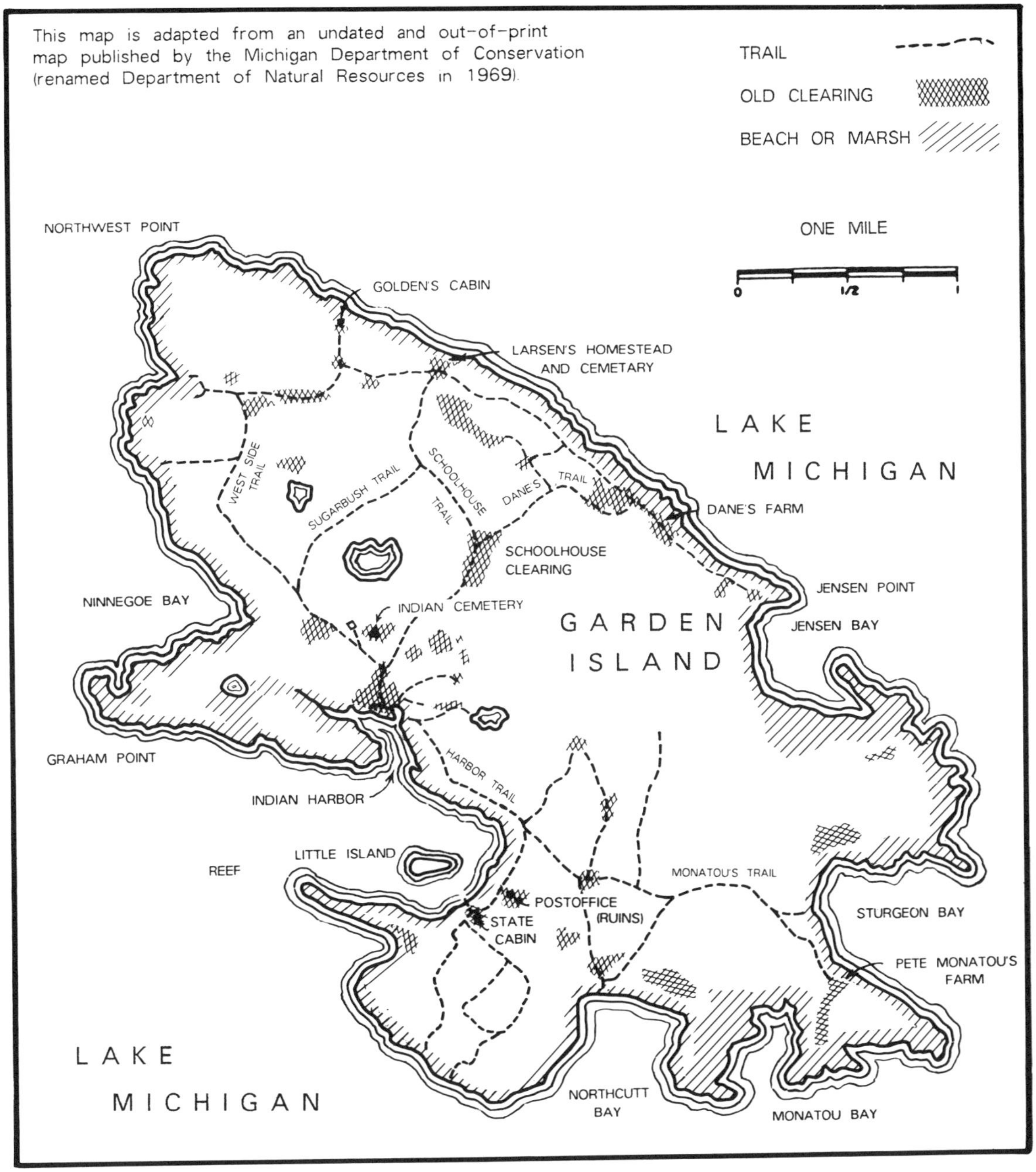

This map is adapted from an undated and out-of-print map published by the Michigan Department of Conservation (renamed Department of Natural Resources in 1969).

Skiing Wildwood Hills

General

Wildwood Hills, about 12 miles east of Petoskey, is located in a snow belt that seems almost guaranteed to have snow on the ground from December through March. Equally important, the area features an excellent trail system totalling almost 11 miles of trail. The terrain and scenery is typical northern Michigan; trails pass through mixed oak-hickory forest and occasional stands of white and red pine. Open meadows are found in the southeast. Terrain is rolling to hilly, and has a pleasant rollercoaster aspect.

Wildwood Hills does not present difficult skiing, but the area is large, so that lone skiers face the danger of becoming lost, although trails are generally well marked. Our respondents recommend that novices stay on loops 1 and 2 unless accompanied by experienced skiers.

A trail, well marked by a Department of Natural Resources sign, leads south from loop 3 to a connection with the Lost Tamarack Nature Pathway. Its trails furnish several more miles of skiing, and give access to a campground that may be used for winter camping. At the time of publication, no trail map for Lost Tamarack was available.

Maps

Emmet and Cheboygan County maps (reference 1). U S Geological Survey Woverine 15' quadrangle. The map printed here is adapted from *Michigan HIking Opportunities* (reference 2).

Other references

Michigan Cross Country Skiing Atlas (reference 11).

Travel from Ann Arbor

Go either to Petoskey or Indian River under guidance of any Michigan road map. From Petoskey, take Mitchell Road east for about 8 miles to the point where it curves to the right to bear away due south. Wildwood Road splits off to the left (east) at the beginning of this curve to continue east. Take Wildwood for about 5 miles to the west parking lot.

From Indian River, take Old 27 south about 3 miles to Wildwood Road. Take Wildwood right (west) for about 3 miles to the east parking lot.

Details

The west parking lot is larger, and permits more options in combining the several loops of the trail network. Loop 1 covers 3.4 miles; loop 2 4.3 miles, and loop 3 4.2 miles. Ream Road, running north-south through the middle of the area, is closed to traffic, and can be used as a shortcut, or as part of an ad hoc loop.

Note that our map has one segment of trail marked "existence doubtful." This caveat comes from a respondent who explored the Wildwood trails in July 1986, and reported that he was unable to find this segment, nor any sign indicating its location.

For snow conditions, call 616-238-9313.

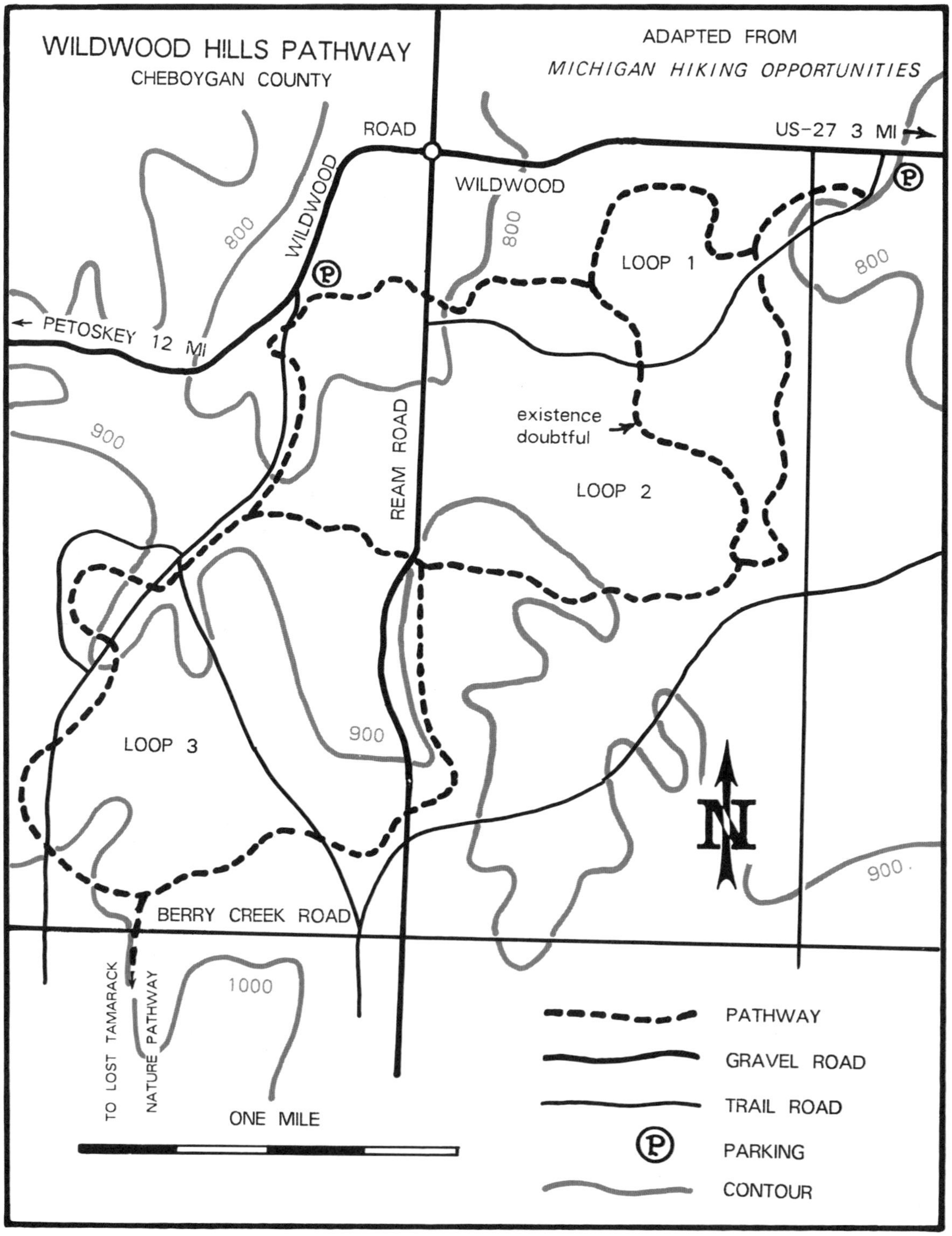
WILDWOOD HILLS PATHWAY
CHEBOYGAN COUNTY
ADAPTED FROM
MICHIGAN HIKING OPPORTUNITIES
ROAD
US-27 3 MI
WILDWOOD
WILDWOOD
800
800
800
LOOP 1
PETOSKEY 12 MI
900
existence
doubtful
REAM ROAD
LOOP 2
LOOP 3
900
900
BERRY CREEK ROAD
TO LOST TAMARACK
NATURE PATHWAY
1000
ONE MILE
PATHWAY
GRAVEL ROAD
TRAIL ROAD
PARKING
CONTOUR

Skiing in the Sand Lakes Quiet Area

General

The Sand Lakes Quiet Area is located just a few miles southeast of Traverse City in northwestern lower Michigan. The area covers about 2800 acres encompassing a trail network that totals about 13 miles.

The area is covered by a mixture of oak and pine forest, and on its southern boundary runs along the edge of the Boardman River valley. A portion of the Michigan shore-to-shore trail passes close to the southern boundary.

Sand Lakes is also a delightful place for winter camping. There is a hike-in, ski-in campsite at the spot marked "wells & toilets" on the map. This site is only about 3/4 mile from the winter parking lot.

Sand Lakes is also suitable for short beginners' backpacking, since there are small hike-in campsites on all of the lakes (not shown on any map).

Maps

Grand Traverse County Map (reference 1). U S Geological Survey Fife Lake 15' quadrangle. The map printed here is an adaptation of the Sand Lakes Quiet Area map included in *Michigan Hiking Opportunities* (reference 2).

Other references

Michigan Cross-Country Skiing Atlas (reference 11).
Michigan Hiking Opportunities (reference 2).

Travel from Ann Arbor

We'll assume you go by way of Traverse City, following the guidance of any Michigan road map. From Traverse City, take M-72 east through Williamsburg. At one mile east of Williamsburg, turn south (right) onto Cook Road. After about 3/4 mile on Cook, jog left for 1/2 mile to Bromhead Road, which is to be taken south (right) for 2 1/2 miles to the Sand Lakes parking lot.

Details

A variety of loops can be taken, but informed opinion recommends the loop trail around the center of the area, as shown by the heavy dashed line on the map printed here. This loop is fairly level, consisting in part of old two-track roads and an old railroad bed. The narrower trails that run east and west across the center of the area go over some very steep hills. Most of the hills have straight downhill runs from which you can continue out onto the frozen lakes.

A detail of possible interest to a hot-weather visitor is a rope swing out into the water of the northernmost lake.

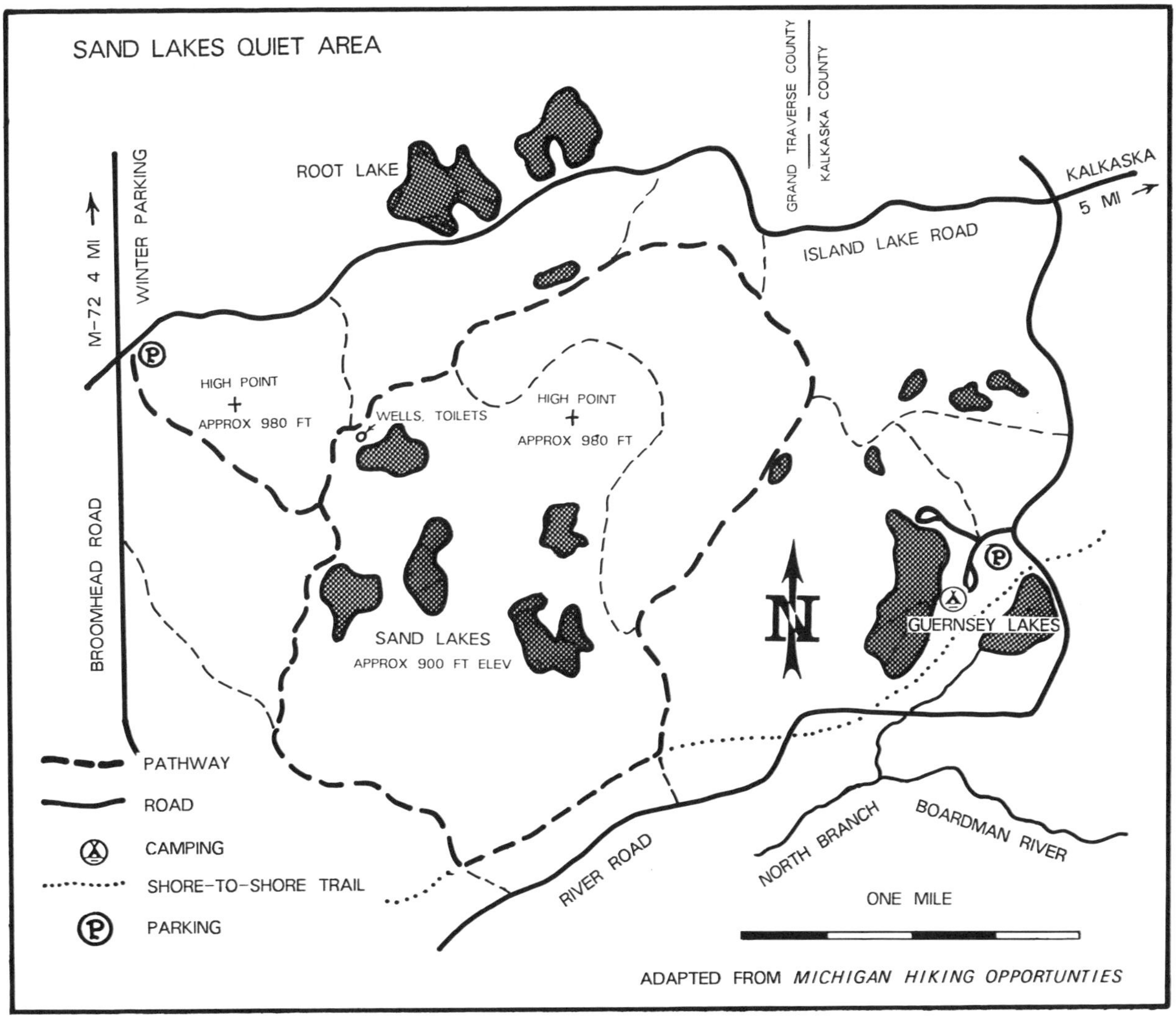
SAND LAKES QUIET AREA
ROOT LAKE
GRAND TRAVERSE COUNTY
KALKASKA COUNTY
KALKASKA
5 MI
ISLAND LAKE ROAD
M-72 4 MI
WINTER PARKING
HIGH POINT
APPROX 980 FT
WELLS, TOILETS
HIGH POINT
APPROX 980 FT
BROOMHEAD ROAD
SAND LAKES
APPROX 900 FT ELEV
N
GUERNSEY LAKES
PATHWAY
ROAD
CAMPING
SHORE-TO-SHORE TRAIL
PARKING
RIVER ROAD
NORTH BRANCH
BOARDMAN RIVER
ONE MILE
ADAPTED FROM MICHIGAN HIKING OPPORTUNTIES

Circumnavigating Lake Charlevoix on a Bicycle

General

This trip is *de rigeur* for any summer visitor cycling in the neighborhood of Charlevoix. And it isn't too difficult for the non-macho cyclist, since the road doesn't deviate too far from the level of Lake Charlevoix. Distance is about 33 miles.

Maps

Charlevoix County map (reference 1), U S Geological Survey Bayshore and Boyne City 15' quadrangles, and any Michigan road map. The map here is made from the county map.

Other references

Cycling Maps of Michigan (reference 5) is certainly a reference, but contains no information not found in the text here plus the county map.

Travel from Ann Arbor

Charlevoix is four to five hours in road time from Ann Arbor. Any Michigan road map will show you the way.

Details

The trip is all on public two-lane highway, and so has its obvious hazards, but traffic is usually light.

The ferry passage across the South Arm of Lake Charlevoix at Ironton (notice that we're describing a ride around only the main part of the lake) is an interesting interlude, and a rest if you should need one. There has traditionally been no toll for pedestrians and bicycles, but we can't guarantee the perpetual continuance of that happy circumstance.

A large city park on the waterfront in Boyne City also provides a good stopping/resting/eating place. Those interested in boats might find modest amusement in viewing the craft docked at the municipal marina that is located in the park.

Such hills as there are occur mainly on the north side of the lake.

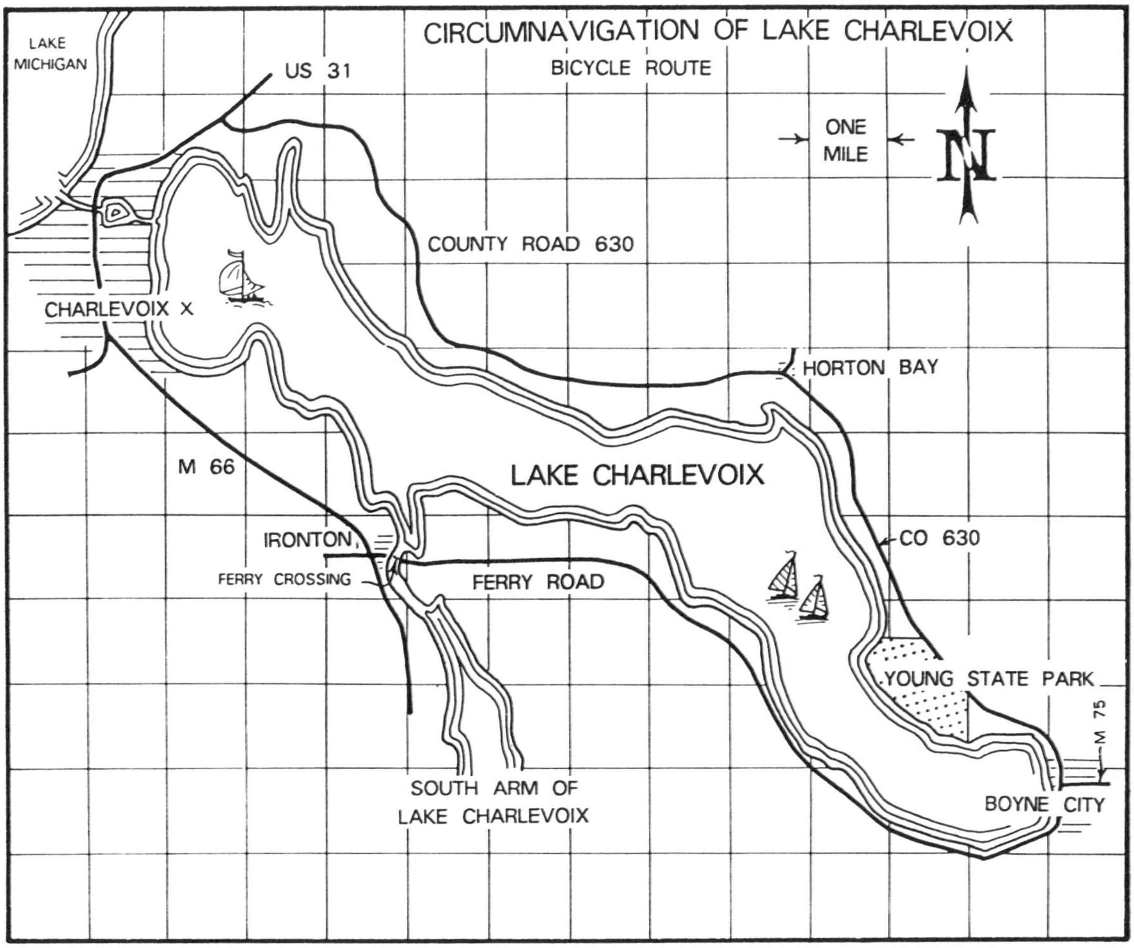

Backpacking on Beaver Island

General

Beaver Island is the main member of a group of islands in the northern reaches of Lake Michigan, lying 40 to 50 miles west (and a little south) of the Mackinac Bridge. (High and Garden Islands, covered in other chapters, are lesser members of the same group.) At its northeastern corner, a spit of land curls around to the east and south to form the harbor of St James, a settlement of several hundred permanent residents, and the only town in the island group. A passenger and vehicle ferry runs between St James and Charlevoix, 35 miles away on the mainland, with two to two-and-a-half hour passage times. The number of trips per day varies with the season and the day of the week.

Beaver Island receives a lot of tourist-media blah about being "Michigan's Emerald Isle" (or even America's). Yes, it is *shaped* somewhat like Ireland, and Irish settlers made up a large fraction of its early white settlement, but it is no more emerald than any other wooded spot in the state. Irish charm, if any, is hard to detect, and St James is only a somewhat bedraggled ex-fishing village (there is some commercial fishing still going on, but only as a faint shadow of a prosperous past), but it does have an air of uniqueness, and even the critic agrees that a trip out on the ferry, if only to walk around a few hours before catching the return trip, is worth the time and cost.

And beyond the limits of St James? The map shows you that a road circles the island, and off the road are the ubiquitous Michigan summer cottages, most of them along the east shore. Fortunately, a big chunk of the island is still undeveloped (as of 1986, anyhow) and wooded so that a backpacking trip is quite feasible. The outing the Huron Valley Sierra occasionally offers starts with a taxi ride from St James to the lighthouse on the southern tip of the island, with a leisurely two-day, two-night progress back to St James along the west shore of the island. See the Details section for a chronicle of one such trip.

Maps

Charlevoix County map (reference 1), and the U S Geological Survey Beaver Island 15' quadrangle. The map printed here is an adaptation of the county map, with a few contours added from the USGS map.

Other references

Beaver Island is renowned in Michigan history as the home (about 1850) of a splinter group of Mormons, led by an autocratic "king," James Strang. The story has been written a thousand times, or so it seems, and if you are interested in the lore of the island, you can surely find a goodly fraction of that thousand on the shelves of any Michigan library. But we can suggest no references that will be helpful on an outing.

Travel from Ann Arbor

Go to Charlevoix, following the guidance of a Michigan road map. The Beaver Island Boat Company dock is located off the main street (Bridge Street) of Charlevoix just south of the bridge over the channel connecting the town harbor with Lake Michigan. You'll need a current ferry schedule, of course. Call the ferry office at 616-547-2311.

Details

The details, beginning with the next paragraph, are simply a chronicle describing a 1983 Sierra backpack on Beaver Island. Most of the points mentioned ae noted on the map printed here. The chronicle begins at the ferry dock in St James following arrival of the morning boat from Charlevoix. The first boat in summer usually sails at 8:30. Such an early sailing demands that the preceding night be spent nearby; if you want to camp, try Fisherman's Island State Park. Park entrance is on US-31

(Bell's Bay Road) about three miles south of the ferry dock in Charlevoix. On to the chronicle.

Called Beaver Island Car Rental for pickup truck, with driver, to take group to lighthouse. Ate lunch (a little late) at the lighthouse. Got water from a tap at the lighthouse.

Hiked west from the lighthouse on West Side Road. After road turned inland, took first left onto a two-track dirt road. After passing a hunting cabin on the right, took left turn toward shore. Trail turned right after a steep downgrade. Abandoned house is landmark.

Camped overnight on lake shore. Swimming poor because of shallow water and numerous rocks on bottom, a condition that prevails long the west shore of the island. [Another respondent reports much better swimming back at the lighthouse.]

During morning of the second day, hiked up west side of island, walking along beach. Landmark is Mrs Redding's house near the end of Redding Road. During afternoon, took side hike to look at Protar's house [Theodore Protar, who acted as island physician in the late nineteenth century. The house is preserved as a historical site.], leaving packs at the "stopping point" noted on the map. On return, stopped at Protar's grave. Continued north on old railroad grade. Potable water found at a spring (pipe in side of hill) on right. Trail became road again, after which went left down to lake shore.

Camped overnight on lake shore near McCauley's point. Retreated a bit south to escape people, dogs, kids from large summerers' subdivision along Donegal Bay, north of the point.

Hiked north through the Donnegal Bay subdivision [ugh!]. Stopped to climb Mount Pisgah, a well-vegetated dune. Continued north to road that passes north of Font Lake. Stopped for lunch on shore of Font Lake. Continued into St James.

In St James, time remaining before afternoon ferry sailing was sufficient for walk north and east along the road that follows the harbor out to the lighthouse. [That's the lighthouse marking St James harbor, not the one where the hike began.] Some quaint sights. Those who had had enough hiking took refuge in the Shamrock Bar. Quaint sights not recorded.

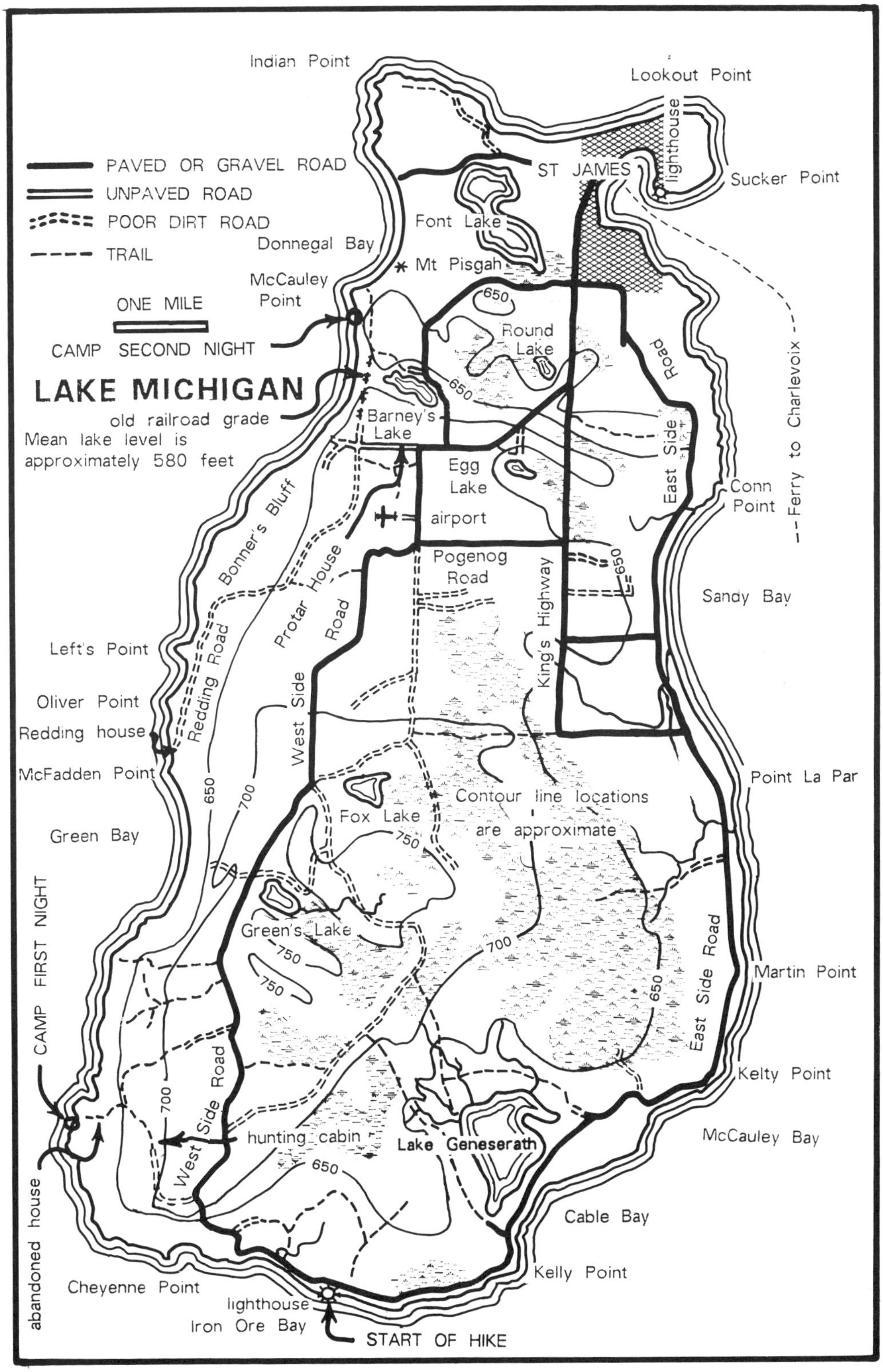
Indian Point
Lookout Point
lighthouse
Sucker Point
PAVED OR GRAVEL ROAD
UNPAVED ROAD
POOR DIRT ROAD
TRAIL
ST JAMES
Font Lake
Donnegal Bay
Mt Pisgah
McCauley Point
ONE MILE
CAMP SECOND NIGHT
Round Lake
LAKE MICHIGAN
old railroad grade
Barney's Lake
Mean lake level is approximately 580 feet
Egg Lake
airport
Ferry to Charlevoix
East Side Road
Conn Point
Bonner's Bluff
Protar House Road
Pogenog Road
King's Highway
Sandy Bay
Left's Point
Redding Road
West Side Road
Oliver Point
Redding house
McFadden Point
Point La Par
Contour line locations are approximate
Fox Lake
Green Bay
CAMP FIRST NIGHT
Green's Lake
Martin Point
East Side Road
Kelty Point
McCauley Bay
hunting cabin
Lake Geneserath
abandoned house
Cable Bay
Kelly Point
Cheyenne Point
lighthouse
Iron Ore Bay
START OF HIKE

A Canoe Trip on the Shiawassee River

General

The Shiawassee River rises in northern Livingston County, then flows northward across Shiawassee County into Saginaw County to join the Saginaw River. The trip described here covers a stretch of about 12 miles in the upper part of the river, beginning in the small town of Byron about three miles north of the Livingston County line, and about an hour's driving time from Ann Arbor. Paddling time should be around six hours.

Our respondent characterizes the river as easy flowing and pastoral, with gentle bends through farms and woodlots, including groves of oak, maple, walnut, aspen, and pine. The word "pastoral" implies a definite rural charm, but it unfortunately also signals a poor water quality caused by agricultural runoff. The river is nonetheless said to be attractive, having the appeal of good scenery, quietness, and easy paddling. Herons, kingfishers, flycatchers, pewees, red-headed woodpeckers, indigo buntings, warblers, and vultures are reported by those who watch for the birds.

The only reported hazard is shallow water in a few spots.

Maps

Shiawassee County map (reference 1).

Other references

Canoe Sport of Ann Arbor (313-996-1393) publishes informal give-away data sheets on several southeastern Michigan rivers. The information you read here is condensed from its Shiawassee River sheets, Upper River, Section 3. Although the present condensed form should be adequate on its own, for all possible details you should ask for Canoe Sport's material.

The Shiawassee is also treated in *Canoeing Michigan Rivers* (reference 19).

Travel from Ann Arbor

Take US-23 north to the Silver Lake Road exit (exit 79) at Fenton, about 35 miles north of AA (beware -- Silver Lakes are scattered all over Michigan, and you will encounter one of these others on an exit sign about 12 miles from AA). Follow this road west for about 12 miles to Byron.

Details

The preferred launching site is at the high school parking lot on the right (heading west) side of Fath Road in Byron. (The Shiawassee County map labels it Bath Road.)

Geeck Park, at about the two-thirds point of the trip, is a convenient lunch spot. Our respondent mentions its picnic tables without criticism, but characterizes the toilets as being poor.

The trip ends at Shaiwassee Dam. A park having much better facilities than those at Geeck Park is located at the dam.

This canoe trip is the only one in this book that encounters an interstate highway (I-69). Not that this is either thrill or hazard, but the water under the I-69 bridge is reported to be too shallow for canoe passage except at the far left. Approach with caution and a sharp eye.

Walnut Hills Camp & Canoe (517-634-9782) provides rental service to the Shiawassee. It is located on Lehring Road, which follows the river westward for several miles out of Byron. See our map.

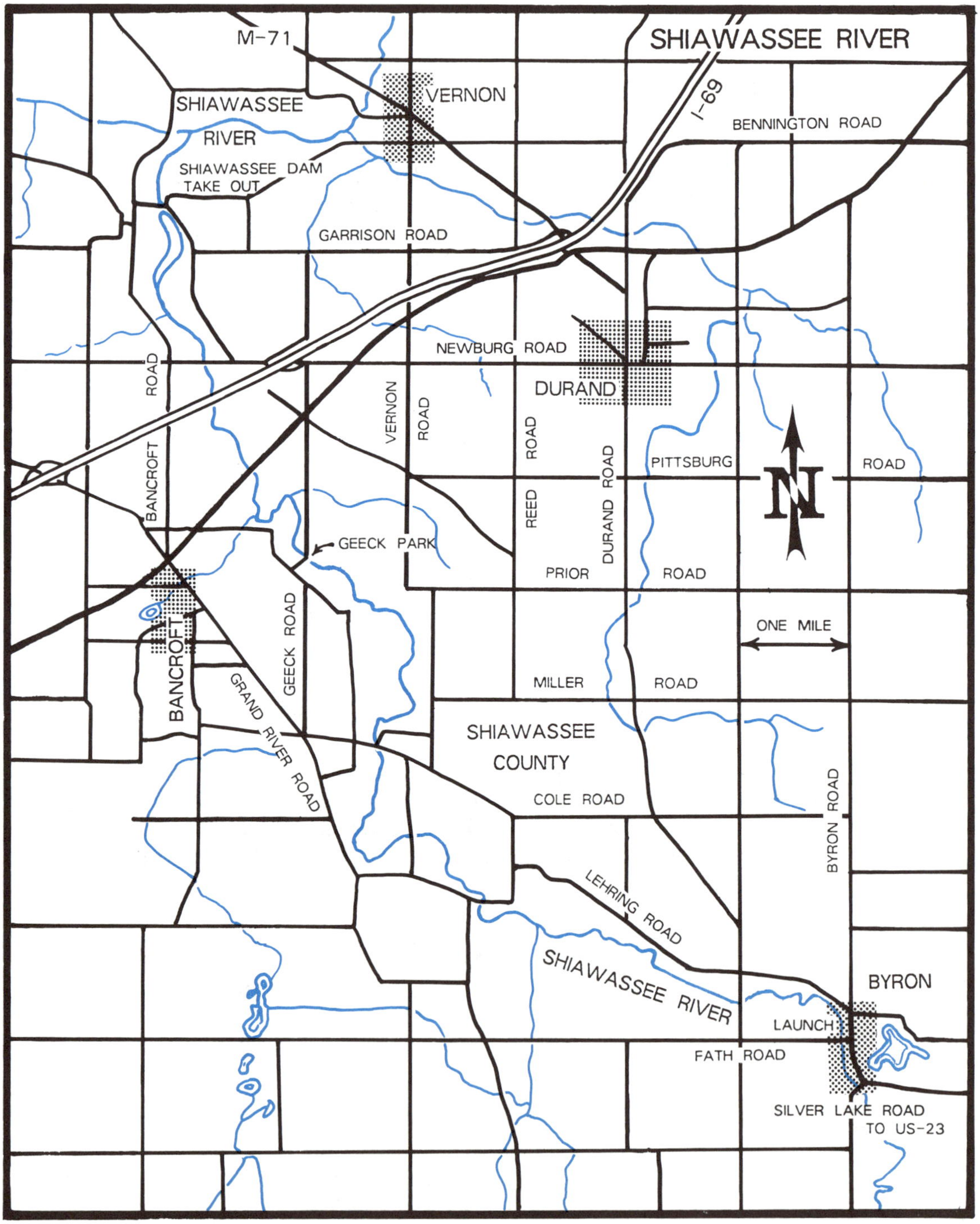
SHIAWASSEE RIVER
M-71
VERNON
SHIAWASSEE
RIVER
SHIAWASSEE DAM
TAKE OUT
I-69
BENNINGTON ROAD
GARRISON ROAD
NEWBURG ROAD
DURAND
BANCROFT ROAD
VERNON ROAD
REED ROAD
DURAND ROAD
PITTSBURG
ROAD
GEECK PARK
PRIOR
ROAD
ONE MILE
BANCROFT
GEECK ROAD
GRAND RIVER ROAD
MILLER
ROAD
SHIAWASSEE
COUNTY
COLE ROAD
BYRON ROAD
LEHRING ROAD
SHIAWASSEE RIVER
BYRON
LAUNCH
FATH ROAD
SILVER LAKE ROAD
TO US-23

Canoeing on The Au Sable River

General

By reputation, a reputation well confirmed by the number of liveries in its watershed, the Au Sable is first among Michigan's many canoeing rivers. It is also highly rated among those who fish, especially among those who do it by wading quietly with a fly rod. There's conflict here - the fishers like to be alone, silent, and to tread softly through the water in their waders, while the canoers shriek and bang their paddles against the aluminum they're sitting in. Only a minority, to be sure, but in its upper reaches, where the fishing is mostly done, the river is just too narrow for unstressful coexistence between fly rod and paddle.

We'll tell you about the river, and tell you that both fisher and boaters are justified in their admiration, but advise that you might enjoy it more at an off-peak time, say on weekdays during the summer, or in the fall.

The Au Sable rises from a swamp just west of Grayling and flows almost due east into Lake Huron at Oscoda. Canoeing begins at Grayling, the site of the largest concentration of liveries in Michigan. It also begins at Roscommon on the South Branch of the river (where there are also liveries), a tributary that joins the main stream roughly 30 miles (by canoe) downstream of Grayling. Roughly 80 miles from both Grayling and Roscommon lies the small town of Mio, and the first of several dams. The favored stretch of the river for all users is upstream of Mio. From the canoer's viewpoint, this stretch has the charm of a helpful current, no great demands upon canoe-handling skill, and the aesthetic of a narrow stream of clear water winding through almost unbroken forest. The scene does not change abruptly at Mio, but the river becomes wider, and at roughly 30 miles below Mio fades into the backwater of the the first of a series of five dams that impede it for most of the remaining course to Lake Huron. Still attractive - save for the possibility of wind on the open waters behind the dams - but not great.

Maps

Crawford, Roscomon, Iosco, Alcona, and Oscoda county maps (reference 1) show the the river; they are especially useful for tracing the roads that lead to bridges and dams where canoes might be launched and retrieved. All liveries furnish maps that are adequate for locating these features from the water. The map printed here was made from a composite of county maps, and though it notes all bridges and dams, and the roads leading to them, does not contain the details found on the original maps.

Other references

Canoeing Michigan Rivers (reference 19).

Travel from Ann Arbor

If you are going to either Grayling or Roscommon, US-23, followed by I-75, takes you to either (just watch for the exit signs). To Oscoda, it's US-23 all the way. To Mio, M-33, which branches off I-75 at Alger, provides a direct route. And M-65, which branches off US-23 shortly after the latter diverges from I-75, crosses the river about half-way between Oscoda and Mio. All points mentioned are nearly equidistant from Ann Arbor, and require three and a half or four hours on the road.

Details

If you would use a livery, there are many to choose from. Most of them are in or near Grayling, but Roscommon, Mio, and Oscoda have them also. There are just too many to list here, but there's an appendix that lists all Michigan liveries.

The usual Au Sable outing organized by the Huron Valley Group is a weekend affair, using livery canoes out of Roscommon. Saturday's run is to Canoe Harbor Campground near Smith Bridge (M-72) on the South Branch in four to five hours. Sunday's run is to McMaster Bridge in another four or five hours. An easy trip, and pleasant, but when run in prime time, may be degraded somewhat by the popularity problem mentioned earlier. For example, one respondent who made this trip on a Fourth of July weekend reports counting 102 canoes sardined against the shore at Canoe Harbor.

Another respondent reports a trip from Alcona Dam (also known as Bamfield Dam) to Five Channels Dam, all well into the lower part of the river downstream from Mio. This was a one-day trip from Ann Arbor (like 6 AM to midnight) with private canoes, and about five-six hours on the river. Surely this is not the prime Au Sable, but he claims to have encountered no other canoes, and only a scattering of flatwater fishers in boats on the dam ponds.

The following is a table of distances and times on the Au Sable as gleaned from livery brochures. From experience, the times appear to be conservative (longer than most people actually require), but more reliable than the distances. Of course, the distances include all the meanderings of the river, and thus are difficult to scale from a map, or to measure in the field. Canoes don't have odometers.

From Grayling:	distance	time
(miles)	(hrs)	
Stephan Bridge	17	4
Wakeley Bridge	25	5.5
McMaster Bridge	40	8.5
Parmalee Bridge	55	11
Camp Ten	75	15
Mio Dam	80	17
McKinley Bridge	102	21.5
US Forest Service Bridge	112	24
Alcona Dam	120	26
Loud Dam	145	31
Five Channels Dam	148	33
Cooke Dam	155	36
Foote Dam	164	40.5
Oscoda	170	44

From Roscommon to McMaster Bridge on main river:

Steckert Bridge	3	1
Chase Bridge	6	1.5
Smith Bridge	28	6
McMaster Bridge	45	10

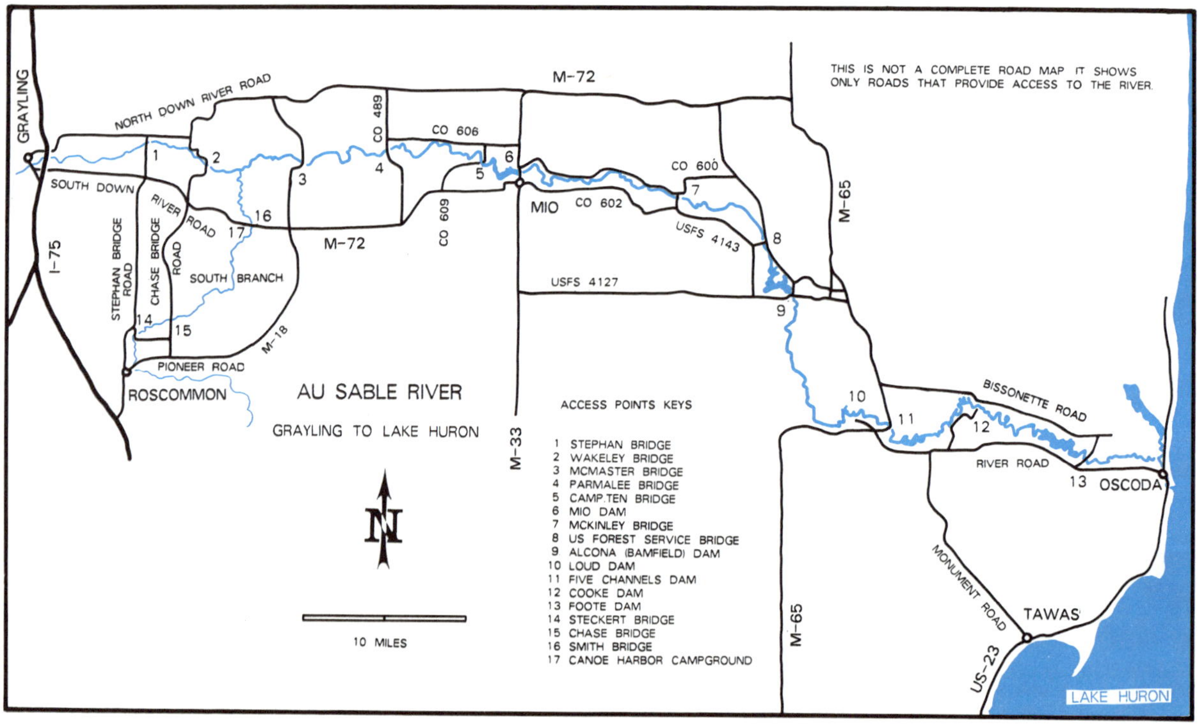

Hiking in the Porcupine Mountains

General

Many a midwestern hummock became a mountain - in name, at least - when downhill skiing boomed in the 1950s. But these Porkies, jewels of the Porcupine Mountains Wilderness State Park in the western Upper Peninsula, *are* mountains, real mountains. The highest, Government Peak, reaches 1850 feet above sea level, or about 1250 above the level of Lake Superior. That wouldn't gain it notice in Colorado, but no matter - 1250 feet gained in a mere three miles makes a genuine mountain.

The park area of approximately 90 square miles encompasses the entire mountain area, but is equally distinguished by being largely virgin forest. The size of the trees impresses the hiker who has been raised on second growth woods. The size of the undisturbed fallen timber even more impressive.

The park has a paved boundary road and a paved road that penetrates a few miles into the interior. There are a few rustic cabins for the use of walk-in campers, and the trails are well marked. Aside from these trifles, the park is true wilderness.

Wildlife testifies to the justice of the wilderness designation. The skunks, the racoons, the squirrels, the porcupines are familiar elsewhere in Michigan, but then there is the bear. The black bear only, thank goodness, but even the black bear is enough to ruin your day by eating its way into and through your pack. Hang it high at night, but if a churlish bruin wants to fang it while it's still on your back, then maybe you had better go home early. You can always buy a new pack.

Hiking is the thing in the Porcupine Mountains. There are 16 trails listed in *Michigan Hiking Opportunities*, with their lengths variying from one to 16 miles. Several of these can be strung together to make loops, with the longest about 35 miles in length. Day hikes that sample vistas from the heights, waterfalls, deep woods, lakes, and the Lake Superior shore can be contrived. Long and footwearying, yes, but rewarding.

Backpacking is an obvious alternative for those who would not do it all in one day. There are no backpackers' campgrounds, but "Adirondack" shelters are to be found along the trails. A limited number of rustic cabins are available for rental, and can be reserved in advance.

Maps

Ontonagon County map (reference 1). *Michigan Hiking Opportunities* (reference 2) has a map that emphasizes the trails, but otherwise is scant on detail. U S Geological Survey 15' White Pine and Carp River quadrangles, and White Pine and Government Peak 7.5' quadrangles. A trail map can be obtained from park headquarters (address later). The map printed here is drawn from all of these sources. It is intended particularly to give an easy overall idea of elevations and trails.

Other references

The Porcupine Mountains and their park, being such a unique feature of Michigan, and indeed of the entire midwestern United States, have been the subject of many writings, mostly in the form of magazine articles. However, as a source of outings information to supplement what is stated here, we recommend only *Michigan Hiking Opportunities*.

Travel from Ann Arbor

It's a long long way from Ann Arbor, somewhat stretching our limit of a day's drive. Road distance to the near edge of the park is about 570 miles, and only about half of that is on interstate highways. Beyond the Mackinac Bridge lie US-2, M-28, then M-64 to Silver City at the eastern edge of the park, all two-laners. An alternative route for driving, available at least through 1986, exploits the Ludington-to-Kewanee ferry across Lake Michigan. A Sierra group from Ann Arbor went that way in 1986. The four-hour lake crossing may have made a pleasant interlude, but in-transit time was longer than via Mackinac.

Details

If you can get there with enough enthusiasm left to jump out and tackle the trails, about all you will need is a map showing them. On the other hand, you will be in a state park, and a park always means rules, and yes, regulations as well. Vehicle entry permits are required, and backpackers must register at the park office (Union Bay, at the park's northeastern corner). Then there are things about fires, littering, and the like, that are to be expected. Copies of the rules are available at the headquarters.

One nice thing about the rules: they do not require backpackers to herd themselves into designated camping areas.

Several campgrounds for motor campers are located around the periphery of the park. The one at Union Bay, hard by park headquarters, offers showers, flush toilets, and other features of home-away-from-home camping. The *Michigan Hiking Opportunities* map and the county map show the locations.

The rustic cabins, accessible only by hiking, are rented on a per-night basis during an April 1 to November 30 season. All contain four bunks, except for one eight-bunker at Mirror Lake. Reservations for the year are taken after January 1. Call or write the Park Supervisor, Porcupines Mountains Wilderness State Park, Ontonagon, MI, 49953, and 906-885-5798.

A personal account (this chapter's map is on page 96)

The remainder of this chapter is a copy of the journal kept by Janet Olszewski of Lansing during a week-long backpacking trip in the Porkies. She begins on Sunday, August 11, 1986.

Sunday This is the third day of our adventure. We departed Friday evening and headed to Ludington to spend the night camping in the Scottville municipal park. We arrived in two vehicles at 11pm and 12am. The trip roster is Dave Plueddemann, Vince Smith, Laura Cross, Janet Olszewski, Charlotte Lawrence, Chris Lawrence, Julie Greiss, Bob Cornish, Larry Taylor, Nancy Shiffler, and Winnie Kerner. We will meet Jim Hewins at the trailhead. The highlights of the Scottville park were the fruit lights adorning the patio of one of the recreation vehicles, and three birch tree trunks, carved and painted to look like giant morels.

On Saturday morning we cleared out of camp at 8am to head for the ferry that will take us to Kewaunee, Wisconsin. After much hanging around, buying donuts and juice for breakfast, the ferry departed at its usual half-hour late departure time. The day is sunny and the lake is very calm, making the crossing very pleasant. It is a nice lazy start to the day, and a nice break from the long drive behind and ahead of us. After departing the ferry we stopped in Green Bay for lunch and supper supplies. Then we drove on for the five hours it took to get to the Porkies. We arrived at the park to thunderstorms, a very soggy campground, and a friendly park ranger who provided helpful hints on the route for our trip. Laura and Janet took one look at the soggy ground and opted for the local motel, conveniently located next to the campground. No need to get really wet until the trek begins. Winnie joined later.

We awoke Sunday morning to gray skies, high winds and some rain. The motel room turned out to be a great place to sort community gear, load and weigh packs. I don't think the cleaning lady will ever get over the sight of 5 people in the hall with gear and food spread all over trying to stuff it into these packs, weighing them after every addition hoping they would be heavy enough not to require any further loading. Finally, we are off to the end of the road to park the cars and start our trek. We have hooked up with Jim. Just as we get out of the cars it starts to rain, no, pour. This is not supposed to happen! We all scramble to find ponchos, pack covers, camera covers, etc. We may never get ourselves going!

We climb to Lake of the Clouds for our first view. Some take pictures; others hope for a better day when we return on the last day of the trip. The trail goes along the edge of the escarpment so we are always climbing, and always on a ridge - really beautiful and different from most of Michigan hiking because of the vistas. Soon the rain stops and we are able to start peeling raingear. We stop for lunch on a high ridge after several of the party made a side trip to the base of the escarpment to see the remains of the Cuyhahoga mining operation. Various pieces of ore crushing equipment are in evidence at the base but we did not locate the actual mine entrance. Studying the map we had lunch on Cuyahoga Peak, and immediately thereafter began our descent to the river. The sun came out in the afternoon making the woods we now trekking through very beautiful. We did go through some swamp reminiscent of the High Country Pathway trip last year. We settle on a great campsite up from the river crossing at a spot where the river and its waterfalls parallel the trail. I am sure we will all be lulled to sleep by the soothing sound of the falls. Our first dinner on the trail was very welcome and finished off with the uncorking of the Jack Daniels (actually uncorking the water bottle that held the Jack Daniels). Suddenly there was a run on the lemonade. Hot water, lemonade, and Jack Daniels to taste. It is guaranteed to soothe sore feet, hips, stiff joints, and any other ailments. (Later on the trip this concoction was named the Fuzzy Backpacker.) So far no injuries, thank goodness - only minor discomforts.

Monday We start our day with a hike sans packs to Union Spring. This spring is the second largest in Michigan, generating 700 gallons of water per minute. You wouldn't know it to look at it. On the way back Chris left the trail, couldn't find his way back, and struck out cross country to find the river and camp. He found his way back to camp, but meantime Charlotte and Bob had gone in search of him. Luckily everyone found everyone else and all were fine. We ate lunch and set off for our next destination, Government Peak or thereabouts. This was a 5 mile hike that we started at 2:30pm. On the way we decided that doing fun hikes first and the work later was a bad idea. People were tired from the first day of hiking, and from the morning's jaunt. Much of the trail was swampy and two veterans of the High Country trip started the regular routine of "Things could be worse...."

We spent a good part of the afternoon leapfrogging with a group of girl scouts who were heading for the same places we were. Singing and full of youthful energy, they managed to run out of steam before we did and camped in mosquito heaven at the bottom of Government Peak. Much to our dismay the lake on the near side of Government Peak was an inaccessble wet spot. This meant we were hiking at least to the top of the peak, and maybe beyond. During our ascent we met up with a hiker coming the other way who told us it got worse before it got better, and that there was accessible water about 3/4 mile down from the peak. Dave, Winnie, and Janet were the first to arrive on the peak and quickly decided this was the evening's campsite. The spot included a very nice view of Lake Superior and what we believed to be the Apostle Islands. Jim scouted the water, which ended up being more like 1/2 mile down the hill. On one of our laundry and water runs we discovered that the source of the stream was a beaver pond created by a 5 foot high beaver dam. It was a great bathing spot.

The day's account would not be complete without a pause to tell of the new piece of equipment we carried along on this trip,

Katahdin giardia filter. It looked like a great idea, cost enough to be a great idea, but proved to be mediocre at best. The filter clogs frequently, requires one's full body weight to get enough pressure and is not conveniently designed to support that weight. The night we spent on Government Peak, we resorted to boiling our water to save some time for hiking the next day. Filtering our water was starting to take all our waking moments.

After bath and supper we gathered on the overlook to watch the sunset, to watch Mars rise and set, and to see the first few stars. One by one the hikers fell into their tents to sleep as the light in the western sky lasted too long for us to see a great star show.

Tuesday Once again we slept until 8am. This is a leisurely trip. Today we only have a 2 or 3 mile hike to Mirror Lake, a piece of cake. We should have known better. Once again, the trail was quite swampy, although getting drier every day. We arrived at our cabin about noon ready to settle in and take a day hike during the afternoon, only to discover that we needed a key for the cabin, and the ranger had not given us one. Bob and Vince ate a hurried lunch and hiked out to the car to find the ranger and the key. In the meantime the rest of us lounged in the sun and decided what projects to undertake. Larry and Chris headed back to a stream we crossed to get water and to follow the stream to its source to see if they could find the spring mentioned to us by the ranger. Dave and Janet borrowed the neighbor's rowboat (there are two cabins at Mirror Lake) to tour the perimeter of the lake and look for signs of the spring. Chris deserted the spring search party when they started bushwacking through underbrush. The tour of the lake did not turn up any signs of the spring, but the swimming was fine.

Given it is the third day of the hike it is time to consider trip awards. The first goes to Charlotte for the best turtle imitation. While traversing one of the many swampy areas we were in today she fell backward into the turtle pose but managed to miss most of the mud in doing so! A fine accomplishment. The second award may go to Janet for best oarsperson of the trip. Circles seem to be her specialty.

The key detail arrived at 4 or 5pm and we were finally able to get in and look at our home.

At dinner we named the drink that has been keeping us going each evening - the Fuzzy Backpacker. The recipe is instant lemonade, hot water and Jack Daniels to taste. After dinner,

Dave, Charlotte and Janet set off on an evening stroll around the lake. Please note that this little walk was Dave's idea. He was going off alone until Charlotte and Janet decided to protect him from himself. So the three hearty hikers set off to find the trail that went around the lake. All was well until we rounded the first inlet of the lake. At that point the trail became fainter and fainter until we were completely bushwacking. This after Dave said "I'm sure there is a trail that goes all the way around the lake." Picture the scene. The sun has set and it is starting to get dark. The three are bushwacking through serious underbrush, always keeping the lake in sight which means some pretty damp underbrush. We cross a couple of inlets, one by a log bridge. Panic begins to set in making Dave walk faster and the two women walk slower. Finally we hear voices calling to us. I might add just in the nick of time as we had just discovered we were only 2/3 of the way around, instead of the 3/4 we were anticipating. Bob and Chris were out for an evening tour of the lake in the rowboat when they heard us crashing through the underbrush, and two women cursing someone. As they were talking us to the shore so they could pick us up Dave was heard to say "I found the trail, we'll meet you up by the rocks." Of course his last words were muffled by the strangle hold he was put in. The three hearty hikers climbed into the boat (we tried to leave Dave behind, but he jumped in before we could get away) - a daring rescue by sea! We all rewarded ourselves with a beautiful moonlight swim. The moral of the story is twofold: (1) never assume there is a trail that goes around a lake, and (2) always hike with at least three hours of light. The third might be never to let Dave talk one into an after dinner stroll!

Thursday Somewhere I lost Wednesday. It gets that way after you have been on the trail for a while. Time and life slow down; dates become unimportant. Things get done because they are there to do - like looking for a walking stick or wading in the rivers, or crossing logs - all just because they are there, and the only goal is to enjoy. I have the feeling of being a child again and of playing. If this is what happens on a week-long trip I can't imagine what would happen on a longer trip, shades of altered states.

Wednesday was a non-pack day because we were spending two nights at Mirror Lake. Consequently, It wound its way toward entropy very quickly. Without a requirement to be on the trail or to get to the next campsite we disintegrated into constant eating and playing. I happen to have a bunk in the cabin, and my pack is going to be declared a disaster area soon. For the first few days on the trail my gear was nicely organized in its pockets of the pack. Now that I don't have to worry about bears or rain it's like a jack-in-the-box spewing contents

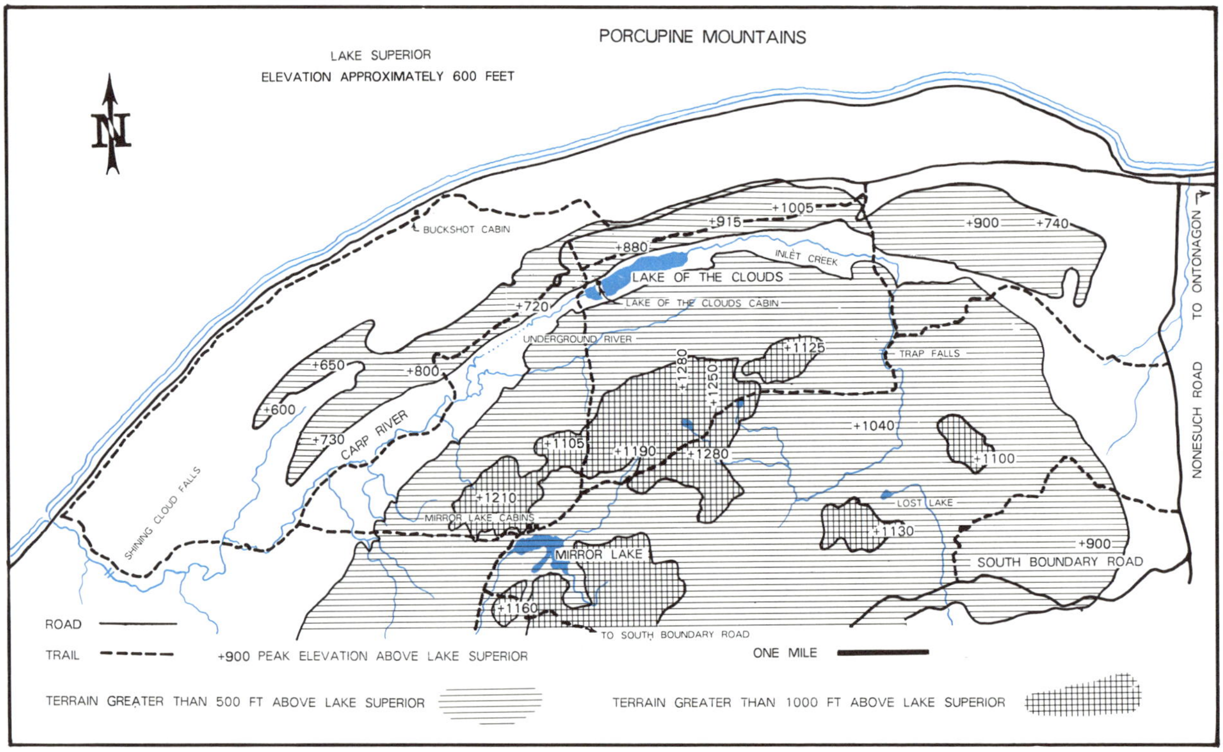

of the pack across several square feet of room. At the pace we are all moving at it may take all afternoon to reorganize it.

In the morning we hiked up to Summit Peak and climbed the lookout tower for the beautiful view. Bob, Jim, and Janet then hiked out of the park to the van which had been spotted closer to the lake on the return trip from picking up the key, to haul out trash and to bring in more fuel. The trash was items we had picked up along the trail or in the back of the cabin. We estimated hauling out 30 pounds of trash. It would be nice if everyone hauled out what they brought in. The fuel represented our decision to give up on the giardia filter and start boiling our water. This was strictly a utilitarian hike, picking up trash all the way out and going over familiar territory all the way back. Many people were on the trail; in general the Porkies appear to be heavily used.

The sunny warm afternoon was given to bathing, hair washing, laundry, as well as a two-hour lunch. Bob, Vince, Dave, Winnie, Charlotte, and Janet headed out on a day hike along Correction Trail to find a waterfall and swim. Some of us are masochists. Even on our day of rest we have to go hiking, not once but twice. We never did find the waterfall. We did find a trickle of a stream, and four turned back not wanting to go any further for so little fun. Bob and Vince continued on the trail to scout the area where we would spend Friday evening. This little trip brought agreement with the ranger who noted that Correction Trail was a mess, lots of downed logs and other booby traps.

Chocolate fondue was the highlight of dinner. Unfortunately, we all ate so much of it we were sugar buzzing for hours afterward. Tomorrow will be our longest hike of the trip and we could use all the rest we could get tonight.

We were on the trail by 9:30 Thursday morning for the 8-mile hike. Threatening skies, but no rain yet. Our trail song was born today, sung to the tune of the themesong for "Rawhide." A sample of the lyrics - "Flip 'em up, head 'em out, raw feet...." Beautiful trail today, very little swamp. We spend most of the day hiking along the Little Carp River, crossing the stream over and over. By the way, we did find the spring so many searched for. It was at Lily Pond, not Mirror Lake - no wonder it was so hard to find.

We had lunch at Greenstone Falls, where several of us swam in the ice cold water. It started to rain in the late afternoon, and we settled on a campsite pretty quickly, which turned out to be about where we intended to stop anyway. After an early dinner the rain stopped and several of us hiked downstream to see what we could see. Waded in the water, crossed logs, etc, all in the spirit of the beginning of this entry. The woods have truly taken over, and the outside world has receded into the very dim background. The geology of the river is very interesting. There is a great deal of conglomerate rock and shale, sometimes together.

Friday The day started with me chasing a toothbrush down the mighty Little Carp River. Mind you, not just any toothbrush, the giardia toothbrush, the one we use to clean the filter that keeps us in drinking water. We never have fully given up on this wonder of modern technology even though it has distinct disadvantages.

Today may not be a good day. Yesterday's rain has stopped, but the air remains very humid and everything is soggy. I can't quite believe that I or my gear will ever be dry again, and that we won't turn into a mushroom in the next five minutes. Not exactly the most desireable start to our last full day of hiking. By the time we reach Lake Superior for lunch, however, we have nothing but blue skies, and all is well again.

On the morning hike Dave and Janet had another adventure. Charlotte was smart enough to to be hiking up ahead. Somehow we missed a river crossing to the east side of the river without realizing it. We climbed a ridge and decided to follow it until we could spot the trail on the other side, or another crossing. A short way down we found trail blazes on the ridge and figured we were home free only to discover when we got to Lake Superior and were on the opposite side of the river from our fellow hikers that we had actually ended up on the Pinkerton Trail. We weren't even looking for adventure and found one.

After a brief rest we began hiking along the Lake Superior Trail. Our hiking was slow because there were so many wonderful thimbleberries to be eaten along the way. This trail is close to shore but not on the shore, and goes through scrub forest. It was here that the realization really hit home about the amount of virgin timber land we had hiked through. The Porkies contain vast areas of virgin timber, and to date we have been in it almost exclusively, to the point of forgetting what scrub forest is like. We stopped for lunch where the Big Carp River flows into Lake Superior. Five of us swam in the big lake. It was surprisingly warm. In fact, it was warmer than the rivers.

There are several other parties of hikers on the trail here, and after lunch we send an advance party ahead to beat them out and claim the explorer's shelter where we plan to spend the night. The beach is so pleasant that it takes a long while for the rest of us to gather our energy and start the uphill trek along the riv er. Along the way we stop at the Shining Cloud Falls, and at a quiet spot for a swim. Charlotte, Dave and I arrive at camp at 6pm to find that Julie and Larry are missing. They were ahead of us but have not yet arrived. Winnie is a late arrival, having done some additional hiking along the lake. She has not seen them either, so we now assume that they took Cross Trail by mistake (the junction is a confusing log crossing, and so might easily be missed) and have ended up at Greenstone Falls. We assume they will hike out of the park close to that point and will meet us tomorrow. Of course, that assumes that they are together, and we do have some concern not knowing exactly what is going on. We are comforted knowing we have swept the trail three times today and they are not hurt and lying along the trail, but we don't know how they have done on Cross Trail. The problem is that sunset is upon us and there is not much we can do this evening.

Larry showed up about dark with half his gear, having hiked the Correction Trail to our camp to let us know that he and Julie had, in fact, mistakenly taken Cross Trail. He left her at Lily Pond and she was heading to Mirror Lake from there, with the intention of hiking out North Mirror Trail to Lake of the Clouds the next day to meet us. Larry had left half his gear at Lily Pond and was planing to hike back there tonight. After some discussion he decided to sleep at camp, get up early and head back to Lily Pond, get his gear, head over to Mirror Lake, and hike out with Julie. In the meantime, we would send our three fastest hikers up ahead early in the morning, and when they reached the end of our trail they would head down North Mirror Lake Trail to intercept and help Julie and Larry. It was good to know there were no injuries or other casualties. This was a little too much excitement.

As the trip nears its end I feel there are many things I have forgotten to record. Perhaps it is just the desire to not lose one moment of the experience that leaves me feeling this way, and the inability ot convey all the perceptions and feeling of the hike.

Saturday It is 12:30pm. It's funny how we start to track time now that civilization is near. We are at the Lake of the Clouds overlook - the end of the line. We have come full circle. We have just sent Jim and Winnie on a beer and potato chip run. Hiking makes you appreciate the finer things of life! Julie and Larry have rejoined us, tired but fine. The trip is now a matter of reflections.

The log would not be complete without a testament to the pesky raccoon who invaded our campsite last night. We were annoyed by his persistent and high speed invasion until this morning when we discovered that he had gotten into Larry's crushed red pepper flakes! Somewhere there is a racoon running through the forest with his mouth on fire. Our hearts go out to him having tested some of Larry's crushed peppers ourselves.

Shingle Mill Pathway
Pigeon River Country State Forest

General

The Shingle Mill Pathway is a loop trail of approximately 11 miles in length (with 10-mile and 6-mile subloops) lying in a heavily wooded area northeast of Gaylord know as the "Pigeon River Country." The area is known for its elk herd, the only such herd east of the Mississippi. It is also the largest contiguous undeveloped wild land in the Lower Peninsula, though it can hardly be called "wilderness" because a network of roads allows the penetration of motored wheels. Hydrocarbon exploration is also an intrusion that has been allowed in some parts of the area, though not in the vicinity of the Shingle Mill Pathway.

The name "Shingle Mill" derives from a shingle-making activity at the town of Cornwall that existed in ancient times (ancient by Michigan standards) along the Pigeon River. The trail now passes through the townsite, but very little evidence of the town is visible other than a spring flowing out of the hillside not far from a beaver lodge in the river.

The terrain is moderately hilly, and in its predominantly upland portions is covered with hardwood forest typical of northern Michigan. There is a modicum of swampy ground marked by the cedars that are typical of such ground.

The pathway forms part of a larger loop, the High Country Pathway, a trail about 70 miles in length. It is described in the next chapter.

Maps

Otsego County map (reference 1) shows the area, but nothing of the pathway. *Michigan Hiking Opportunities* (reference 2) has a trail map. This map is the source for the one printed here.

The trail area lies within the U S Geological Survey Hetherton quadrangle.

Other references

Michigan Hiking Opportunities (reference 2)

Travel from Ann Arbor

Your likely starting point with the Pigeon River area is the Pigeon Bridge campground on Sturgeon Valley Road, 11 miles from I-75, which you exit at Vanderbilt, about 10 miles north of Gaylord. Our respondents estimate four to five hours driving time from Ann Arbor.

Details

It's an easy and pleasant walk through the woods, and 11 miles isn't a bad length for a day hike, especially since the elevation changes are minor. You might see some of the elk.

The Pathway is also used for backpacking, especially those who come from distant parts of the state. It works out easily as half a day to get there, the remaining half to load up and walk a few miles to a spot for a night on Michigan's bone-easy forest soil, etc. The map shows two campgrounds, the Pigeon Bridge and the Pigeon River State Forest campgrounds, and one undeveloped camping spot just south of Grass Lake. A respondent also reports camping at the Cornwall village site, where water from a spring is available. Another reports camping in a small clearing in the woods near the overlook just north of Grass Lake, although there was no water source at hand. Potable water sources are to be found only at the two campgrounds and at the Cornwall spring.

Backcountry camping is also possible at other places out of sight of the trail in the vicinity of the two campgrounds. One such spot can be found about 400 yards south of Sturgeon Valley Road near the Pigeon Bridge campground. Pine duff and lush grass are a refreshing change for hikers who have been lying on the hard and bare ground of the established sites.

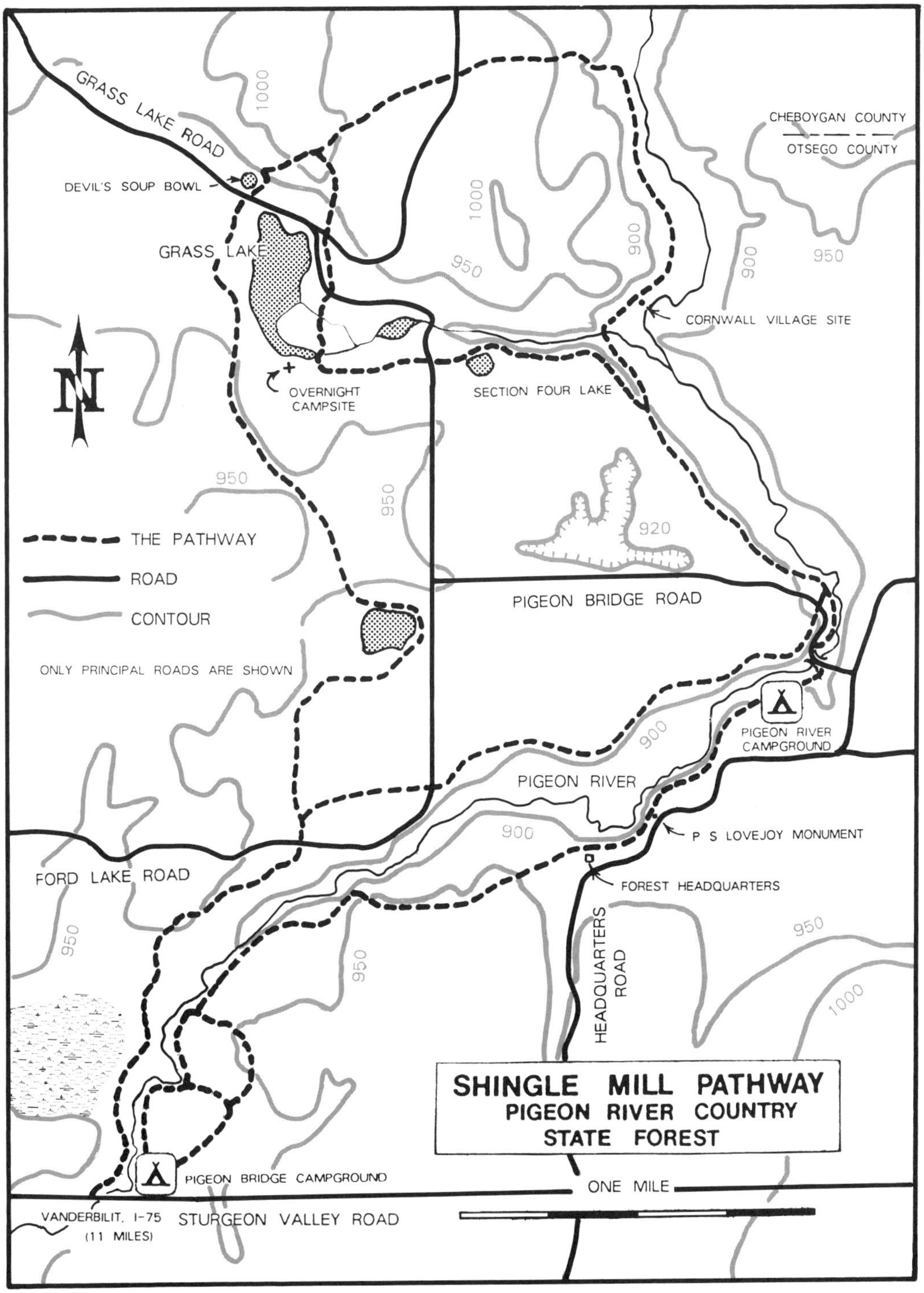

Backpacking the High Country Pathway
Pigeon River Country State Forest

General

The High Country Pathway is a 75-mile loop lying mostly within the primitive forest lands of the Pigeon River Country State Forest in northern lower Michigan. Both published guides and experience indicate that a week should be allowed for doing the full loop at a reasonable pace. However, the trail is intersected by roads at several points, so that cars can be spotted to arrange shorter hikes.

The area is nearly all forest land, but offers a variety of experience provided by wetlands, beaver floodings, man-made floodings, remains of lumbering or Civilian Conservation Corps camps, abandoned railway grades, sinkhole lakes, areas of recent clearcuttings, state forest campgrounds, and vistas from the high ground.

The state forest campgrounds offer primitive pleasures such as well water and pit toilets, but they are not distributed well enough to provide for every overnight stop. On the other hand, camping is permitted anywhere on state forest land, subject to the rules that the gentle camper would follow without being told. But water supply may be a problem in the wild spots, so plan carefully.

The map printed here gives the general aspect of the trail, but is not sufficient for field use. The essential document is *Field Guide to the High Country Pathway,* a pamphlet that contains maps in detail, accompanied by notes. The *Guide* is sold by the Pigeon River Country Association, Box 122, Gaylord, MI 49735, mail order price of $2.50 (1985 report). The 1980 edition, the latest available when this book was published, contains errors and inadequacies that caused difficulties for our respondents who hiked the trail in 1985; the major trouble spots are noted on the map here.

Maps

County maps (reference 1) of Cheboygan, Montmorency, Presque Isle, and Otsego Counties, and US Geological Survey 15' quadrangles Hetherton, Atlanta, and Tower. Maps are also found in *Michigan Hiking Opportunities* (reference 2) and the *Guide* discussed in the preceding section. The map printed here is based on the *Michigan Hiking Opportunities* map, with some additions from the topographic maps.

Other references

Michigan Hiking Opportunites (reference 2) and *Field Guide to the High Country Pathway* (see above).

Travel from Ann Arbor

Your most likely starting point is the Pigeon Bridge State Forest Campground, which is approximately 10 miles east of I-75 on Sturgeon Valley Road. Take US-23, I-75 to the Vanderbilt exit north of Gaylord, guided by any Michigan road map. Driving time should not be more than five hours.

Details

Let's begin by annotating the map with comments made by respondents who hiked the entire trail in 1985. Numbers here correspond to the circled numbers on the map.

1. Detour around a recent beaver flooding may be difficult to find if trail blazes have not been renewed. Watch for a sharp left turn from the still-blazed trail.
2. Detour around a clear-cut may be difficult to find for the same reason. Skirt the left-hand edge of the clear cut until you come to the trail again, up the slope to the east.
3. A recent clear-cut has no apparent detour. Nasty climb over debris.
4. Another clear-cut where a detour may be difficult to find.

5. Trail overgrown in this area.
6. Trail departs from old railway bed, but point may not be marked.
7. Trail hard to pick up east of vista.

A personal account (the map for this chapter is on page 111)

The remainder of this chapter is a copy of the journal kept by Janet Olszewski of Lansing during a ciruit of the Pathway by a Sierra outing in July 1985.

Day 1 After a long lunch at Big Boy in Houghton Lake we hit the trail at Pigeon Bridge at 3:30 PM. Hiking was great, though very warm [this was July]. Just as we were feeling our oats about how well we were doing and how we'd be at camp in an hour a beaver changed our plans by having built a dam that flooded an extensive area. We spent an hour and a half working out different strategies to get around the "lake." Finally backtracked to a rerouting of the trail we had passed - too cocky, I guess. Saw lots of gnawed trees and possible elk droppings. Also saw a red-throated humming bird. Back on the trail again at 9:05 PM we seemed sure we had only a mile to go. We finally rolled into campground at 10:30 PM. Broke into efficient work gangs to to make dinner, pitch tents, bear-pack food, etc - all in the dark, I might add. We finally gave up and asked three beer-drinking fishermen to stow our food for us in their car. They are good for something.

Stars put on a most beautiful show.

Day 2 Woke to the natural musical strains of something from the Eurythmics - our friends the fishermen brought their ghetto blaster and proceeded to play it throughout breakfast. I might add that this was at 6:30 AM. We all creaked and groaned, made it out of the tents and started the day. The luxuries of an established campground: running water.

On the trail at 9 AM. Half-mile up, literally, from camp was one of the prettiest river views I've ever seen - Pigeon River from 50 feet up - a bend that over the years has caught many logs and must be the home of some big trout. Soon after, we hit a clear cut - the first of our adventures for the day. Lost the trail in the clearing and spent a half hour scouting to find it again. Once found we continued to trudge through the rough terrain of downed logs everywhere. Saw bear scat, a deer, and fighter jets - some combo.

Today we noticed our speed was slower and our rest breaks more frequent. After that initial setback of the clearcut, the trail seems endless. It wasn't too well marked, and we went through a lot of scrub forest. Our inital schedule of having lunch at Dog Lake went by the wayside in the first hour. Found a pretty place - the first of the day - to have lunch. A welcome relief. Saw Indian pipes. Had a lot of obstacles on the trail, and just as we were excruciatingly tired we had another clear-cut area blocking the trail. Everyone was sporting serious scrapes. Hiking afterwards was very pretty, through pine and mixed forests. I led for a while and put up a few woodcock. Renewed but exhausted, we stopped for a rest and discovered we were either real close to camp, or had another hour to go. Luckily the sign beckoned us at the end of the first hill. With shouts of alleluia we headed up the spur trail to McLavey Lake - the Promised Land, Children. First thing eveyone did was head for the lake - swimming and washing clothes. Truly a welcome relief after sweating all day. Lake water was warm, but the air from a cold front that moved in was cool - also a welcome relief. An osprey watched from on high as we invaded his own private lake. Tents pitched, supper on the stove, clean clothes on, we're set for a relaxing evening. We can only hope that there are no surprises tomorrow - 14 miles is surprise enough.

Day 3 We made it! Shoepac Lake campground by 8 PM at least. The trip plan said 14 1/2 miles - we probably did more like 16. Got a good start at 8:30 AM and never lost the trail or hit a new clearcut. The day was sunny and cool. Those facts alone probably saved us today. First few miles were swamp with many fallen trees, so we had a few obstacles to challenge us. Then we started climbing up and down. My legs started screaming. The two miles to the Black River felt like 3 1/2. Might have been. Took us through an old clear-cut area or two - just enough to give us lots of moguls. The scenery today was beautiful all day, climaxed by a great view overlooking Canada Creek. Forgot lunch - it was had by the Black River where we contemplated hyjacking a beer truck on the nearby road while soaking our feet.

Lost ourselves toward the end when we tried to take a shortcut.

It wasn't really, but we intersected the trail and came on home. Shoepac Lake is lovely. Our camping neighbors are terrible and the sinkholes are fascinating. I can't believe we're going to do this again tomorrow! We are nuts.

Camping at Shoepac Lake was quite the experience. We had camp neighbors who ran over the dog with their bicycle and the parents kept shooting fireworks after dark as we lay in our tents taking inventory of the sore muscles. I took a walk by the lake after dark - beautiful moon and stars, and saw a heron and lots of fish breaking the surface. Also heard loons calling.

Day 4 On the trail again by 9, hoping to reach our next stop by late afternon so we'll have time to play. Of course we know it's hopeless. No matter how early we rise we leave at 9; no matter how few miles we always arrive at 7 PM. Today will only be 12 1/2 miles - a cake walk. One clearcut, but we found our way around it. Walked on the railroad grade, and Charlotte saw pitcher plants. Then there were the African grasslands we crossed, hot, sunny, late afternoon bake, and of course we lost the trail. Found it with relative ease. Ended up walking along M-33 to Clear Lake State Park where we camped for the night. Lots of high ridges and pretty scenery today. Lunch was in a semi-shaded meadow where a butterfly landed on Vince's finger, and tried to get nectar from the flowers on Chester's shirt. As soon as we hit our campsite at Clear Lake, after we had no car license number to give the ranger and after he told us if we didn't like our campsite we could walk back to complain, we headed for a swim. Wonderful after a hot grueling day on the trail. Each of us had a shock when we went into the bathroom and saw ourselves in the mirror. Betsy, Charlotte, and I commandeered the sinks in the bathroom to do our laundry. We were watched by 3 teenaged girls who were checking their eye makeup and smoking cigarettes, and wondering where these crazy women came from.

We bought firewood and barely had the energy to stay awake to build the fire. Luckily we had a friendly neighbor who allowed us to use the trunk of his car for our food, saving us another bear bag night.

Day 5 Woke to a sunny sky again today. This is unbelievable Michigan weather. Could we possibly make it through the week with no rain? Allowed ourselves a very late start today - 11 AM. It was welcome, too, after two very long days of hiking. Trail was well marked today - no incidents of lost blue blazes or clearcuts. This is getting too easy - we really have been in the woods too long. We now thoroughly understand the trail marking! One member's trail injury began to take its toll today. Dave sustained a knee injury while catapulting over a guard rail at the Black River (day 3). It has begun to cause him serious pain on the day we're to climb Rattlesnake Hill. We come to the hill before we can imagine, and after some consultation and application of an ace bandage to Dave's knee we begin the ascent. For once the trail is well graded and marked and we complete the climb with less difficulty than we had thought possible. Stopped at what we believed to be the highest point, only to find the trail taking us to the next ridge for an even better vista. Clouds had rolled in but the view was still great. It became awesome as we calculated that we had walked around or through everything we could see. This trek is definitely something to take pride in doing. Filled our water bottles at the East Branch of the Black River after our descent from Rattlesnake Hill, and walked about 1/2 mile to a suitable campsite. No facilities tonight - this is a back country stop.

The night was hot and humid. A squall line came through during the night, followed by a cool rainy front.

Day 6 The rain abated long enough for us to have breakfast, pack up, and decide that it would clear as we hit the trail. As soon as we hit the trail it began to rain. As if things weren't bad enough, every time Chester would state that he saw some "clearing clouds" it would rain harder. About 5 minutes onto the trail my feet were sloshing in my boots. Shoe breaks took on new meaning until we decided that taking breaks only heightened and prolonged our misery. I don't know if anyone kept track, but I think we stepped up our pace from our usual 1 1/2 mph. We were relentless in our misery. In retrospect, what was our hurry? A soggy campsite with no hope of drying tents and gear awaited us.

When we did get to camp Vince began a heroic effort to build a fire using birchbark, wet wood, and finally a candle. Huddled under the tarp, the rest of us watched, figuring the cause was hopeless. Vince prevailed and certainly deserves highest praise for what became a well established, comforting, and drying fire. Meanwhile Chester and I tested Town Corner Lake by swimming and doing laundry in a downpour. Hopefully, no one will never see this account. That action alone could get us entry to a psych ward. The rain finally let up before dark, but no clearing yet. We crawled into our damp tents before dark, hoping for a better day tomorrow.

Day 7 Vince received his award for firestarting today. We awoke to bright sunshine and proceeded to try and dry our gear as we ate breakfast and broke camp. By the time we hit the trail we looked like a walking laundromat - clothes hanging from every backpack. Today was to be the last day of hiking, but we have decided to do a side trip to Round Lake instead of going straight to Pigeon Bridge. This gives us a better swimming spot and generally better ambience for our last day on the trail.

Today is our fun day. We reach camp by 4 PM - plenty of time to dry gear, swim and relax. The end of the trail is close and everyone begins to shift gears. It's a sad and glad time. We have accomplished a good deal. It's almost over. Lunch conversation centered around where the next trip should be - sounds like the Porcupine Mountains. Two days ago - even yesterday - we talked of burning our boots and packs at the end of the trail. Today we're planning another marathon!

Dave did the distance to Pigeon Bridge today, rounded up his car, and drove back to meet the rest of us at Round Lake. His knee was as bad or worse and this was his shot to complete the trail. He begins our reintroduction to civilization by bringing us beer. It was so welcome he and Chester ventured to the store a second time for more. Chester returned with tales of civilization and its pitfalls - driving, stores, making change, etc.

Day 8 Woke to sunshine again. Ate all the remaining food possible for breakfast. Hoisted our now light packs over our heads for the last time and set off on the last 1 1/2 miles of the trail. We reach the cars at 10:30.

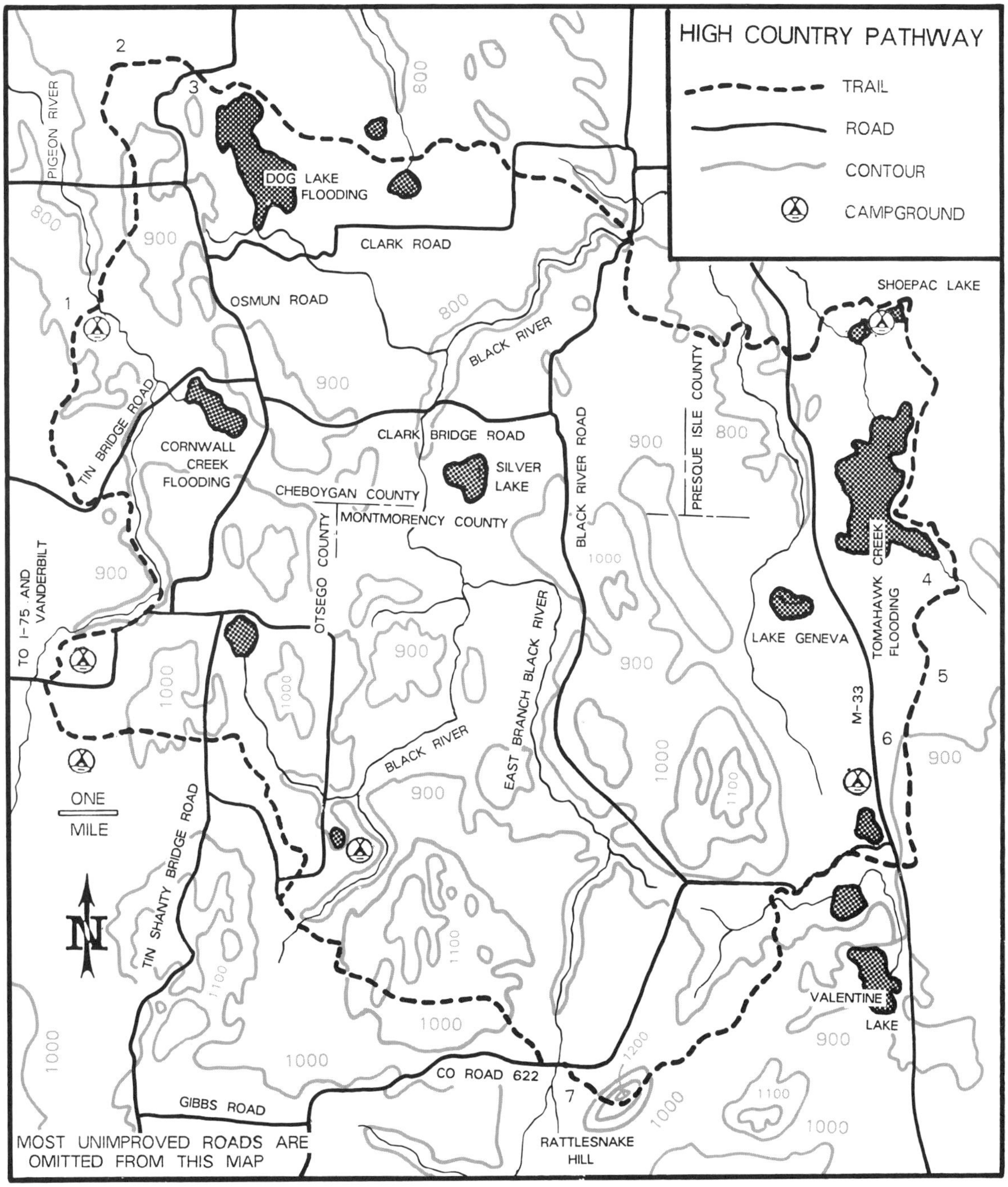
HIGH COUNTRY PATHWAY
TRAIL
ROAD
CONTOUR
CAMPGROUND
PIGEON RIVER
DOG LAKE FLOODING
CLARK ROAD
OSMUN ROAD
BLACK RIVER
TIN BRIDGE ROAD
CORNWALL CREEK FLOODING
CLARK BRIDGE ROAD
SILVER LAKE
CHEBOYGAN COUNTY
MONTMORENCY COUNTY
OTSEGO COUNTY
PRESQUE ISLE COUNTY
BLACK RIVER ROAD
SHOEPAC LAKE
TOMAHAWK CREEK FLOODING
LAKE GENEVA
M-33
TO I-75 AND VANDERBILT
EAST BRANCH BLACK RIVER
BLACK RIVER
ONE MILE
TIN SHANTY BRIDGE ROAD
VALENTINE LAKE
CO ROAD 622
GIBBS ROAD
RATTLESNAKE HILL
MOST UNIMPROVED ROADS ARE OMITTED FROM THIS MAP

Skiing Muncie Lakes Pathway

General

Muncie Lakes is close to Sand Lakes - about five air miles southwest - and offers a possible alternative to the latter after a heavy snowfall, since the Department of Natural Resources maintains the Muncie pathway.
The pathway is actually a set of six overlapping loops, with a total trail length of about 10 miles.

Muncie Lakes is quite close to Ranch Rudolph, a private resort that has a trail network of its own, but which is connected to the Muncie Lakes trails. The Muncie trails are therefore sometimes crowded by overflow on weekends when large groups are using the Ranch Rudolph lodge.

Maps

Grand Traverse County map (reference 1). U S Geological Survey FifeLake 15' quadrangle. The map printed here is an adaptation of the Muncie Lakes Pathway map included in *Michigan Hiking Opportunities* (reference 2).

Other references

Michigan Cross Country Skiing Atlas (reference 11).

Travel from Ann Arbor

We'll assume you go by way of Traverse City, following the guidance of any Michigan road map. Take Garfield Road south out of Traverse City. (Garfield Road intersects US-31 in Traverse City roughly a half-mile east of the Holiday Inn) for about 8.5 miles to Hobbs Highway. Take that road east 1.5 miles to Ranch Rudolph Road, on which you will find the Muncie Lakes parking lot after about three miles.

From the south, the trip can be shortened several miles by avoiding Traverse City. One might go north through Kingsley to Hobbs Highway, say. See the county map.

Details

The pathway covers rolling-to-hilly terrain in mixed pine/oak forest, with occasional meadows. There is only one steep hill. It is located on the westernmost loop of the pathway, at a point where the trail descends into the Boardman River valley near Fork's Campground.

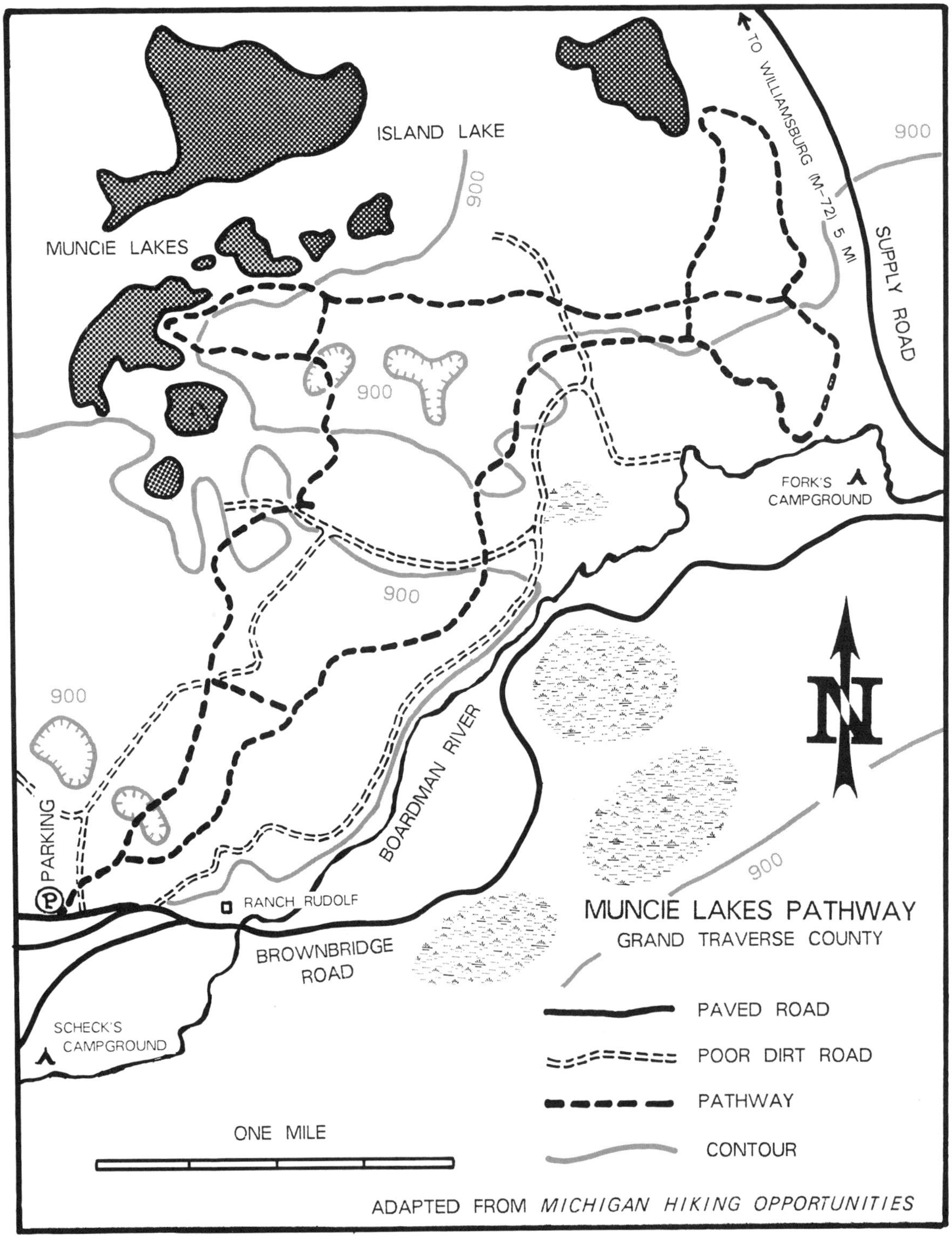
ISLAND LAKE
MUNCIE LAKES
TO WILLIAMSBURG (M-72) 5 MI
SUPPLY ROAD
900
FORK'S CAMPGROUND
PARKING
BOARDMAN RIVER
RANCH RUDOLF
BROWNBRIDGE ROAD
SCHECK'S CAMPGROUND
N
MUNCIE LAKES PATHWAY
GRAND TRAVERSE COUNTY
PAVED ROAD
POOR DIRT ROAD
PATHWAY
CONTOUR
ONE MILE
ADAPTED FROM MICHIGAN HIKING OPPORTUNITIES

Nordhouse Dunes
Manistee National Forest

General

Sand dunes dominate much of eastern shore of Lake Michigan (Michigan's "west coast"). The Sleeping Bear National Lakeshore is probably the best known dune site, and more kids and other people scramble up and down the exposed sands of Sleeping Bear than at any other place. Other parks provide these hills to the pleasure of feet and wheels; Ludington State Park, virtually contiguous to the dune area we speak of here, is one of these. Some are in private hands, even to the extent of being owned by those who would shovel their substance into trucks for sale as foundary sand. And then there's Nordhouse Dunes, maybe not truly unique, but our principal respondent proclaims the area to be "one of the last of the really beautiful places. Could be.

In the broad sense, we are speaking of a 20 square mile (roughly) chunk of the Manistee National Forest that lies just north of Hamlin Lake (which is roughly 10 miles north of Ludington), and west of US-31, the principal north-south highway along the Lake Michigan shore. This part of the Forest is densely wooded with recent-growth mixed pines and hardwoods; it has about two miles of shoreline of sandy beach backed by the dunes. A paved two-lane road runs from its intersection with US-31 for about eight miles to a national forest campground laid out among the woods just behind the dunes. The dunes themselves are mostly wooded, especially on their inshore slopes, but if you like sand, or swimming in Lake Michigan, there are access trails to the beach. For access to the pleasures of the woods, several trails lead southward behind the dunes. The trail closest to the shore also bring you to larger areas of inland open sand caused by "blowouts," i.e places where storm-blown sand from the shore has overwhelmed the vegetation.

An alternative access is via Nurnberg Road, which runs along the southern edge of the National Forest land. From a parking area at its end, trails lead to the dunes (about a mile away), and to the campground mentioned in the preceding paragraph.

Maps

Mason County map (reference 1). U S Geological Survey Manistee 15-minute quadrangle. *Michigan Hiking Opportunities* (reference 2) provides a map. The county map is preferred for local road information, the *Hiking Opportunities* map is the only one of the three to show the trails. The USGS map is, of course, the best source of topographical information. The map printed here is a composite that shows the principal features from all three. You will also find trail maps posted at the trailheads and trail intersections.

Other references

None. *Michigan Hiking Opportunities* contains only the map just mentioned.

Travel from Ann Arbor

Aim for Ludington. Your road map shows you two alternatives: US-23 to Brighton, I-96 to its intersection with US-31 near Muskegon, then north; US-23 and I-75 to Bay City, then US-10 to its intersection with US-31 seven miles east of Ludington at Scottville, then north. These alternatives are of about equal length, but the latter has the longer stretch of two-lane road. The forest service road to the national forest campground leaves US-31 just a little more than 11 miles from the center of Scottville; it's the second left after crossing the Big Sable River (called Grand Sable River on some maps). A large Forest Service sign near the road junction announces a Lake Michigan recreation area. The sign makes no mention of Nordhouse Dunes, but you're there. After another eight miles through the woods, that is. Allow five hours from Ann Arbor.

Nurnberg Road originates in the same neighborhood, but does not intersect US-31. When checked in 1986, this road was not blessed with a sign at its origin, but was readily found by noting intersections and distances on the access map.

Details

The campground at the end of the access road is the only feasible camping spot, unless you're a lie-down-by-the-trail person. (See the personal account following this section for a comment by someone who is.) This campground is typical of the campgrounds found in national forest recreation areas. The roads are paved, and each camping spot has a paved off-road parking area. There are picnic tables and grills. The "bathrooms" are about as good as you can expect far down in the woods. And the whole ground is in the woods, so that the camping spots are fairly well screened from their neighbors. Showers, electricity, and like amenities of home are not available.

The Forest Service does not offer a reservation service, so you take your chances. Experience has shown that spots are usually available for those who arrive decently early, even on summer holidays. Nordhouse Dunes is a place of gentle pleasures (well, you could throw frisbees on the beach), and hence does not attract the more rampant recreationists, like those that take their outdoor joys from internal combustion engines.

The maps show a network of primitive roads (presumably old logging roads) throughout the area between US-31 and the Lake; you will probably observe some of these from the access road as you drive in. They seemingly offer extensive hiking, though we have no respondents who can give any guidance on this opportunity.

The trails shown on the map printed here, and on any other map you are likely to come across, should be regarded as approximate in their location, especially in the dune area where shifting sand may have forced *ad hoc* shifting of trails. Shortcuts taken by some of the many people who visit the area apparently have caused trails to develop where none are shown by the maps.

A personal account

One of our respondents offers the comments quoted in the following paragraphs.

I have led several trips to Nordhouse Dunes in which I used the Nurnberg Road access. (These were "introduction to backpacking" trips, but they also attracted old regulars who wanted to spend a day on the beach.) I avoided the national forest campground, using it only for source of water on the first night while camping off one of the fire trails in the area. On the following morning we drove to the end of Nurnberg Road and hiked through the woods from there. After a mile or two it was up onto the high dunes, then on to Lake Michigan. We camped in a wooded area at the base of one of the dunes, spent an afternoon on the beach, and then on the following morning hiked south on the beach to Ludington State Park, where we had spotted a car on the morning before. End of trip.

But two warnings about this scheme. First, the southern dune area has been turned over to the federal government by the Nature Conservancy since my last trip. If the feds' prohibition against camping "on the dunes" has been extended to the wooded area about a half-mile from the lake (where we camped the second night), then some spot farther to the east may have to be used.

[Another respondent who checked in 1986 found a list of rules posted at the Nurnberg Road trailhead, but it did not include any such prohibition.]

Second, the car spotted in Ludington State Park was in a "day use only" area, and so required permission from the ranger for parking overnight.

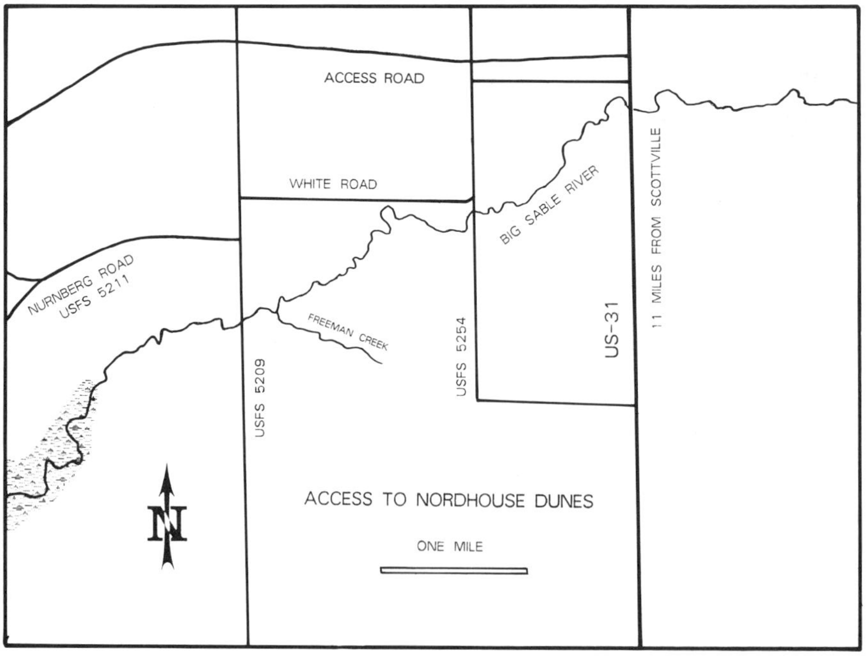

Nordhouse Dunes

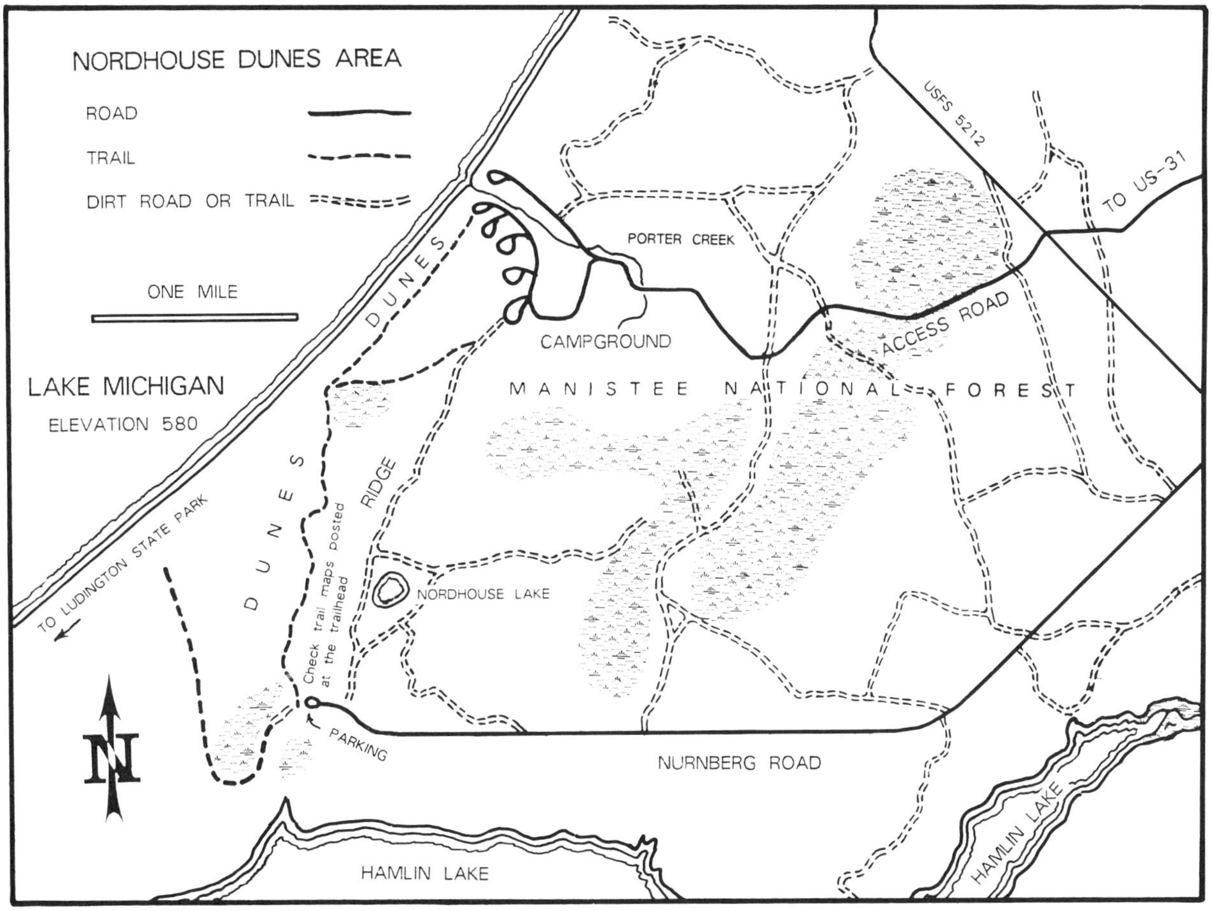

A Pastoral Hike in Charlevoix County

General

This is called a "pastoral" hike because its major ambience is that of farmland - several cornfields, a pasture of horses, a dairy farm, perhaps the chug of a tractor, and a whiff of pigsty. Removing it further from the wildwoods category is the circumstance that it is entirely on public roads. (Vehicular traffic is light, and indeed so light that our respondent claims to have once accomplished the hike without encountering a single vehicle.) The region traversed is hilly, lying as it does in the physiographic region known as Charlevoix Oriented Hill-Land. Several creeks flow generally northward toward Lake Charlevoix, and between them lie the ridges that constitute the hills. At one point the way passes through woodland, and you will note here that you are walking along a narrow ridge, with the land sloping away to swampy ground on both sides.

Not worth a special trip from very far away, but a pleasant divertissement of, say, two hours for someone in the Charlevoix area.

Maps

Charlevoix County map (reference 1), and US Geological Survey Central Lake quadrangle. The map here is drawn from the county map.

Other references

None.

Travel from Ann Arbor

Go to Charlevoix, following guidance of a Michigan road map. Take US-31 south to Barnard Road, which diverges to the left close by the Buick-Chevrolet dealer on the outskirts of Charlevoix. Take South Barnard Road to the left at about 3.5 miles after leaving US-31. Park outside the cemetery that lies just a few hundred yards from Barnard Road.

Details

Follow the route marked on the map. A counterclockwise direction might be favored, but mostly just because it gets the paved part of the route out of the way first. Length is approximately six miles.

The same route is feasible for bicycling, though some of the way is unpaved road.

Charlevoix County Hike

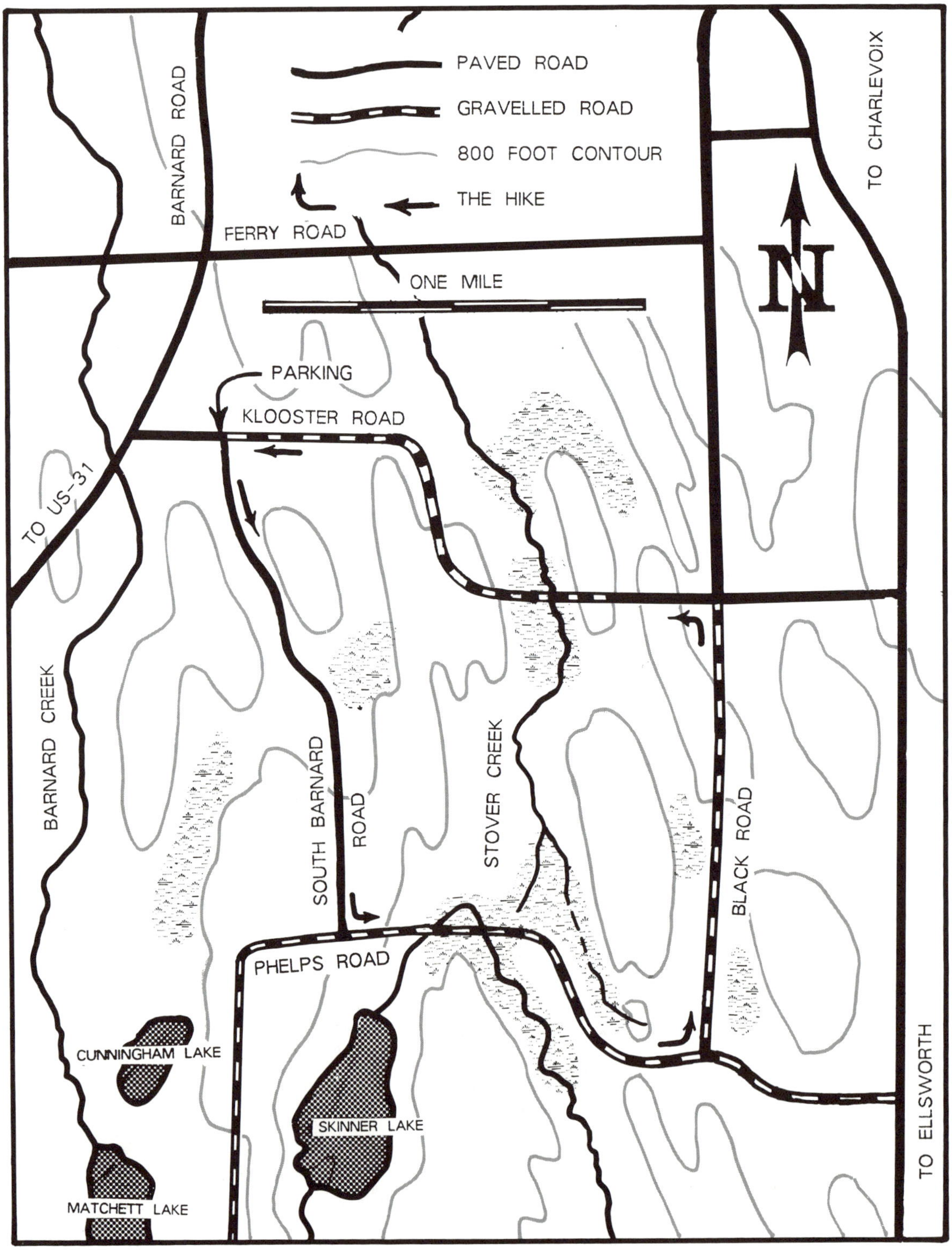

Day Hikes in the Jordan River Valley

General

The Jordan River is the principal feeder of the south arm of Lake Charlevoix in northwestern lower Michigan. It's cool and clear, and offended by only a few cottages along its lower reaches. It's emminently canoeable down from Graves Crossing, just off M-66 as you drive north from Mancelona. The trip to a takeout point where Rogers road crosses the river, just above its debouchment into Lake Charlevoix, requires only about three hours, for it is but a small stream. There are no hazards beyond the mild threat of overhanging branches, and the possibility of a downed tree. See the appendix for name of nearby canoe liveries.

Before its near intersection with M-66 in the vicinity of Graves Crossing, the river loops through an almost-totally wooded valley that has no human habitation within a mile of the river. A dirt road (variously labelled Pinney Bridge Road, Piney Bridge Road, Penny Bridge Road) runs along the north bank from M-66 to an intersection with Old State Road (which continues on to M-131) to provide access for fishermen, hunters, hikers, and the like. Within the surrounding state forest (Jordan River State Forest), and crossing the river in two places, is the Jordan River Pathway, an 18-mile loop that is occasionally used by the Sierra members for weekend backpacking. See *Michigan Hiking Opportunies* (reference 2) for a map and information.

The principal interest of this chapter is day hiking in the upper valley, plus some contiguous area, on the north side of the river. There is one "official" hiking (and crosscountry skiing) trail - the Warner Creek Pathway - that is dignified by a sign and parking lot on highway M-32, by a posted trail map at the trailhead, and by blazes along the trail. Mostly, however, the area we speak of is one of narrow dirt roads that are good enough for access by car, yet primitive enough for pleasant walking, plus a network of unmarked tracks (old logging roads?) that beg for joyful exploration. Many of the tracks of this kind are shown on our map; in part their location comes

from higher sources, such as the Geological Survey topographic map, but also in part from experience of our respondents. You may find others.
The country is heavily wooded in second-growth hardwoods. A few cleared areas - apparently surviving from old farms - can be found, and you may stumble into patches where clear-cut lumbering has obviously been done. And hills. You will note on the map a span of 300 feet in its contours, a span which can't justify any claim to mountainous terrain, but as you stand in one of the clearings admiring the surrounding wooded ridges, the feeling of being among mountains will require only a little help from your imagination. A place where the deer and the antelope play (your imagination will have to help with the antelope also). If you like exploring wild country, here's an easily accessible place to unleash that primitive urge.

Maps

Antrim County map (reference 1), and US Geological Survey Boyne Falls quadrangle. The map here is drawn from the county map, with elevation data from the USGS map.

Other references

Michigan Hiking Opportunities (reference 2) will serve you well for the Jordan River Pathway, but no reference covers the area and trails discussed by this chapter.

Travel from Ann Arbor

US-23 and I-75 take you to Gaylord. From Gaylord follow M-32 west to the intersection with US-131. From this intersection turn south for a few hundred yards to the intersection of US-131with Old State Road (Maps call it by this name, but in 1986 the sign at US-131 said "Jordan River Road"). Go west on Old State Road for approximately 3 miles to parking area P1, or continue from here on Pinney Bridge Road to other parking areas. If there are no road signs (don't expect them), Pinney Bridge Road can be identified as the only driveable alternative at P1. Marsh Road is approximately 3.5 miles from the Old State - Pinney Bridge intersection, and is the first driveable turnoff after you leave that intersection.

An alternative is to continue westward on M-32 past its intersection with US-131. The parking area for the Warner Creek Pathway is about 2.5 miles from that intersection, and is marked by a sign. At about 6 miles from US-131, Marsh road leads south into the area shown on the map (about 2.5 miles to P5).

If approaching from the west, take Pinney Bridge Road or Old State Road from their intersections with M-66, or take M-32 from East Jordan to its intersection with Marsh Road at about 8 miles from East Jordan, or continue to the Warner Creek parking lot.

A caveat: Except for P6 (Warner Creek lot) none of these parking "areas" or "lots" are that in any formal sense. They're just places where a few (like two or three) cars can pull off the road without climbing the trees. Primitive.

Details

If you would first like an overview - in quite a literal sense - of the the Jordan valley and its surroundings, go to the Deadman Hill overlook. This hill is a cliff that borders the valley for a stretch of a mile or so, and is reachable by a short excursion from US-131 over a paved road. The hill, the road, and the parking area for an overlook show in the lower right corner of our map. The intersection of the road with US-131 is approximately two miles south of the intersection of the latter with M-32. The view is better in the morning, since the view is to the west.

Deadman Hill is also a starting point for the Jordan River Pathway, which runs down into the valley and westward on the south side of the Jordan River. Part of this pathway therefore lies within the area mapped here, but we have elected not to show it on the map, an omission to avoid encouraging anyone from attempting to reach it from the north by wading the river. Oh, it's but a small and shallow river, but the muck it flows through sucks at feet and might swallow blundering humans. So says a respondent who got it up to his bellybutton in an attempted wade-across. For information on the Pathway, see *Michigan Hiking Opportunities* (reference 2).

The 3.8-mile Warner Creek Pathway is another good beginning excursion, since its entry is marked by a sign, it has a capacious (though unpaved) parking lot, and its course is marked by blue paint blazes. Warner Creek is not a tributary of the Jordan, and hence the Pathway doesn't take you into the Jordan valley at all, but the terrain and its aspect are quite Jordanian. In addition, departure from the Pathway at the west end of O'Brien Pond (shallow, almost grown into marsh) is feasible by crossing the low earthen dam that impounds the pond onto a trail that leads into the Jordan Valley. See map.

With the exception of the Warner Creek Pathway, the trails shown by our map are not marked by signs at beginnings or junctions, nor by trustworthy blazes (don't be deceived by occasional paint spots on trees), and the roads are signed only at their junctions with the neighboring highways. The trails are tracks through the woods, roads of a sort, but seemingly of a type that only a jeep could love. The trail that appears to be a continuation of Old State Road is found on the Geological Survey map, but the others shown on our map have been found by our respondents. Given the uncertainties of estimating distances in the woods, their locations must be regarded as approximate. And there may be other tracks that could be mistaken for the mapped ones. An enthusiasm for exploration, modified by caution and compass, is recommended.

An interesting objective is the large cleared area near the center of the map, outlined by a dotted line. The area appears to have once been farmland, now (1986) in the process of becoming pine forest. Meanwhile it affords a fine view of the surrounding hills.

A second clearing - also outlined by a dotted line - is adjacent to the intersection of Old State Road and Marsh Road. It was once a farm, a fact made obvious by the remnants of farm buildings. The house is more than a remnant; it appears to have been restored, perhaps as a summer cottage. Whatever, there is a gate is front of the house at the point where Old State Road degenerates into a woodland track, and on the gate is a sign of unwelcome. A respondent reports that this closure was done by the State, and therefore not by the nearby landowner, and that the track is similarly blocked near its emergence into the clearing mentioned in the preceding paragraph.

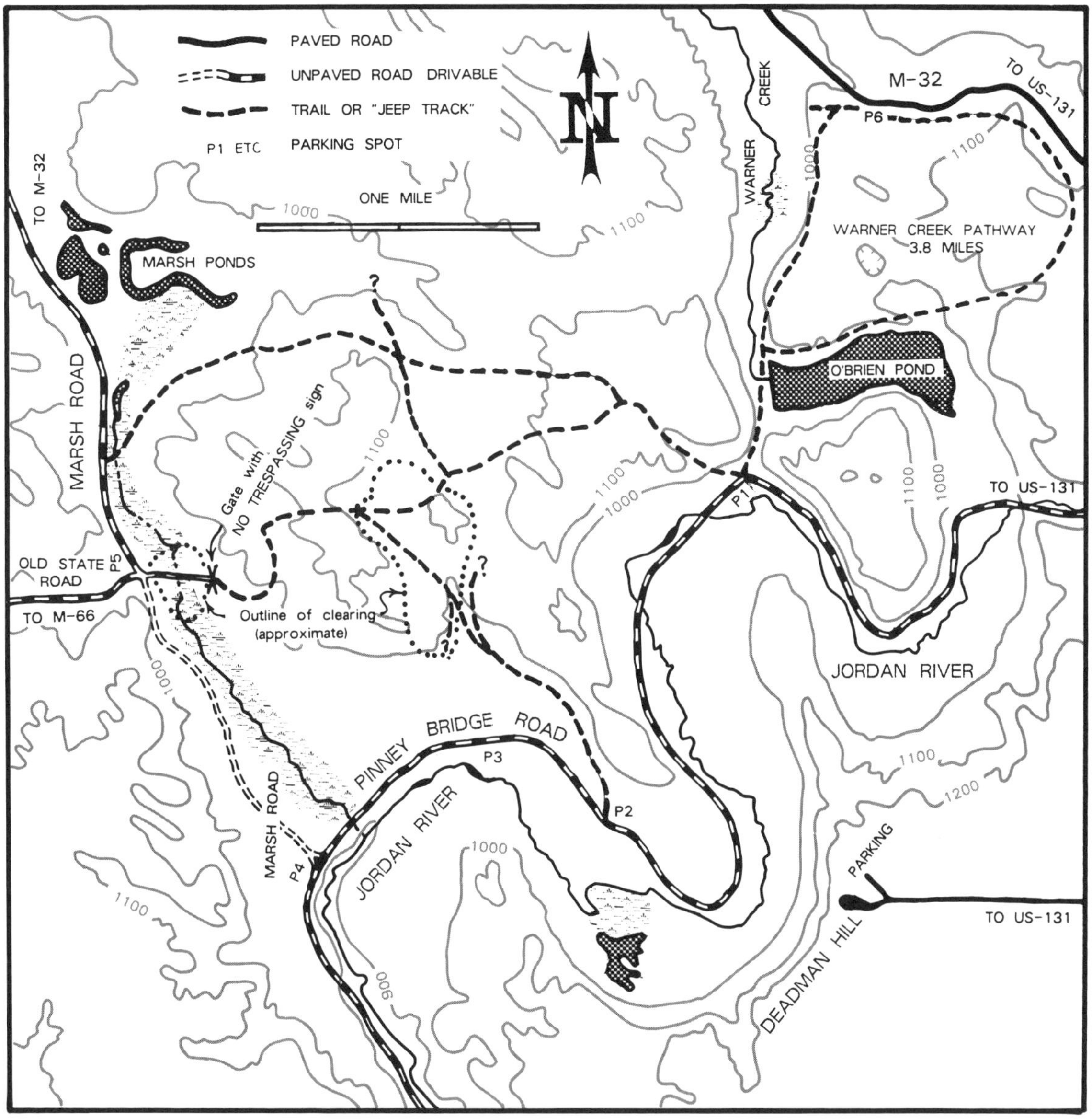

Canoeing and/or Hiking, Two Hearted River and Lake Superior Shore

General

The Michigan shore of Lake Superior and its hinterland are rich in opportunities for outings. For example, even a casual admirer of pretty rocks could spend a lifetime picking up all that lie on a few miles of the Lake beach. The woods have a primitive charm, even if they are in many places interrupted by the recent devastation of clear-cut lumbering.

Among places of well-deserved popular renown are the Pictured Rocks National Lakeshore and the Porcupine Mountains State Park. The place described here is not designated by such a well-known name, but is fairly defined by natural boundaries, and has those rocks and that primitive charm even if there is nothing so impressive as the Porcupines or the Pictured Rocks. You will encounter a few people because of several state forest campgrounds and a few private cabins, but hikers and canoeists seem to be rare.

The area in question lies in Luce County within the narrow triangle of land formed by Lake Superior, the Two Hearted River, and the road (a dirt track, really) that runs from the Reed and Green (yes, it really is ***Reed***, and not the ***Red*** that seems to belong here) Campground to the Lake. See the accompanying map. The river provides a pleasant canoe trip of about three hours from that campground to the mouth of the river, and if you are not being serviced by a canoe livery, a hike of about six miles back to the start to pick up your car. Given the pleasures of hiking in this area, the time taken to spot a car at the downstream point isn't worth the trouble, and you might even refuse a livery's ride in order to sample the beach and the woods.

Canoeing, day hiking, backpacking are all possible singly or in combination.
For instance, you might canoe down the river, set up a camp on the beach or in the edge of the woods along the beach (or in the campground at the mouth of the river if you admire pit

toilets), spend the rest of the day hiking eastward down the shore to admire the boats in Little Lake harbor, return to spend the night in your camp, then hike back to your car at Reed and Green campground the next morning. The alternative at the other end of the spectrum of possibilities is to cover all of this on foot during a single day - quite feasible if you start early.

Maps

Luce County map (reference 1), and US Geological Survey quadrangles Muskalonge Lake East, Betsy Lake NW, and Betsy Lake North (the last only if you want to take that side excursion to Little Lake). The map printed here is drawn from the county map.

Other references

The North Country Trail, which traverses this area just inland from the beach, is described in reference 2.

Travel from Ann Arbor

Any Michigan road map will show you how to get to Newberry, the metropolis of Luce County. About four miles north of Newberry on M-123, take county road 407 to the left. (This road is shown on the typical road map, but all maps do not list its number.) After approximately 17 miles, 407 crosses the Two Hearted River at High Bridge; at about 1.5 miles beyond this crossing, turn right onto county road 410. This road leads to the mouth of the Two Hearted River, and at the intersection signs proclaiming this are much more in evidence than the little board saying 410. After 5-6 miles take the road to the left that leads to the Reed and Green campground within a few hundred yards. If you cross the river while on 410, you've just missed the R and G road. An alternative is to go on to the mouth of the river on 410, 412, and 423 (there are signs) and start your adventure from there.

A warning: The road from 410 to the R and G campground

continues through the campground to Lake Superior, just as the map printed here shows. However, only four-wheel drive vehicles should risk going beyond the campground.

Details

The map here, and the county map from which it originates, are fairly accurate in showing the roads (sandy tracks, really) extending from Reed and Green campground to the lake, and to the mouth of the river, but they cannot show many important details.

The road leading most directly to the lake shore is easy to follow from the campground, but there are no signs of any kind to identify it. Coming westward along the beach and looking for this road, you may be troubled in identifying its beginning. The best way of identifying it is to have a rough idea of where you are on the beach, and to watch for a rough track (with tire tracks, very likely) debouching from the woods. There are no other such debouchments for several miles along the beach east of here (true in 1984).

The other track may be difficult to identify from the beach also, but you can surely find it by means of brief explorations of tracks leading inland in the vicinity of the river mouth. No signs. Along the way you will encounter branchings that no map shows. If you are heading for Reed and Green, then a safe rule is to take the left at any branching, except for the few that will obviously lead to cabins along the river.

This area has been subject to clear-cut lumbering for many years. You are likely to encounter recently cut patches, and others that have been replanted and are once again well wooded, though perhaps with rather small trees.

The Two Hearted River is narrow and moderately swift, but over the stretch from Reed and Green to the mouth, it presents no significant difficulties to a canoeist. Trouble with downed trees is a possibility, but none has been reported. A canoe livery is operated by the Rainbow Lodge, located at the mouth of the river. Its telephone is 906-658-3357. (None of our respondents has experience with this livery; the information here is taken from a roadside sign.)

The North Country Trail parallels the beach just a short distance inland. This trail is copiously marked with blue blazes on the trees. See reference 2 for further information. The trail enhances this small area in only a modest way. Its principal virtue is that it offers an alternative to walking on the beach.

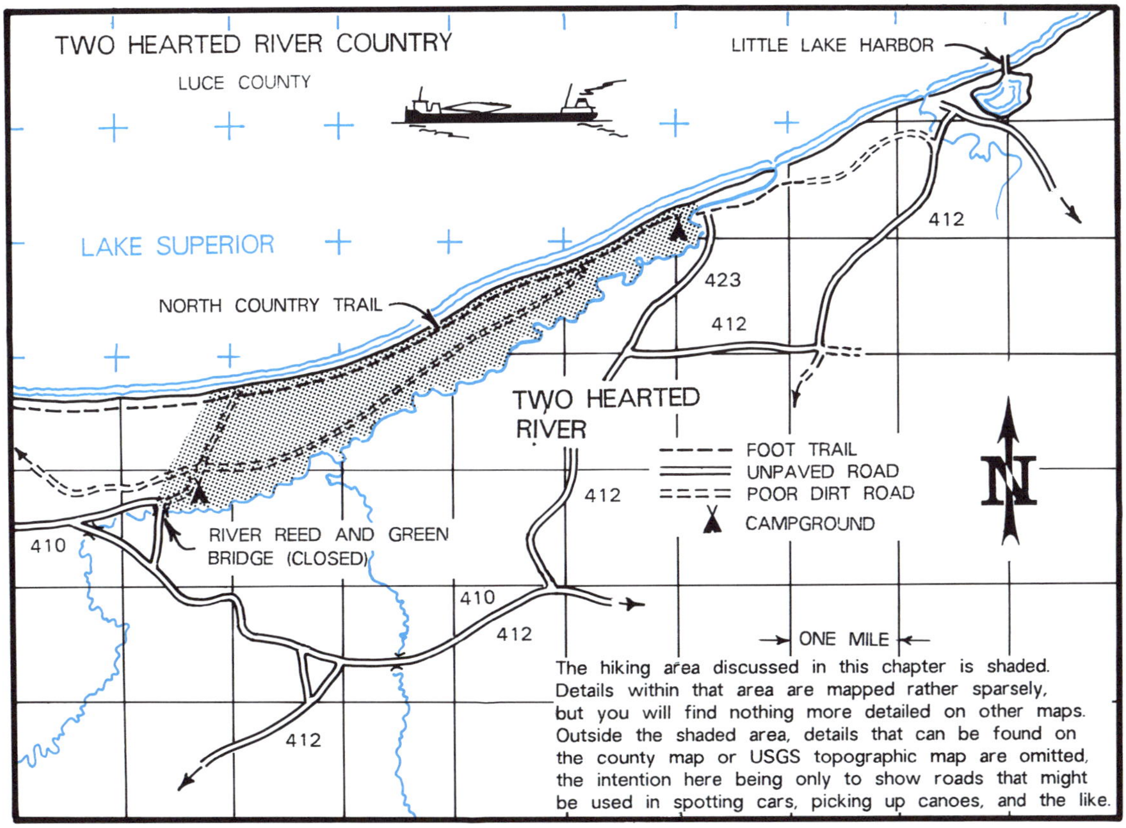

Day Trips or Canoe Camping on the Pine River

General

The Pine River is in most ways typical of many canoeing streams in the northern part of the Lower Peninsula. It is narrow, winding, imbedded in attractive forest (though with occasional cabin or cottage evident), and in many places bordered by high sand bluffs on one side, low swampy ground on the other. The unique feature of this river is its reputation for being the best Lower Peninsula river for those who like their water fast, and like at least some challenge from rapids. It is by no means dangerous at normal water levels to canoeists of reasonable skill and experience. Novices might better practice elsewhere, and families with small children aboard might prefer a tamer river.

Several day trips are easily arranged. A one-night camping cruise is also quite feasible.

Maps

Lake and Wexford County maps (reference 1), and canoe livery maps. The last are the most useful, since they show access points, distances, predicted travel times between access points, and campgrounds. The map printed here is copied from a livery's map.

Other references

Brochures distributed by canoe liveries are a handy source of information. They can be gotten in many ways: picked up at highway rest stops, from roadside restaurants, by calling the Michigan Tourist Council in Lansing (see Appendix 1 for phone number), or by call the liveries mentioned here, or other liveries that you may find in the state list of liveries that constitutes Appendix 2. The Pine is also treated in *Canoeing Michigan Rivers* (reference 19).

Travel from Ann Arbor

Your point of aim is Cadillac, a city about 185 miles from Ann Arbor. See a Michigan road map for routes. The river is reached by taking M-55 west or US-131 south from Cadillac. The map here shows the routes off M-55 to several access points and liveries. From Cadillac the distance is roughly 20 miles, depending, of course, on the particular destination.

Details

A table at the end of this article lists distances and estimated paddling times between access points (taken from a livery brochure). Trips to suit a variety of time budgets are obviously possible. The time column adds to 14 hours, surely a bit long for a single day, but about right for an easy two-day trip. Note that the map shows several campgrounds along the middle stretch of the river. (Just to the left of the map, the river flows into the Manistee River for a long day's paddle to the city of Manistee on Lake MIchigan.)

This is a popular river; it is supposedly very crowded on summer weekends. Campgrounds likewise. An entry permit for the river may be required on summer weekends. Liveries are empowered to issue these; if they rent you a canoe, the permit comes with it.

The map printed here and the times listed below are adapted from brochures distributed by Horina Canoe Rental and Marrik's Canoe Service . Their locations are noted on the map; addresses, phone numbers are in Appendix 2.

ESTIMATED CANOEING TIMES IN HOURS

Access Point	Time from Preceding Point
Edgetts Bridge	0
Skookum Bridge	3

Lincoln Access	3
Dobson Bridge	3
Peterson Bridge	2
Low Bridge	3

We have noted earlier that from the standpoint of the canoeist with moderate skills, the river is challenging but not dangerous. Of course, some spots will obviously present more challenge than others, and spots do come and go (thinking of downed trees). The essential response of paddlers is to remain alert and on duty at all times when the boat is underway. For the canoeist who had the moderate skill and attends to duty there are no special hazards. Just don't be pawing in the beer cooler while going 'round a bend.

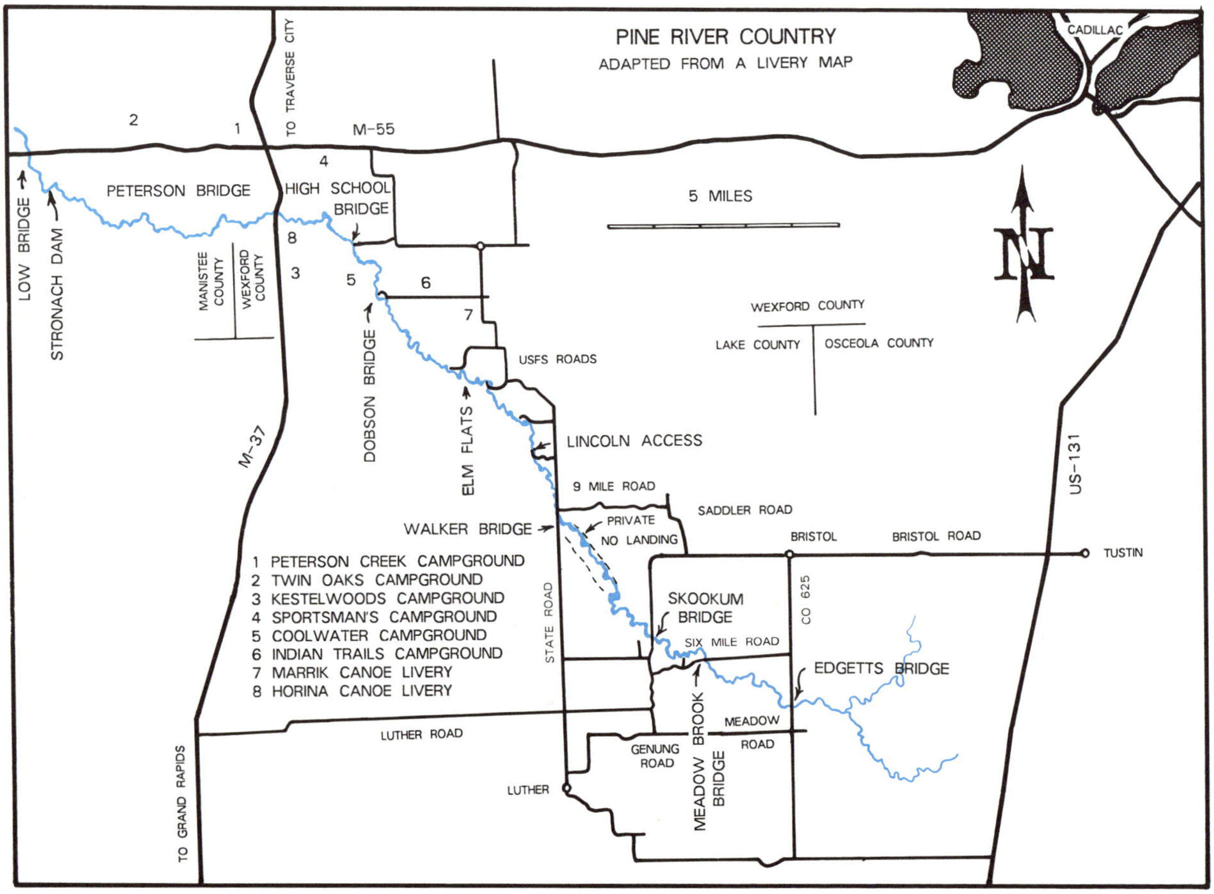

Skiing the Corsair Trails

General

One of the best cross-country skiing trail networks in Michigan is located in the Tawas area, only three hours from Ann Arbor. Both beginners and experts enjoy the well laid-out, groomed, and marked tracks of Corsair Trails. Over 35 km of trails are groomed twice weekly by the U S Forest Service, and by the Corsair Ski Club.

The area is attractive to groups of skiers in which the members have different skiing abilities since there is a good mix of easy and intermediate trails that allow the group to split up according to ability.

Another highlight of this area is the 18 km annual Silver Creek Challenge Citizens Cross Country Race, usually held around the second week in February. It is a great way to become acquainted with cross-country racing, yet the race is short enough that participants usally have the energy to enjoy recreational skiing for the remainder of the day. For details, contact Nordic Sports in East Tawas (517-362-2001).

Maps

Iosco County map (reference 1) and U S Geological Survey Tawas City 15' quadrangle. The map printed here is adapted from *Michigan Hiking Opportunities* (reference 2). Trail maps that show more detail are posted at all trail junctions, and at the parking lot. Copies of the map may also be obtained from Nordic Sports in East Tawas.

Other references

Michigan Cross Country Skiing Atlas (reference 11).

Travel from Ann Arbor

US-23 takes you to East Tawas. From there take monument road about 12 miles northwest to the Corsair Trails parking lot.

Details

The trail network is bisected by Monument Road. Terrain to the east of the road is generally more hilly, with some long downhill runs. There are several large open fields on the southernmost loop. This loop, named the Lost Lake Loop, is said by one respondent to be the best skiing trail in the Corsair area.

West of Monument Road the trail parallels the banks of Silver Creek in several places, with some short, steep runs down the walls of the creek valley.

The eastern side of the trail network is mostly in mixed pine and oak forest. There are lowland conifers along Silver Creek, and some larger stands of pine on the western side of Monument Road.

The Tawas area often has snow when other parts of the state, especially Ann Arbor, do not, so that it may be the haven for the frustrated skier in scant-snow areas. For a report on snow conditions, call Nordic Sports (517-362-2001).

Corsair Trails

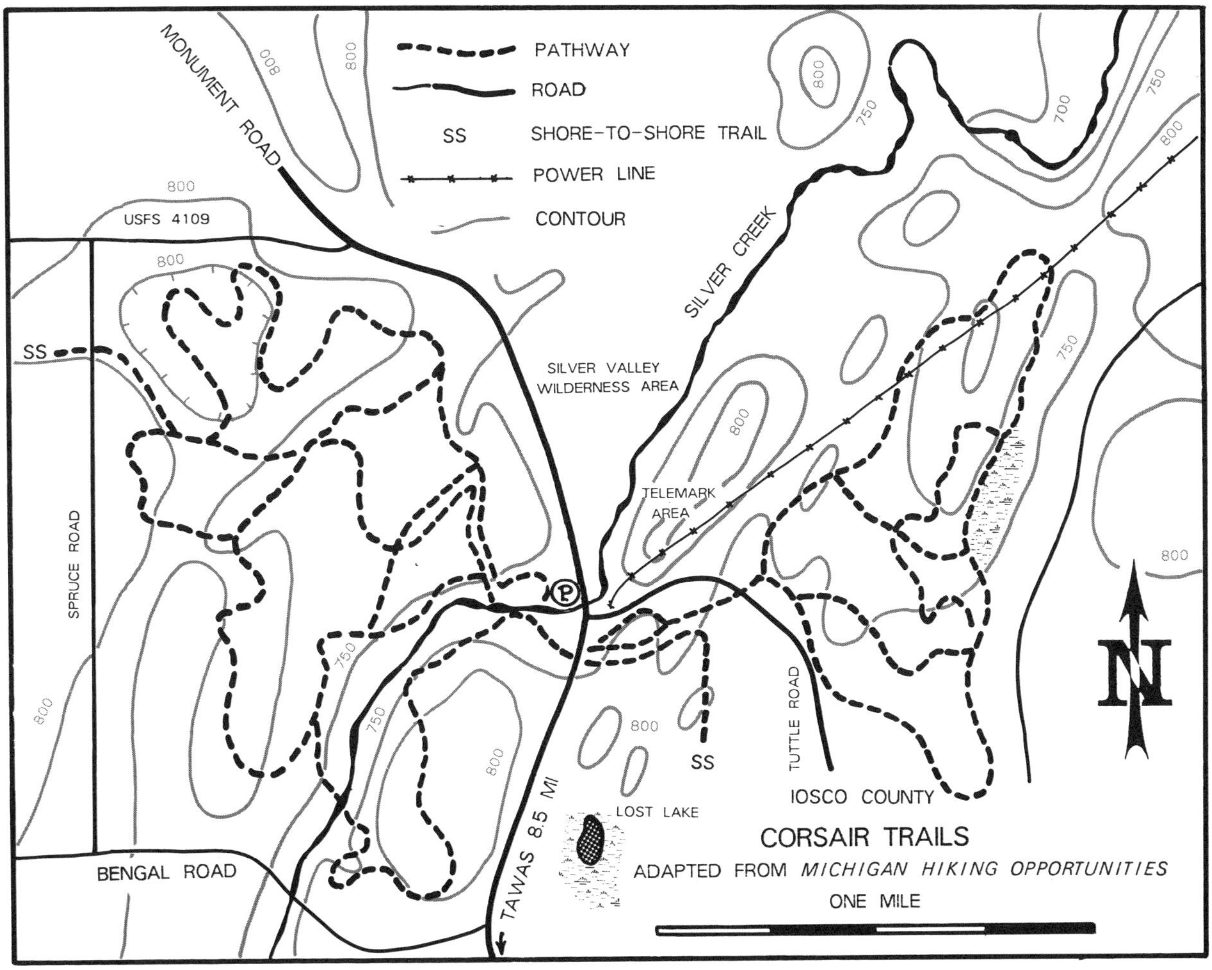

Canoe Camping at Tahquamenon Lower Falls

General

The falls of the Tahquamenon River (Chippawa County in the Upper Peninsula) are probably the largest in Michigan in terms of water volume and of tourist visits. A large state park campground spreads along the north bank of the river at the lower falls, and a paved road gives easy access to the campground, so that a visit to these falls - and to the nearby upper falls - is an easy matter. On the other hand, the lower falls can be the objective of an overnight canoe camping trip originating at the point where the river enters Whitefish Bay (Lake Superior). The river has a current, to be sure, so that paddling upstream demands its exertions, but in the typical late summer or fall that current is not a great burden. A respondent states that he once made the trip in August in a 90-lb canoe, loaded with camping gear and three children (a ten-year old was the bow paddler), and covered the 15-mile passage from river mouth to the falls in eight hours. And he stopped for lunch.

The river is wide as canoe streams go, and offers little impediment from shallows, rapids, or downed trees. There is a hint of rapids just below the falls.

There are no good intermediate camping spots along the river, but primitive camping is possible along the south bank at the falls. The campground on the north bank at the falls is an obvious facility.

Maps

Chippewa County map (reference 1). The map printed here is adapted from the county map.

Other references

None.

Travel from Ann Arbor

From the Mackinac Bridge continue on I-75 approximately eight miles to M-123. Follow this route north to the mouth of the river. Should be about seven hours driving time from Ann Arbor.

Details

There is a state park campground at the mouth of the river, providing a launching ramp and parking area. (Since there appear to be no canoe liveries nearby, you are likely to be bringing your own canoe.) Load up and paddle. The passage to the lower falls is approximately 15 miles, and if the current is not unusually strong (has it rained a lot lately? snow melted recently?), paddlers of average strength can expect to make the trip in seven to eight hours.

There are no good access points between the river mouth and the lower falls.

The river water is deeply stained by vegetation. Even with purification pills, you will probably not want to drink it. Well water is available at the campgrounds that lie at both ends of the trip.

Our only camping reports are from people who have camped in primitive style on the south side of the river at the lower falls. This area is wooded, but not thickly enough to preclude pitching tents. If you don't need a tent, or don't need to drive pegs for the one you need, camping right on the rocks beside the falls is possible. The water makes a goodly bit of noise, but it's 100-percent natural. Natural enough to drown out the unnatural noises from the campground across the river.

Above the falls the river is too swift for upstream paddling, and dangerous because of the falls. You probably won't want to try a portage.

In spite of the occasional cottage and the nearness of the road to the Lower Falls campground, the river flows through wild country. It's Upper Peninsula, after all. Owls, osprey, and maybe a bald eagle will stare unblinking as you pass.

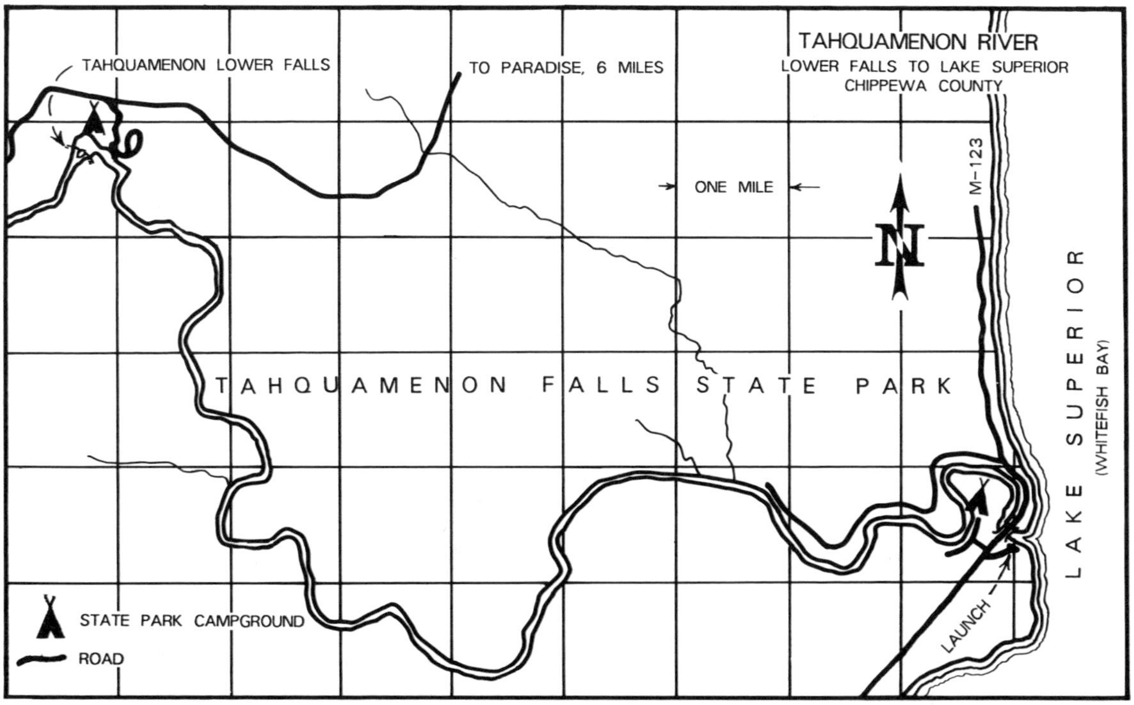

North Manitou Island

General

North Manitou lies close to the Lelanau County mainland, on the order of 10 miles offshore from the town and harbor of Leland. In some ways it is much like the other islands of northern Lake Michigan, High and Garden, that are treated in other chapters of this book. The greatest similarity is that it was not so long ago inhabited by a population that supported itself by farming and lumbering, and was large enough for a while to justify a school and a post office. The similarity continues in that it has been deserted by its people, and is reverting to wilderness through the natural encroachments of forest on abandoned fields and orchards. Meanwhile, the decaying remnants of human activity remain to intrigue the curious visitor.

One element of contrast is that North Manitou has known summer cottagers, something never reported on either Garden or High. A similarity is that all of these islands are now publicly owned. But Garden and High are owned by the state, and dedicated by the state to wildlife research, with not the slightest provision made for the hiking/camping visitors who may find their way ashore from private transportation. North Manitou, quite in contrast, is now part of the Sleeping Bear Dunes National Seashore, National Park Service in command. A ranger is stationed on the island, and at the landing (known as "The Village") where you may put ashore from public transportation, there is a maintained campground. However, the remaining 99.8% of the island not to be developed, rather is "managed as wilderness" under the provisions of Public Law 88-577.

Camping is permitted (ah, but the feds always have their "rules and regulations") virtually anywhere on the island, and the island is laced with trails that make easy the hiking through forest, old fields, to two inland lakes, and up and down the dunes. The highest dune point is approximately 420 feet above the level of Lake Michigan.

A public boat service operates from Leland on the weekend, but because it makes only two trips -- one on Friday and one on Sunday (substitute Monday on our three-day holiday weekends), a visit to the island by this means has to be a camping visit. Other arrangements with charter boat operators out of Leland are said to be possible.

The public boat (Manitou Island Transit) leaves Leland 10am Friday; leaves the island about 11am Sunday. Phone is 616-256-9061.

Your own boat? Yes, a private boat may dock to load and unload at the ranger station on the east shore of the island (see map), but for no longer than 15 minutes. But there is not the slightest protection from the possible rage of Lake Michigan.

Maps

Lelanau Conty map (reference 1). U S Geological Survey North Manitou 15' quadrangle. The Park Service furnishes a map that shows about everything there is to show, including topography at 100-ft contours. The map printed here is a copy of the Park Service map.

Other references

The Park Service issues a brochure (the map mentioned above is included) that contains a wide range of current information, plus a brief (very) sketch of island history. We know of no other reference relevant to the island as an outing destination.However, we have been told that the one of the two remaining long-time summer residents of the island is writing a history.

Travel from Ann Arbor

Traverse City, metropolis of northwestern lower Michigan is the major objective, approximately 230 miles from Ann Arbor. Leland, the ferry port, is another 25 miles up the Leelanau

Peninsula. Given that leave the interstates far short of Traverse City, five hours travel time seems like a minimum. See earlier statement on the public boat schedule and phone number.

Our respondents recommend the D H Day campground in the Sleeping Bear Dunes area as a good spot to camp the night before catching the ferry to the island.

Details

The Park Service is generous in that it allows you to camp anywhere, though with certain limitations and restrictions. They are (quoting from the brochure)

1. Camps are not to be set up within sight or sound of a designated trail, building, another camp or the inland lakes.
2. Camps may not be set up within 300 feet of the Lake Michigan high water mark or 200 feet of water sources.
3. Open fires are prohibited. However, there are two fire rings for open fires in the village campground near the ferry landing.

There is no refuse disposal. Take it back to Leland.

There is no potable water source, save for a few springs that are difficult to find. Purification of surface water (i.e. from lakes) recommended.

Deer are numerous, and perhaps an attractive element in the wilderness scene. They are too numerous, much too numerous however. They eat everything they can reach, giving the forest a park-like aspect. Pretty in a way, yes, but unhealthy since no seedling can grow to be a tree. The Park Service (which had owned the island only two years at the time of our publication) allowed a hunting season in 1985 that is reported to have restored some flora-fauna equilibrium, and 1986 visitors saw evidence of new vegetation on the forest floor.

Raccoons, curse the thieves, are a problem that requires campers to hang their food at night. And to keep an eye on it all the time. The remaining summer residents say (1986) that the red fox is a large element of the animal population, but that skunks, porcupines, and poisonous snakes are not present.

Pets not allowed.

Lake Manitou is suitable for swimming. The south and west beaches are preferred (less rocky) for Lake Michigan swimming.

Old Baldy dune blowout gives a spectacular view from its top.

The "Frederickson Place," a clearing at the edge of a cliff above Lake Michigan on the southwestern shore of the island is an attractive camping spot.

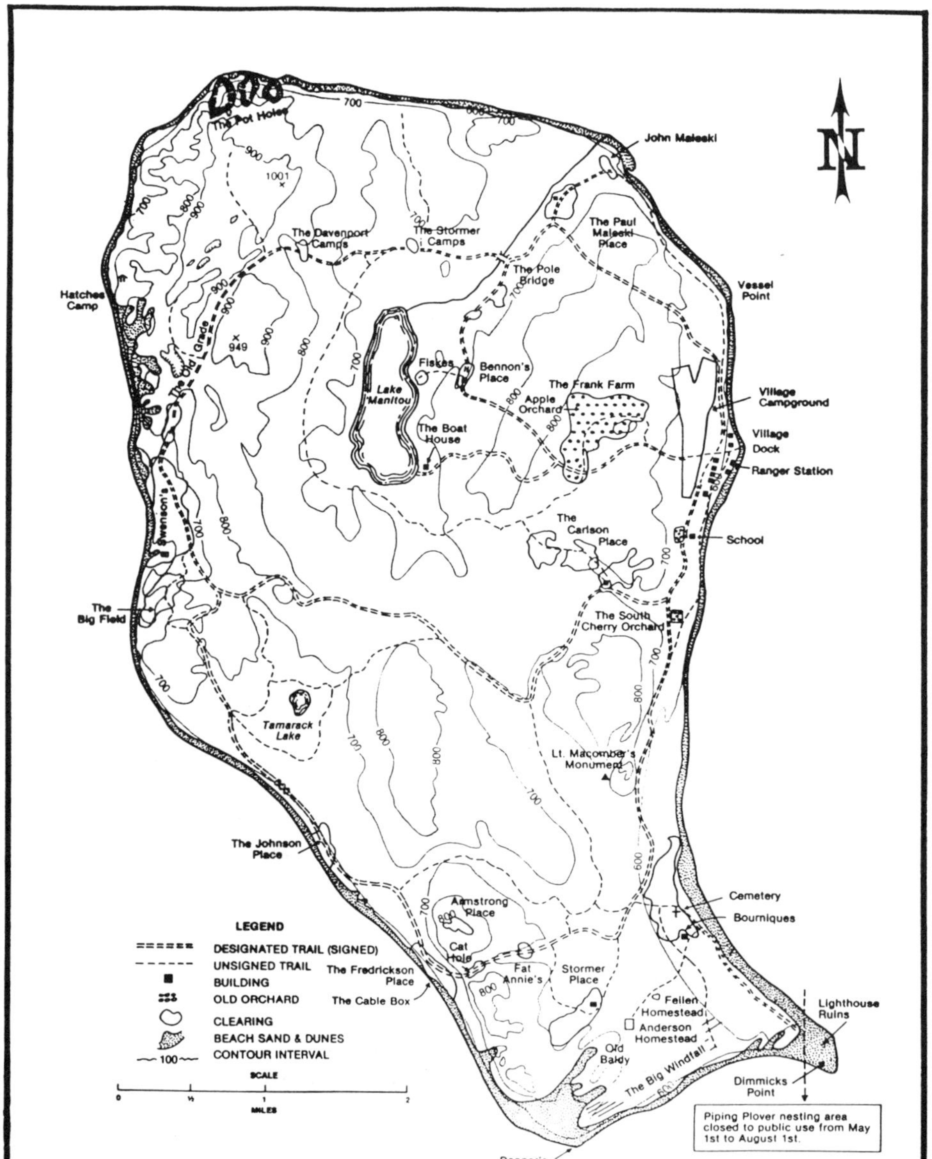

North Manitou Island
Sleeping Bear Dunes

COPIED FROM THE PARK SERVICE BROCHURE

Distant Outings

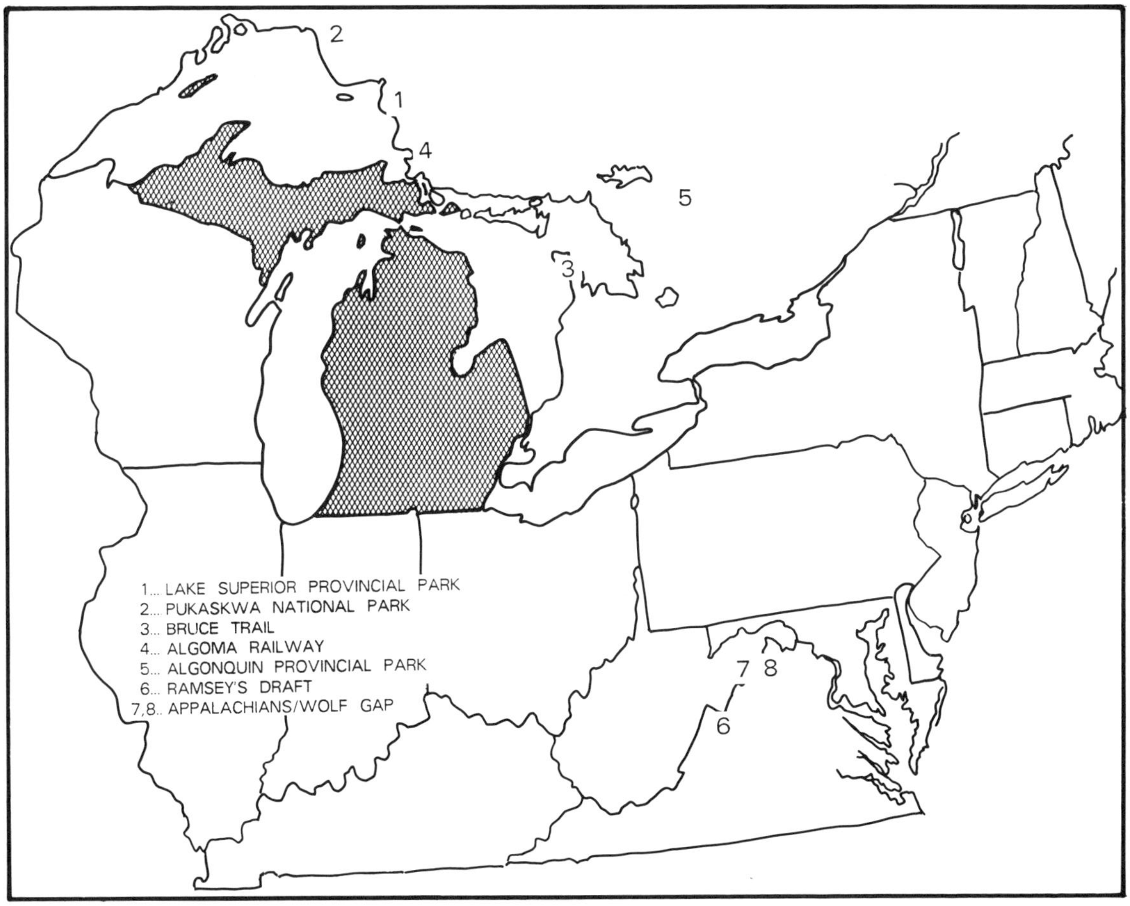

Distant Outings

Michigan is a great place for outings of many kinds (just count those Ohio license plates speeding north on I-75), but, yes, there are other places that have things that Michigan doesn't, or have more of them. Canada is wilder, Colorado is higher, Virginia (and all of Appalachia) have more more more of mountains than those sand dunes and occasional Porcupines of the Great Lakes country. We aren't ashamed to go to these other places when time, budget, and inspiration fall into place.

Here, much more than in the earlier parts of the book, we must not attempt to be all-inclusive. Even Michigan's outings are too much for one volume, and giving the same density of coverage to the balance of North America, say, is entirely impractical. So we have picked only the few places that Huron Valley members have visited since 1980, have volunteered information on, and certify that they can drive to within our 12 hour limit.

Camping, Hiking, and Canoeing in Lake Superior Provincial Park

General

Lake Superior Provincial Park is a heavily forested tract of steep hills and numerous lakes lying along the eastern shore of Lake Superior, north of Sault Sainte Marie, Ontario. Those who have been there love it. No words can convey.... Moose, black bear, wolves, coyotes, lynx (and innumerable other creatures) suggest the ambience.

Although day visits based on Sault Sainte Marie are practicable, camping in one of the several campgrounds, overnight canoeing, or backpacking are more typical. Visits to Agawa Canyon, on the southeastern edge of the park, are most feasible by rail, a trip usually made within a single day from SSMarie. This activity, being a somewhat distinct from other park uses, is discussed in a separate chapter.

Maps, Other references

The map Of the park reproduced here is based on one published in a park brochure, and is intended only for armchair use. Park authorities publish a brochure *Hiking Trails* for the hiker, and two for the canoer, *Canoeing in Lake Superior Provincial Park,* and *Old Woman/Sand River Canoe Routes.* These, and a brochure describing the general features of the park, can be obtained from either of the following:

Lake Superior Park Superintendent
22 Mission Road, Box 1160
Wawa, Ontario P0S 1K0
705-856-7396

Ministry of Natural Resources
Communications Services Branch
Whitney Block, Queen's Park

Toronto, Ontario M7A 1W3

Literature, including a much more detailed map than that reproduced here, can also be picked up at the park entrance.

Travel from Ann Arbor

US-23 and I-75 to Sault Sainte Marie. Ontario Route 17 leads north close to the shore of the Lake, and passes through the middle of the park. Nine hours driving time from Ann Arbor is said to be typical.

Details

Day hikes on the trails leading to the Lake Superior beaches have been reported with enthusiasm. (Swimming from the beaches is only for those who like it cold.) See, in particular, the Warp Bay and Orphan Lake trails.

At the time our respondents made their most recent visit to the park there were no long trails to challenge the backpacker to a multi-day excursion into the interior. Most of the trails are intended for day hiking from the highway, although several lead to hike-in campgrounds where the backpacker can lay the burden down (or hang it in a tree, Br'er Bear), pitch the tent, and then continue to seek the hiker's pleasure in the neighborhood. On the other hand, we have been informed of the development of a coastal trail that is lengthy enough for two-to-three-day backpacks. The map printed here does not show that trail, but surely the map you obtain now from park headquarters will include it.

As an alternative for those who would experience the country far from a roadhead, the park offers a number of lengthy canoe trails via its lakes and rivers. Numerous canoe routes appear on the map printed here. One respondent speaks of canoeing for three days in the Mijinemungshing Lake area without encountering other humans. Canoes can be rented at park headquarters, and at the Agawa Bay campground.

One respondent speaks with enthusiasm of the Rabbit Blanket Lake campground at the north end of the park, saying that it is the most rustic and least populated of the campgrounds.

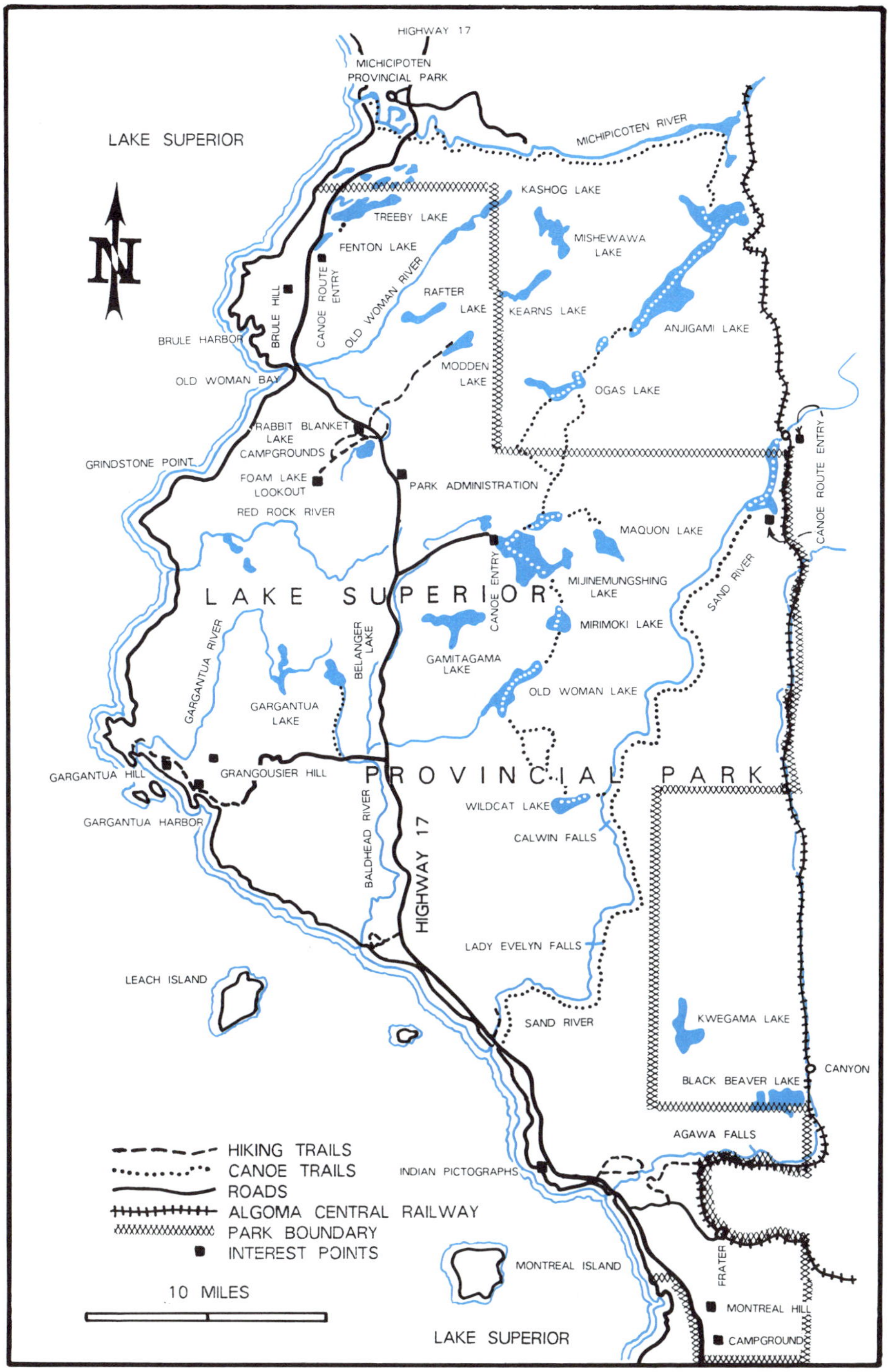

Camping, Hiking, Canoeing in Pukaskwa National Park

General

Pukaskwa National Park is an almost completely wild area of about 1880 sq km lying along the northeastern shore of Lake Superior. Its entrance is 408 km by Ontario Route 17 from Sault Sainte Marie, Ontario. It features the rock of the Canadian Shield, boreal forest, white-water rivers, and in quite typical generality, the plants, animals, and scenery of the Canadian North.

The only entrance to the park is a road branching from Route 17, entering the extreme northwestern corner in the neighborhood of Hattie Cove. The area near the entrance is developed with local hiking trails, restrooms, a visitor center, campgrounds, and a dayuse (picnic tables, swimming access) area. The only other artificial feature of the park is the coastal trail, originating at Hattie Cove, and following the shore toward the southern extremity of the park at the Pukaskwa River, a distance of about 100 km. The several rivers that flow into Lake Superior along this coast are bridged, and numerous primitive camping places are provided, but otherwise the wilderness of forest and shore is unaltered. (When this was written, in 1985, the trail had not been completed to its intended destination.)

No trails penetrate the interior (again, as of 1985), but Park literature states that interior trails will be constructed after the coastal trail is finished.

The White River and the Pukaskwa River are said to be canoable, though the latter usually has sufficient water only during spring runoff. Neither is the sort of river you are likely to test by upstream paddling, so you presumably would enter them from their intersections with Route 17 outside the park. We have no reports from anyone who has canoed this area, but canoeing guides to both rivers are offered by the park headquarters. See address later.

There are many small harbors along the Lake Superior shore (poorly shown by the map published here), so that a camping cruise down this shore by prudent canoeists seems possible.

Approach by water is also feasible, and is practiced by a few venturesome yachtsmen. Hattie Cove is too shallow of entrance for offshore boats, but there are numerous wild coves along the Pukaskwa shore. We'll say nothing about them here, but a cruising guide to Lake Superior is listed among the references (reference 8).

Maps

The map published here is based on the general park brochure, and is intended for illustration only. Detailed maps of the coastal hiking trail are included in a booklet *Coastal Hiking Trail*, available from the park office. Address is

Superintendent
Pukaskwa National Park
Box 550
Marathon, Ontario P0T 2E0
807-229-0801

The canoe guides can be obtained from the same source.

Other references

A brochure describing the park can be obtained from the source listed just above, and a Lake Superior cruising guidebook has been noted already. A source for the canoeist is *Canoe Routes of Ontario* (reference 9). For general acquaintance with the north shore of the Lake, you might try *Geology and Scenery, North Shore of Lake Superior*, reference 10.

Travel from Ann Arbor

The village of Marathon, roughly 15 miles north of the park entrance, has passenger rail service, but we'll assume that you're motoring via Sault Sainte Marie, about seven hours from Ann Arbor over US-23 and I-75. From there it's 406 km (231 miles) to the park entrance over a two-lane road (Route 17). Dawdlers might not make it within our 12-hour time limit.

Details

We have one respondent who has backpacked a short distance along the coastal trail, spending one night on the trail. He is charmed by the experience, but otherwise reports that the trail literature mentioned here is quite adequate as a source of information.

One nettling note, to close: even the park literature points out the nuisance of biting insects from spring through early August. Would that the black flies ate mosquitos instead of people!

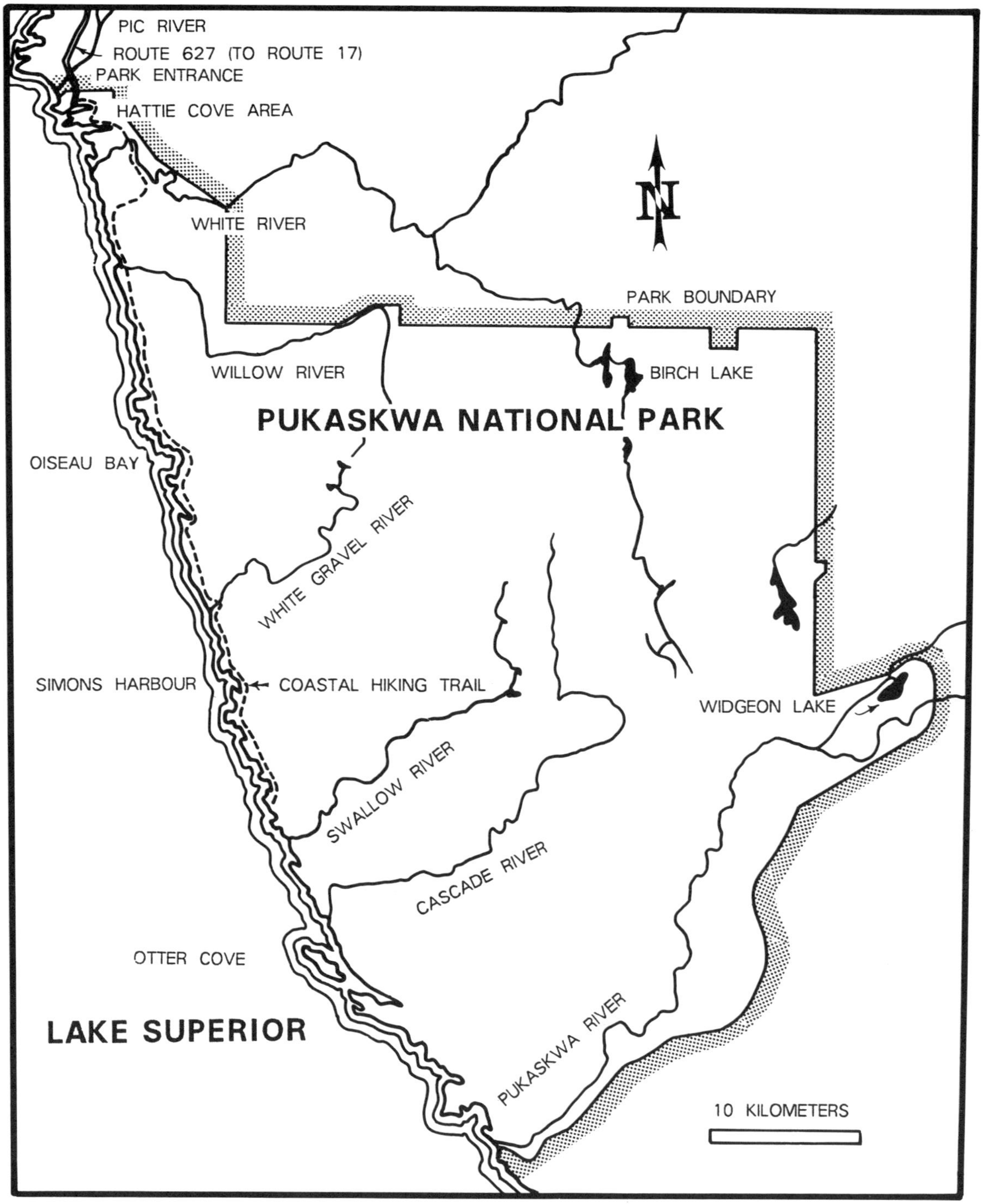
PIC RIVER
ROUTE 627 (TO ROUTE 17)
PARK ENTRANCE
HATTIE COVE AREA
N
WHITE RIVER
PARK BOUNDARY
WILLOW RIVER
BIRCH LAKE
PUKASKWA NATIONAL PARK
OISEAU BAY
WHITE GRAVEL RIVER
SIMONS HARBOUR
COASTAL HIKING TRAIL
WIDGEON LAKE
SWALLOW RIVER
CASCADE RIVER
OTTER COVE
LAKE SUPERIOR
PUKASKWA RIVER
10 KILOMETERS

Backpacking on The Bruce Trail

General

The Bruce Trail is a footpath that follows the Niagara Escarpment through Ontario from the Niagara River to the tip of the Bruce Peninsula at Tobermory. There must be those that have hiked its entire length, and now wear a shoulder patch or teeshirt telling of it to those who read other people's shirttales. On the other hand, the Sierra enthusiasts of Michigan have preferred to limit their experience to the part of the trail that traverses the Bruce Peninsula itself, and most often to a stretch that runs for 20 miles or so from the northern terminus at Tobermory. This is the segment of the trail treated in this chapter. Allowing for seven to eight hours on the road each way, the trip can be accomplished between a late Thursday afternoon departure from Ann Arbor and a Sunday night return.

The Bruce Peninsula is mostly flat farm and woodland, sprinkled with a few small urban centers, such a Tobermory, Wiarton, and Lion's Head. To some extent it's quaint and tourist-oriented. Many of the tourists are just passing through, since ferry service from Tobermory to Manitoulin Island (which is connected to the mainland farther north by a bridge) provides the best route to more northern parts for many people in southern Michigan and the adjacent parts of Ontario. But its shoreline with Georgian Bay (to the east of the peninsula) is the abrupt face of the Niagara Escarpment, providing a rugged, rocky strip of country that's near-wilderness in quality, and offering repeated high-point vistas over the Bay. And rugged hiking.

Rocks, rocks, the Escarpment is rocks. Bones of the Earth, as one or our respondents labeled them. You have to walk on them, and they are suggestive of bones, being in many places the weathered edges of sharply uptilted strata. The weathering has rounded what might otherwise be knife edges, but not enough to keep the feet from longing for a nice sandy - or even muddy - path. And the trail goes up and down: from the edge of the escarpment, in places several hundred feet above the water, to the beach. Then up again.

So the walking itself is not the easiest thing you ever did, but presents neither great distress nor great difficulty for the experienced backpacker. The scenic appeal of the escarpment, spectacular in places, and the panoramas of Georgian Bay, override the obstacles for anyone whose feet and muscles are in good shape.

Day hikes are quite feasible as well. A good access point is Cyprus Lake Provincial Park. The Park is marked on the map here, and you will note on it park trails (shown dotted) that connect with the main trail along the shore. One could camp in the Park and from it experience some of the Bruce Trail unencumbered all the weights and stuffs of backpacking.

The map printed here shows the segment of the Bruce Trail being spoken of in this chapter.

Maps

The Bruce Trail Guidebook, published by The Bruce Trail Association, Box 857, Hamilton, Ontario L8N 3N9 in frequently updated editions, contains a series of fold-out maps, each covering 10 to 15 miles of trail. These are the maps you should have. Topographic maps are sold by the Canada Map Office, Department of Energy, Mines, and Resources in Ottawa. Those that cover the area in question are Dyer's Bay and Dorcas Bay (both Bruce County). The topographic maps aren't much help with the trail, but they do show the roads that lead from the highway (Route 6) to an intersection with a branch of the trail leading inland at the end of the hike we are describing here. Unfortunately, the *Guidebook* maps don't show these roads.

Other references

The Bruce Beckons, by W Sherwood Fox, published by the University of Toronto Press, and *The Bruce*, by Lindsey Brown, published by the Mariner Chart Shop of Tobermory, are paperback books that offer a lot of local lore. The latter, which is small enough to fit in a pocket, appears to be better for a hiker. It has some flora/fauna information, and contains street maps of the towns.

Travel from Ann Arbor

I-94 to Port Huron/Sarnia. A short hitch on Route 7 (about 20 miles), then north on Route 21 until it intersects Route 6 at the base of the Peninsula. In all, about 310 miles to Tobermory. The Canadian portion (about 220 miles) is all two-lane road, and hence may offer slow going to those accustomed to reaching Anyplace via an interstate highway. Allow eight hours.

Details

The Huron Valley Group stages a Bruce Trail expedition whenever enough mutual desire surfaces, typically once every year or two. The trip might be staged something like this: leave Ann Arbor via carpool late Thursday afternoon; arrive Cyprus Lake Provincial Park about midnight to camp overnight; spot car at trail exit early Friday, then drive to Tobermory to start hike about 10 AM; camp Friday night at Driftwood Cove; hike Saturday to High Dump; hike Sunday morning inland to the trailend car. (All places mentioned here are on the map, the last denoted by a car symbol.)

The trail begins in Tobermory itself, at the shore of Little Tub Harbor. Look for the trail marker. There's a parking lot close at hand.

There are no formal campgrounds, so that the stops at both Driftwood Cove and High Dump are a matter of pitching the tents in the edge of the woods along the beach. Primitive, but then you're unlikely to be disturbed by the squawlings and blarings of the run-of-the-mill "campers." Bad 'cess to 'em, eh? By the way, the "dump" here refers to the dumping of logs over the cliff into the water, not to the disposal of noisome solid wastes.

The Friday and Saturday hikes described in this section are of roughly six and twelve miles, respectively, and a body of opinion has it that a more even split could be better because twelve miles is quite wearying, given the constant walking over rock, and the frequent ups and downs of the trail. However, shortening Saturday by lengthening Sunday is not as attractive because there is no source of water between Halfway Dump and High Dump, the trail being just too isolated from the Bay by high and rugged cliffs. Although this barrier is broken at Halfway Dump, camping at that spot is prohibited. One Sierra group has reduced Saturday at the expense of a longer Friday by camping Friday night at Loon Lake, which is shown on our map.

In summer the Bruce Peninsula can be hot enough to make you wish you were tough enough to jump into the chilly water of Georgian Bay, but it can also be cool, and especially along the trail, exposed as it often is to wind off that water. Be prepared for either condition.

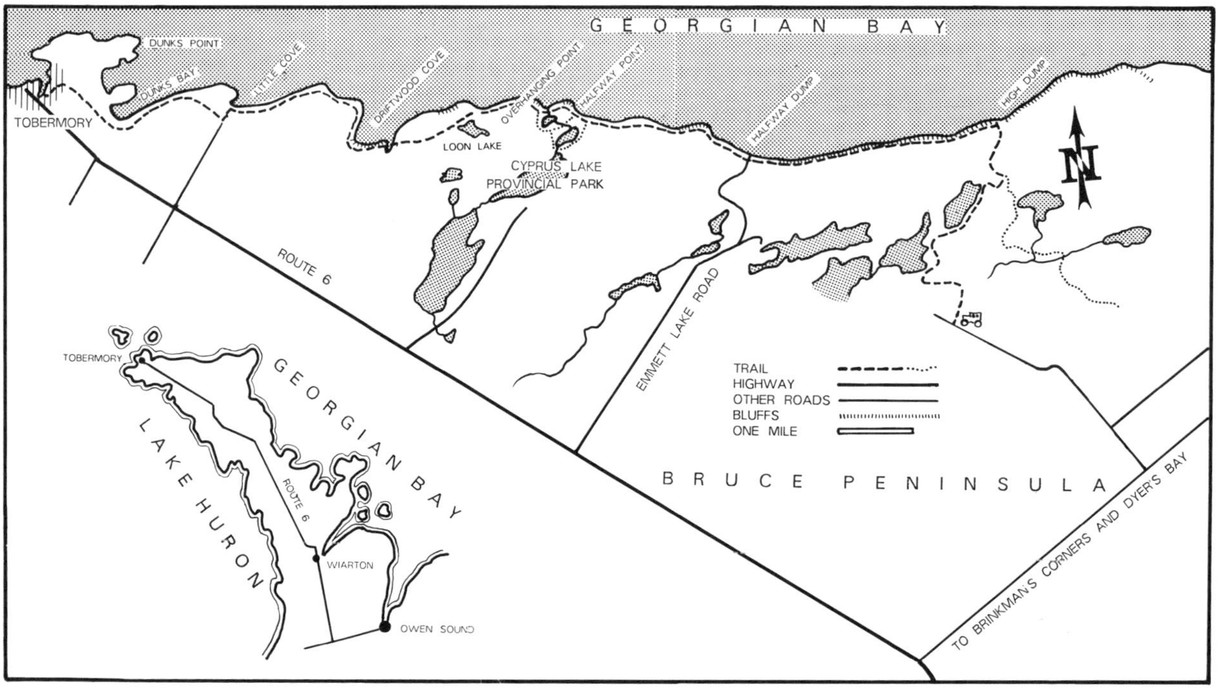
GEORGIAN BAY
DUNKS POINT
DUNKS BAY
LITTLE COVE
DRIFTWOOD COVE
OVERHANGING POINT
HALFWAY POINT
HALFWAY DUMP
HIGH DUMP
TOBERMORY
LOON LAKE
CYPRUS LAKE PROVINCIAL PARK
ROUTE 6
EMMETT LAKE ROAD
TRAIL
HIGHWAY
OTHER ROADS
BLUFFS
ONE MILE
BRUCE PENINSULA
TO BRINKMAN'S CORNERS AND DYER'S BAY
TOBERMORY
GEORGIAN BAY
LAKE HURON
ROUTE 6
WIARTON
OWEN SOUND

Excursions North from Sault Sainte Marie, Ontario, on the Algoma Central Railway

General

Train trips don't fall within the "outings" definition used in assembling this book, but this one comes close. The trip is through wilderness, and you can, in the warm part of the year at least, hop off to savor the wilderness *mano e mano* for a few hours while the train waits for you. And you can go deeper into the woods, backpacking, and catch the return train on a later day.

The Algoma Central Railway is a line that runs northerly from Sault Ste Marie, Ontario, for almost 300 miles to the small town of Hearst, Ontario. From late spring to early fall, it operates an excursion train on a 8:00 AM to 5:00 PM round trip to Agawa Canyon, a river gorge of great scenic appeal about 130 miles north of the Soo. A two-hour stopover at the canyon is made to allow picnic lunch, short hikes, and the like.

The winter excursion runs on an 8:30 AM to 4:30 PM schedule on weekends from late December to late March, but with no stopover.

Maps

The map accompanying our chapter on Lake Superior Provincial Park shows the rail line running along the park's eastern edge, and shows the location of the canyon. The road map published by the Province of Ontario shows the rail line also. No map accompanies this chapter.

Other references

The railway distributes brochures describing these trips. Contact Passenger Sales, Algoma Central Railway, 129 Bay Street, Sault Ste Marie 13, Ontario P6A 1W7. Phone is 705-254-4331. The Algoma Kinniwabi Travel Association, 616 Queen Street East, Suite 303, Sault Ste Marie 1, Ontario P6A 2A4, phone 705-254-4293, distributes literature on the area traversed by the trains.

Travel from Ann Arbor

US-23 plus I-75 lead directly to the Soo area in about six-seven hours (maybe more in winter). Since the "roadhead" in this case is a large city (large for its part of the world), public transportation can serve. There's both air and bus service. You probably won't like the bus.

Details

Both the winter and spring-through-fall trips are very popular, making reservations important. See address/phone information given earlier.

The trains have meal service.

The winter train is known as "The Snow Train," with its *raison d'etre* being the beauties of wilderness covered by deep snow. You press your nose against the windows, and are charmed. The warm weather train has similar purpose, sans snow, but also provides the opportunity at its layover of the contact experience. (The layover is effected by an exchange of the excursion cars between a regular northbound train and a southbound.)There's two hours between the leaving of the first and the arrival of the second.) You could extend that experience by hiking away into Lake Superior Provincial Park, with return on a later day. See our chapter on the Park for sources of information that you will surely need if planning to leave the rail line.

It is also quite feasible to use the regular passenger service for access to the park. A respondent reports buying tickets to Mile 131, which is beyond the layover point mentioned in the preceding paragraph, camping in the northeast corner of the park, then returning on the next day's southbound train. Mile 131 is nowhere, just a flag stop.

The information you are reading here was assembled in 1985. At that time it was known through press reports that Algoma Central was losing money on its passenger service, and that the equipment was causing problems because of its age, with replacement by new cars being unreasonably expensive from the railway's point of view. Demise of the service at some near-future time was therefore a recognized possibilty. Check before you cry All Aboard.

This isn't really an outing either, but many of the Huron Valley Group play softball in the Ann Arbor co-rec leagues. In this action view, the catcher of the Sierra Sluggers, one of the popular diamond squads, shows classical form in "putting the tag on" an opponent who is attempting the "crossing the plate" maneuver.

A Day Hike or Backpack in the Appalachians, George Washington National Forest

General

The area in question lies almost due west of Washington city along the boundary between Virginia and West Virginia. In fact, the trail passes for almost half its length along the crest of the ridge that forms the boundary between the states. The trip length is approximately 15 miles, with about 1750 feet in elevation change between highest and lowest points. Sounds a bit much for a day hike, but a respondent who is no great athlete reports doing it in seven hours without distress to foot or muscle.

Oh, it's mountains all the way! Not the Sierra, nor Colorado, but a beautiful wooded wilderness nonetheless. From the high points, views are, well, what you have the right to expect from the tops of mountains in the midst of other moutains. From some vantages the view extends eastward over the Shenandoah Valley toward the Massenutten and Blue Ridge ranges. The viewing is especially impressive from the apex of Big Schloss, a major outcropping of rock that towers from the ridge crest.

It's an outing for all seasons, especially to the hardy Michigander who thinks of a 20 F temperature in January as being "warm." However, the locale is not so far south that you can ignore the dangers of winter weather. An East Coast winter storm, brewed up by the exotic collisions of warm and cold that occur off Cape Hatteras, and blasting north to deluge New York and Boston can dump an awful lot of its snow in these mountains as it passes.

Although fairly distant from large population centers, the trails of this area are well known and well used, in part at least, because of the publications of the Potomac Appalachian Trail Club, publications that have made the trails easy to find and to use.

Maps

U S Geological Survey Wolf Gap and Woodstock (Virginia - West Virginia) 15' quadrangles. The map here is drawn from the USGS maps, as is the map in the Potomac Appalachian Trail Club guide book (referenced below).

Other references

Circuit Hikes in Virginia, West Virginia, Maryland, and Pennsylvania (reference 6), published by the Potomac Appalachian Trail Club, details five contiguous circuit hikes in this area. Hike10 in *Circuit Hikes* is in part coincident with the hike described here. Information in this reference adds little to what is given here, but the descriptions and maps of the contiguous hikes will be of interest if you aspire to covering more than 15 miles. (Also see our next chapter.) The book is a small paperback, making it more suitable for carrying on the trail than this one. Address of the Trail Club is 1718 N Street, N W, Washington, DC, 20036. *Hiking Trails of the Old Dominion* (reference 15) also is a source of information.

Travel from Ann Arbor

Ohio Turnpike, Pennsylvania Turnpike, and I-81 bring you in about 10 hours to Woodstock in the Shenandoah Valley of Virginia. Then VA-42 takes you to Columbia Furnace, and from there VA-675 winds westward and upward toward Wolf Gap, a low place in the ridge that forms the border between Virginia and West Virginia. A national forest campground at Wolf Gap (Wolf Gap Recreation Area) is the place to park, to unwind from the car, and to camp for the first night. Eleven hours from Ann Arbor, if you haven't dawdled too long over eating along the way.

A respondent reports doing this hike as an addendum to a business trip (by air) to Washington. His travel time in a rented car from Washington National Airport was about 2.5 hours, all within the speed limit.

Details

A start from the Wolf Gap campground in the counterclockwise direction is preferred because the trail that cuts downhill to FR (fire road) 92 from Wolf Gap is faint and unmarked (1986 report), and much more difficult to locate at the FR 92 end. At the other end you can locate it by noting that the map shows it intersecting VA-675 at the first sharp bend downhill (east) from the campground. The trail may not be marked, but if you can't be sure of the trail, well, a downhill bushwack will get you to the fire road without much trouble. Follow that road to Stony Creek Trail as the map indicates. Stony Creek Trail, at its lower end, is too broad to miss, even if some klod has vandalized the sign.

Sugar Knob Cabin, near the end of Stony Creek Trail, is a dark cabin, reeking of smoke, maintained for the shelter of hikers by the Potomac Appalachian Trail Club. It is padlocked when not in use, with key obtainable only from that Club.

The trail intersections are well marked by signs giving trail names, and distances to significant points. The exceptions are several shortcut trails, such as the several that are mentioned here.

Mill Mountain Trail passes close by the base of Big Schloss. A parallel branch passes over the top of this feature, but is said to be very steep and scrambly on the north side of Big Schloss. Going up and returning via the south side is much easier.

The last mile or so of Mill Mountain Trail into the Wolf Gap parking lot is very steep downward, and therefore is a bit dangerous with snow or ice covering it.

There are no campgrounds along the trail, other than the Wolf Gap Recreation Area, but backpackers will have no trouble finding flat spots to lie down. The area at the top of the map traversed by the Half Moon Trail is best in this respect. Water sources are only those shown on the map.

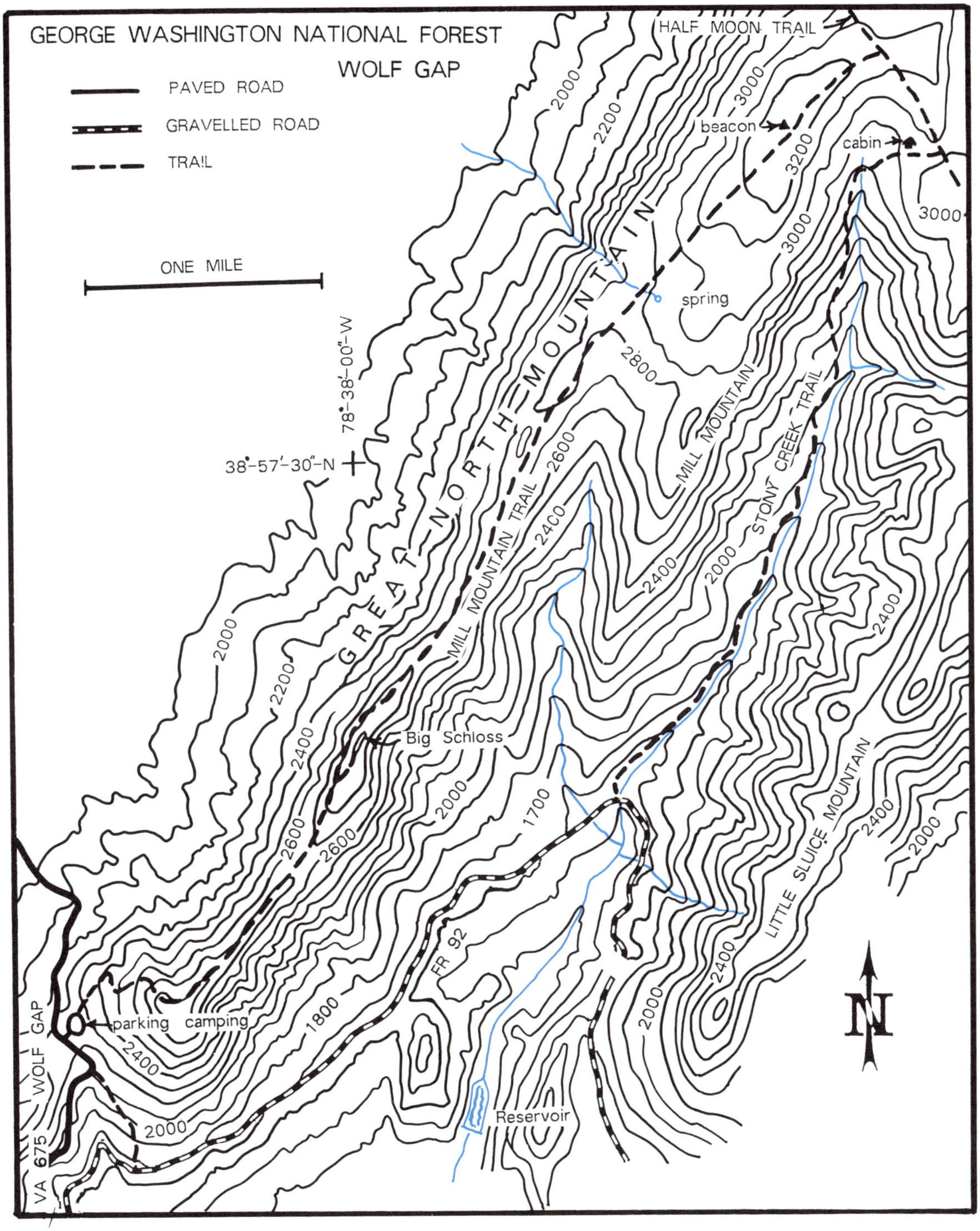
GEORGE WASHINGTON NATIONAL FOREST
WOLF GAP
PAVED ROAD
GRAVELLED ROAD
TRAIL
ONE MILE
78°-38'-00"-W
38°-57'-30"-N
HALF MOON TRAIL
beacon
cabin
spring
GREAT NORTH MOUNTAIN
MILL MOUNTAIN TRAIL
MILL MOUNTAIN
STONY CREEK TRAIL
LITTLE SLUICE MOUNTAIN
Big Schloss
FR 92
parking
camping
WOLF GAP
VA 675
Reservoir
N
2000
2200
2400
2600
2800
3000
3200
1700
1800

Hiking North from Wolf Gap
George Washington National Forest

General

The preceding chapter describes a circuit hike of approximately 15 miles in the George Washington National Forest, Virginia and West Virginia, with roadhead at the Wolf Gap Recreational Area. Our prime reference, *Circuit Hikes in Virginia, West Virginia, Maryland, and Pennsylvania* (reference 6) describes a number of such hikes. A glance at their maps shows that the hikes overlap, and thereby form a set of interlocking circuits that together frame a hiking area in which a backpacker can spend four or five days in constant motion on fresh trail. The map printed here is a composite map showing all of the principal trails on one sheet.

Circuit Hikes tells of several roadheads for the area, but the national forest campground at Wolf Gap appears to be the best access point, especially since it provides the only paved parking lot, and also an immediate camping spot for someone dragging in at sunset from a day on the road out of Michigan.

One hiking plan is to pack to a base camp along the Half Moon Trail near Sugar Knob (plenty of flat ground for tents, and a spring a short distance down the Stony Run Trail).Then for as many days as may please, one can explore the several loops, burdened only by lunch and water bottle.

Another is to establish the base camp right at Wolf Gap (no backpacking!), drive on day one to another roadhead, hike back to Wolf Gap for the night, hike back to the other roadhead on day two, following a different route, then drive back to Wolf Gap to gather tents and flee. Or the process can be repeated several times with different distant roadheads.

Maps

U S Geological Survey Wolf Gap (VA), Baker (WV),

Woodstock VA+WV), and Wardensville (VA+WV) quadrangles. Trail maps of the individual loops are to be found in reference 6.

Other references

See the preceding chapter.

Travel from Ann Arbor

See the preceding chapter for travel to Wolf Gap. The finding of roadheads other than Wolf Gap is detailed in reference 6, though the directions are for travel from the Washington neighborhood. Routes between roadheads are not described in the reference, nor are they evident on our map, but can be easily picked out on the USGS maps.

Details

Details discussed in the preceding chapter also apply here in a general way, and in particular to the loop Stony Creek Trail, Half Moon Trail, Mill Mountain Trail that is treated in that chapter.

None of our respondents have covered all of the the trails shown by our map. We do have a 1986 report from a group who established a base camp on the Half Moon Trail as suggested in the general section of this chapter, and then spent a day on the Waites Run Trail. This trail passes down into Wilson's Cove, an area of pasture that is closely surrounded by mountains, giving an interesting contrast to the wild woods of the mountain tops where lie most of the trails. In fact, the trail passes right through a farmyard where one may speak to cows and the like. The trail passes out of Wilson's Cove through a narrow pass along an unpaved road (mud in season) that gives access to one of the Cove farms. The road leads to Wardensville, which should hold no fascination for hikers, but shortly before reaching the first straggle of houses, hikers can turn into the woods along Waite's Run to visit the remains of a nineteenth-century iron furnace. (Reminds somewhat of the furnace at Fayette in Michigan's Upper Peninsula.)

The furnace is not shown on our map, nor on those in *Circuit Hikes*, but is marked on the USGS topographic map. In fact, there are several other remains of the primitive iron industry that can be found around the periphery of the hiking neighborhood we speak of here. See the topo maps.

The hike descriptions in *Circuit Hikes* are rather terse, but are adequate for guidance in the field. They list trail junctions and points of interest, with distances from the point of origin (in kilometers).

North from Wolf Gap
George Washington National Forest

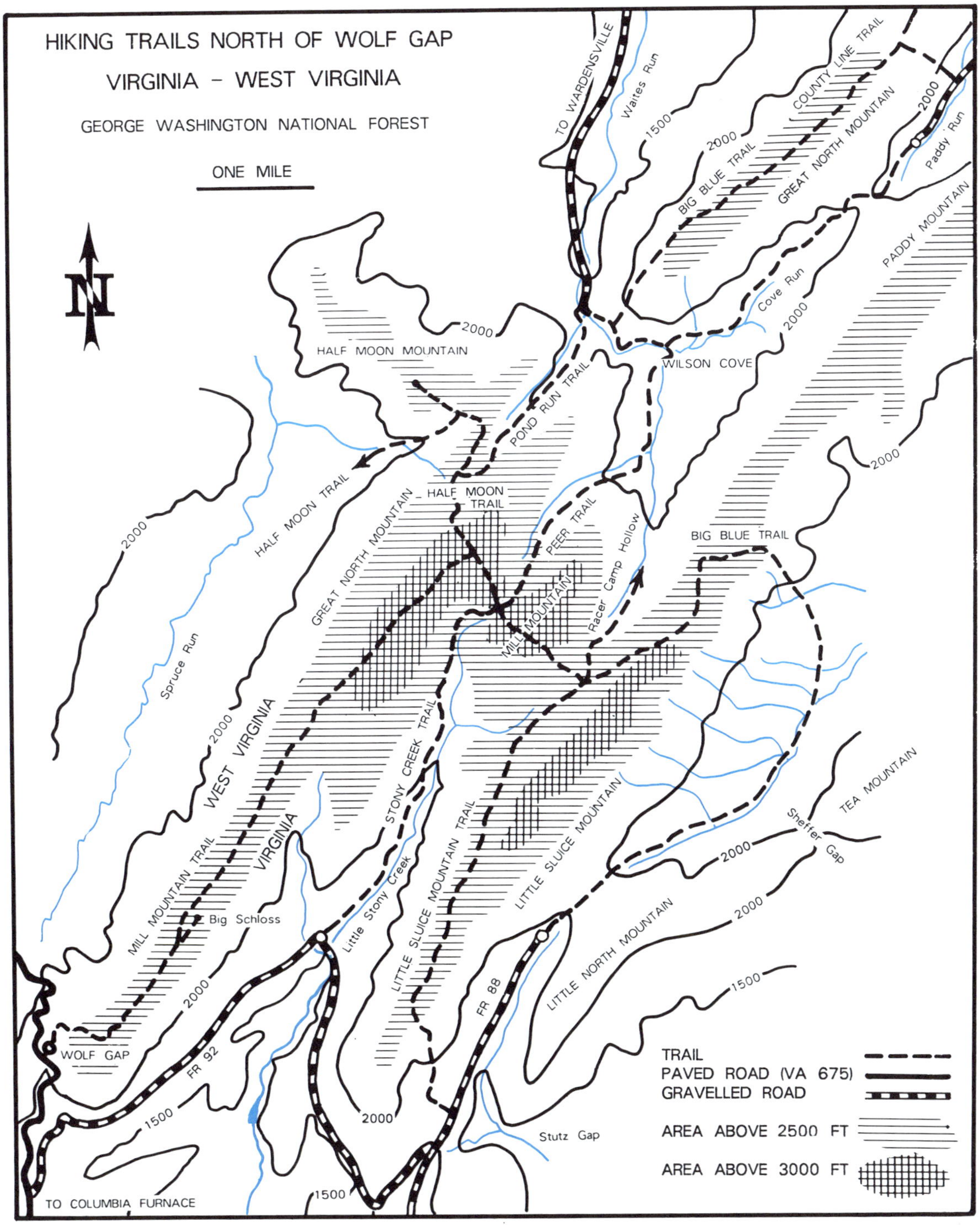

Algonquin Provincial Park

General

Algonquin Park provides pleasures both tame and strenuous in an area close to the center of gravity of Canada's population. Lying no more than a half-day's drive from Toronto, Ottawa, Montreal, and other large Canadian communities, it is immensely popular, and in some places a bit crowded in season. Michiganders think it's a great place also, although it lies a day's drive from the southern crossings into Canada.

Algonquin is largely a blend of forest, hills, bogs, lakes, and animals. It is by no means true wilderness, having been thoroughly logged, but its interior is largely inaccessible except by canoe (plus quite a bit of portaging), and hence wild and wooded. Bear, wolves, moose, and smaller mammals live there. Logging is still going on, but supposedly under rules that keep it aethetically inoffensive.

The Park's major uses originate along the only highway (Route 60) that crosses its boundaries, and it is close to this road that you find the tamer pleasures. Picnic grounds and campgrounds lie along the road, accessible by car without expenditure of energy of backpacking magnitude. For pleasant but not strenuous diversion, 10 (as of 1986) walking trails originate along the highway, ranging in length from about one km to about 20 km. Each is described by an interpretive brochure that can be bought at the park gates, its information center, or ordered via mail.

The walking trails are not for backpacking, and indeed, backpacking is rather limited for an area so large and so primitive. Two backpacking trails - the only backpacking trails - originate at the highway. The loops that constitute these trails range in length from 19 to 71 km. A park brochure describes them.

At the high end of the tame-to-strenuous spectrum of pleasures lies canoeing, the only means by which the Park's interior can be explored. That interior is speckled with lakes large and small.

Of course, paddling a canoe on a calm day doesn't tax one's resources excessively, but carrying one on your head over a long and rocky trail surely does. Portaging: that's where the strenuous part comes in. Short excursions from the launching sites can be accomplished entirely in the boat, but exploring the interior requires lengthy portaging from lake to lake.

The canoe routes are described in a brochure which includes a large-scale map. The map shows the portages, campgrounds, and also access sites. Many of the access sites are along Route 60, but others are located around the periphery of the park, reachable by primitive roads from paved routes that lie outside the park boundaries.

All overnight activities in the Park require permits. This necessity, and other regulations, are explained in the appropriate brochures.

Maps

Maps that are part of the several brochures have all details, including topography in the case of the hiking maps. See list in our Details section. The map printed here is a simplified copy of the park map found in the general brochure.

Other references

Day-Hiking and Backpacking in Ontario (reference 13), *Canoeing in Ontario* (reference 12), and *Canoe Routes of Ontario* (reference 9) may be helpful, although we know of no information in them that is not also in the park brochures.

Travel from Ann Arbor

You should equip yourself with an Ontario road map. The most likely route shown there (from Windsor) is Route 401 to

Toronto, 400 to Barrie, 11 to Huntsville, 60 to the park. The distance from Ann Arbor to the park boundary is approximately 425 miles. One of our respondents reports a nine-hour drive.

Details

Details are beyond number. At least, beyond reproducing here. Whatever your interest, the recommended prior step is to obtain the appropriate brochure by mail. The list of those available in 1985 follows:

Algonquin Provincial Park Canoe Routes
Algonquin Provincial Park Backpacking Trails
Fishing in Algonquin Provincial Park
Birds of Algonquin Provincial Park
Mammals of Algonquin Provincial Park
Reptiles and Amphibians of Algonquin
Pictorial History of Algonquin
Wildflowers of Algonquin
Geological Guide to Highway 60
Whiskey Rapids Trail
Hardwood Lookout Trail
Peck Lake Trail
Hemlock Bluff Trail
Two Rivers Trail
Lookout Trail
Booth's Rock Trail
Spruce Bog Boardwalk
Beaver Pond Trail

These publications are sold by The Friends of Algonquin Park, Box 248, Whitney, Ontario, K0J 2M0. The prices are not given here because the possibility of their change after 1985.

In general, information about Algonquin Park can be gotten from the Park Superintendent, Algonquin Provincial Park,

Ministry of Natural Resources, Box 219, Whitney, Ontario, K0J 2M0. Information telephone is 705-633-5572.

We'll close with a small note of interest from one of our respondents: several canoe liveries offering day or long-term rentals are located in Whitney at the east end of the park, and they will even hoist the canoe onto your car.

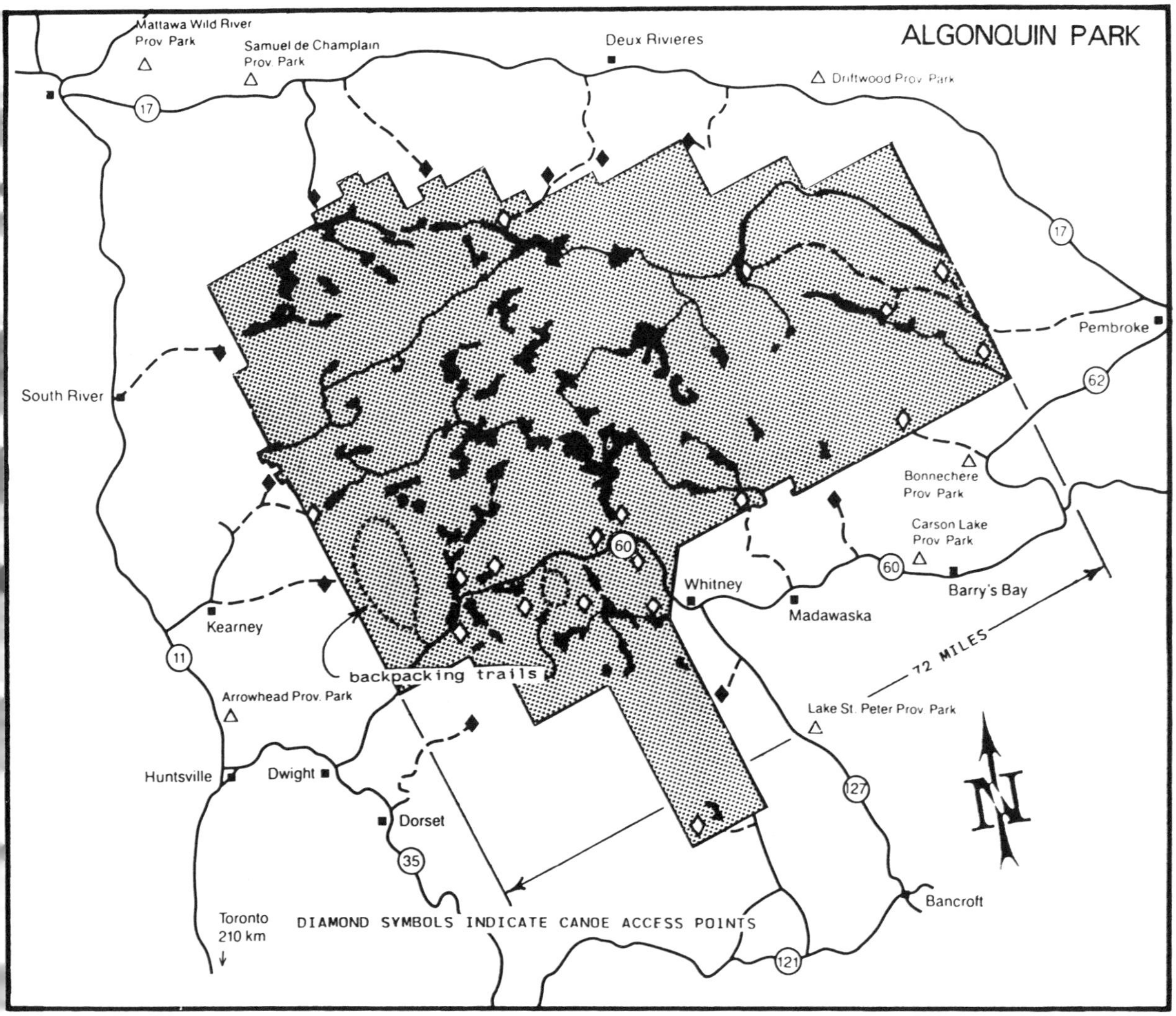

Backpacking in the Ramsey's Draft Wilderness Area, George Washington National Forest

General

Ramsey's Draft is a mountain stream that has its source in springs near the crest of Shenandoah Mountain, a ridge with elevations exceeding 4000 feet that lies along the boundary between Augusta and Highland Counties in western Virginia. The word "draft" is correctly applied only to the stream, but by obvious association it also is attached to the narrow valley in which the stream lies. The "area" to which we refer is part of the National Wilderness Preservation System, consisting of 6,725 acres, administered by the U S Forest Service Southern Region, Suite 800, 1720 Peachtree Road, NW, Atlanta, Georgia 30367.

The Ramsey's Draft valley (at least, that part of concern here) extends from highway U S 250 for about four miles (upstream) to the base of Hardscrabble Knob, one of the peaks of Shenandoah Mountain. Although there is an increase of about 700 feet in elevation over this stretch, walking is easy along a hard-packed gravel road. The ease is broken, however, by numerous fords of the Draft, so unless the water is low or you enjoy wading, the hike is rather arduous. There are pleasures, nonetheless. The greatest is perhaps the admiration of the primitive nature of a forest that has never been logged. The woods are dominated by hemlock and white pine of impressive size, leading one respondent to compare the valley to Muir Woods. No, the trees aren't really as big as those redwoods, but the comparison is appropriate. (Because of the ban on motor vehicles, the accompanying map shows the Ramsey's Draft "road" by a trail symbol.)

The Shenandoah Mountain trail, passing along the crest of that mountain from US-250 to North River Road, provides a pleasant hike of a different sort. It provides extensive vistas from the ridgeline, has no streams to ford, and is at a nearly uniform elevation except for a change of about 1000 feet within approximately one mile near North River Road. Other trails (see map) connect this high-level trail with the Ramsey's Draft trail. The map highlights a three-day hike that begins at the south end of Shenandoah Mountain trail (there's a parking lot off US-250), proceeds via Jerry's Run down to Ramsey's Draft, then up to a camping spot for the first night near the spring (Hiner's Spring) near the top of Hardscrabble Knob. The second day's passage is a loop (leave the lumpy backpack behind, eh?) via Camp Todd trail, North River Road (pleasant walking, even if it is a road), and a part of Shenandoah Mountain Trail back to the spring. The third day's passage is a hike back to the beginning via Shenandoah Mountain trail. A more detailed description of the hike is given in the **Details** section.

Maps

Most of the area is covered by the U S Geological Survey West Augusta (Virginia) 7.5 minute and the McDowell 15 minute quadrangles. The map printed here is based on those quadrangles, and though it lacks the accuracy and detail of the originals, field experience has shown it to be adequate for use by the hiker.

Other references

Hiking Guide to the Old Dominion (reference 15) gives some information, but nothing in addition to that here.

Travel from Ann Arbor

Highway US-250 provides the only road access. In driving from Ann Arbor, you will encounter 250 as it crosses the Ohio Turnpike between Toledo and Cleveland, and thenceforth can follow it all the way to the mountain. However, several respondents from Ann Arbor prefer to follow the Ohio Turnpike, the Pennsylvania Turnpike, and I-79 to an intersection with 250 near Fairmont, West Virginia. Although longer than the first alternative, this way appears to be slightly faster, and avoids a wearying, winding stretch of 250 in West Virginia (though there's plenty of that remaining after you leave I-79). The distance is just a few miles more than 500 miles, and should require about 12 hours without fracturing any speed limits, and with reasonable meal and rest stops.

Details

We supply most of the details by reproducing the notes supplied by a group of respondents who made the hike traced by arrows on the accompanying map in late February 1985.

> Arrived from Ann Arbor 6:00 PM at parking lot, crest of Shenandoah Mountain ridge. Camped in woods nearby. No camping facilities, no water available. Used water carried from AA. Next day hiked to spring near top of Hardscrabble knob via Jerry's Run and Ramsey's Draft, requiring about 9 hours. All trail junctions found to be marked by signs. Impeded by many fordings of the Run and the Draft. Some crossings made on logs, some avoided by bushwacking along banks until trail recrossed, but some accomplished only by wading. Water high from recent thaw, but kneedeep at maximum. No formal campgrounds or camping facilities anywhere, but primitive camping appears feasible at many places, particularly along the Draft. Extensive level (well, almost) area around the spring, but also much wetness from multiple openings of the spring. Camped for the night; left tents here next day. Camp Todd trail (marked by sign) leads down to North River Road from this point. Road end of this trail not marked by sign, so may be difficult for first-time user to locate if going in the reverse direction. North River Road is compacted crushed stone, scenic, and no vehicles evident (but this is February, remember). Beginning of Shenandoah Mountain trail is not marked, and found only by estimating its location from the map. No competing trails, however, so little chance of making wrong choice. Trail not blazed. Intersection of this trail with Camp Todd trail, which leads back to the spring, marked by sign. Hike required seven hours. Returned to car the next day, hiking along crest of Shenandoah Mountain. Required about 6 hours.

The trails are maintained by one of the Appalachian Trail clubs with junction signs and blazes, but two sections shown on the accompanying map are apparently not included: the section of Shenandoah Mountain trail from Hardscrabble Knob to North River Road, and the Shaw's Fork trail. In fact, our respondents report failing in a search for the upper end of the latter trail, even though a sign at its supposed junction with Shenandoah Mountain trail points to it.

Ramsey's Draft,
George Washington National Forest

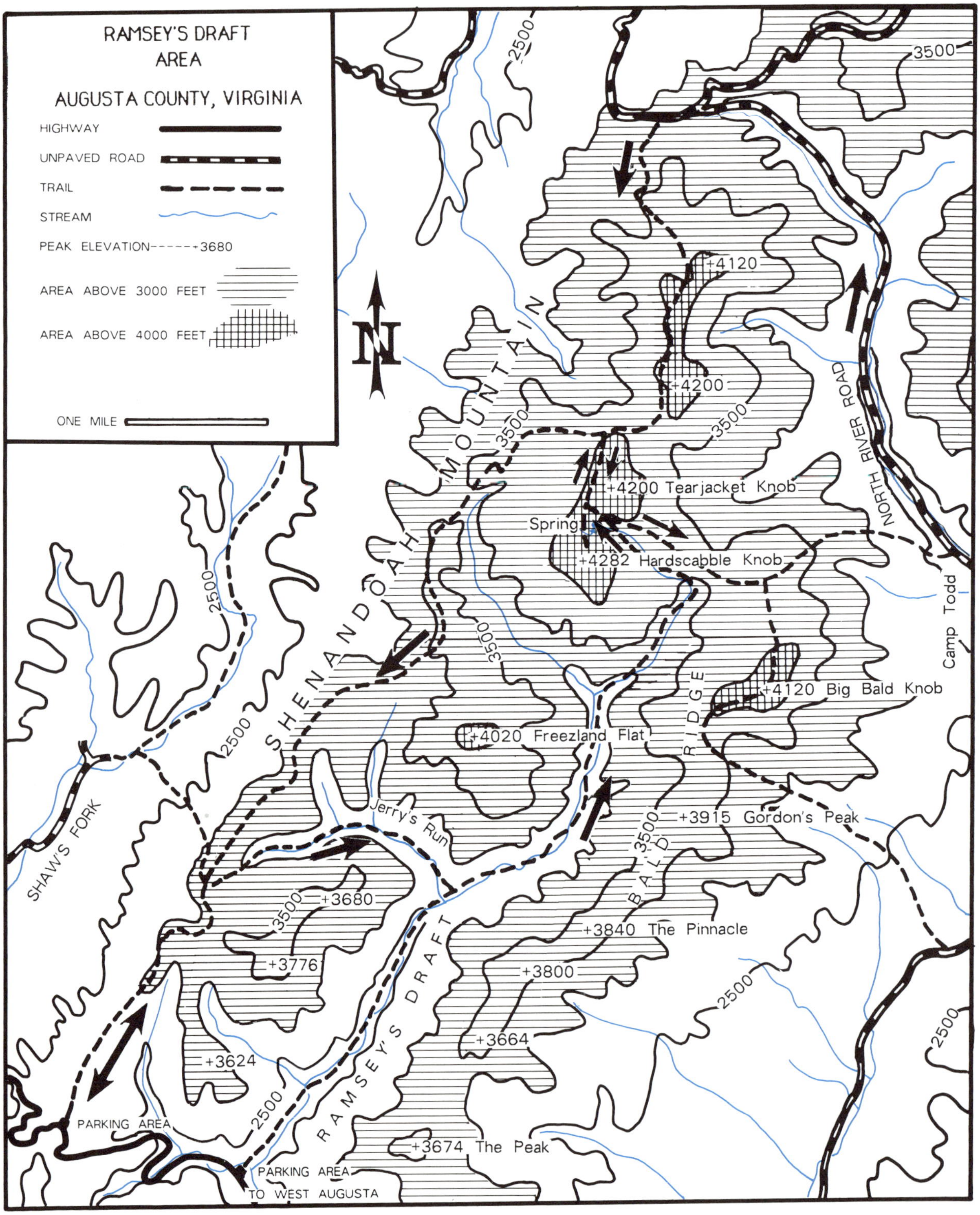

REFERENCES

1. MAPBOOK OF MICHIGAN COUNTIES
Michigan Natural Resources Magazine
Department of Natural Resources
Box 30034
Lansing, MI 48909

2. MICHIGAN HIKING OPPORTUNITIES
Michigan Natural Resources Magazine
(see reference 1)

3. FOOTLOOSE IN WASHTENAW
The Ecology Center of Ann Arbor
417 Detroit
Ann Arbor, MI 48104

4. GREAT LAKES CRUISING GUIDE
The Great Lakes Cruising Club
Chicago
(Available only to members)

5. CYCLING MAPS OF MICHIGAN
Michigan Natural Resources Magazine
Box 30034
Lansing, MI 48909

6. CIRCUIT HIKES IN VIRGINIA, WEST VIRGINIA, MARYLAND, AND PENNSYLVANIA
Potomac Appalachian Trail Club
Washington, DC 20036

7. BIKE RIDES IN WASHTENAW COUNTY
Washtenaw County Parks and Recreation Commission
4133 Washtenaw Avenue
Ann Arbor 48104

8. THE SUPERIOR WAY - A Cruising Guide to Lake Superior
Bonnie Dahl
Inland Sea Press
Ashland, WI 54806

9. CANOE ROUTES OF ONTARIO
Cannon Books
1205 Bathurst Street
Toronto M5R 3H3

10. GEOLOGY AND SCENERY NORTH SHORE OF LAKE SUPERIOR - Guide Book 2
E G Pye
Ontario Department of Mines

11. MICHIGAN CROSS COUNTRY SKIING ATLAS, third edition, 1981
Denis R Hansen
Hansen Publishing Company
Grosse Pointe Farms, Michigan

12. CANOEING IN ONTARIO
Ian Scott and Mavis Kerr
Greey de Pencier Publications
Toronto, 1975

13. DAY-HIKING AND BACKPACKING IN ONTARIO
Ellie Roddick
Greey de Pencier Publications
Toronto, 1976

14. A GUIDE TO BIRD FINDING IN WASHTENAW COUNTY AND SURROUNDING AREAS
Washtenaw Audobon Society

References

15. HIKING THE OLD DOMINION
Allen de Hart
A Sierra Club Totebook
Sierra Club Books
San Francisco, 1984

16. BACKPACKING IN MICHIGAN
Pat Allen and Gerald de Ruiter
University of Michigan Press
Ann Arbor, 1985

17. HIKING TRAILS IN THE MIDWEST
Jerry Sullivan and Glenda Daniel
Contemporary Books
Chicago, 1980

18. CANOE TRAILS DIRECTORY
James C Makens
Doubleday & Company
Garden City, NY, 1979

19. CANOEING MICHIGAN RIVERS - A COMPREHENSIVE GUIDE TO 45 RIVERS
Jerry Dennis and Craig Dale
Friede Publications
Davison, Michigan, 1986

Oh, ah, Miss Snibbles, I know where there's this real private little camping spot, and I was kind of wondering if you....

APPENDIX 1

Information Sources

The information printed here consists mainly of addresses and phone numbers of organizations from which outings information may be sought. If a name is given without address or phone number, the organization is one without a permanent staff. Ask around.

This list is confined to the state of Michigan, or in the case of local organizations, to the Ann Arbor area. One exception, because of its general interest, is the Canadian Ministry of Natural Resources. Information sources for other places outside Michigan are given in the main text at the appropriate spots.

Sierra Club
Huron Valley Group
(Washtenaw, Lenawee, and
Monroe Counties)
Call Mackinac Chapter for
current contact person

Sierra Club
Mackinac Chapter
115 W Allegan, Suite 330
Lansing, MI 48933
517-484-2372

Michigan Department of
Natural Resources
Information Services Center
Box 30028
Lansing, MI 48909
517-373-1220

Michigan Department of
Natural Resources
Detroit Information Office
1120 State Fair Avenue
Detroit, MI 48653
313-348-4410

Michigan Trail Riders Association
1179 Garn Road
Traverse City, MI 49864
(for the Shore-to-Shore Riding and
Hiking Trail)

Sleeping Bear Dunes
National Lakeshore
400 1/2 Main Street
Frankfort, MI 49635
616-334-4017

Pictured Rocks
National Lakeshore
Munising, MI 49862
906-387-2607

Canadian Ministry of Natural
Resources
Communication Services
Whitney Block
99 Wellesley Steet, West
Toronto, Ontario M7A 1W3

Isle Royale National Park
87 North Ripley Street
Houghton, MI 49931
906-482-2890

Porcupine Mountains Wilderness
State Park
Star Route
Ontonagon, MI 49950
906-885-5798

Forest Supervisor
Ottawa National Forest
Box 468
Ironwood, MI 49938
906 932 1330

Forest Supervisor
Hiawatha National Forest
Escanaba, MI 49829
906-786-4062

Forest Supervisor
Huron-ManisteeNational Forest
421 South Mitchell Street
Cadillac, MI 49601
616-775-2421

Michigan Travel Bureau
Department of Commerce
Box 30226
Lansing, MI 48909
517-373-1195
800-292-2520

Upper Peninsula Travel and
Recreation Association
Box 400
Iron Mountain, MI 49801
906-774-5480

Southeast Michigan Travel and
Tourist Association
27777 Franklin, Suite 350
Southfield, MI 48034
313-357-1663

East Michigan Tourist
Association
1 Wenonah Park
Bay City, MI 48706
517-895-8823

West Michigan Tourist Association
136 Fulton East
Grand Rapids, MI 49503
616-456-8557313-961-5865

Huron-Clinton Metro Authority
3050 Penobscot Building
Detroit, MI 48226

MNR Reference Library
Box 30034
Lansing, MI 48909

City of Ann Arbor
Parks and Recreation Dept.
City Hall
Ann Arbor, MI 48104
313-994-2780

County of Washtenaw
Parks and Recreation Commission
4133 Washtenaw Avenue
Ann Arbor, MI 48104
313-994-2575

Michigan Audubon Society
409 West East Avenue
Kalamazoo, MI 49007

North Country Trail Association
Box 311
White Cloud, MI 49349

Ann Arbor Bicycle Touring
Society
Box 2854
Ann Arbor, MI 48106

APPENDIX 2
Michigan Canoe Liveries

This list is furnished by the Recreational Canoeing Association, 5042 Scenic Drive, Honor, Michigan 49640.

	NAME	LOCATION	RIVER	PHONE
1.	AAA Canoe Livery	Rockford	Rogue	616-866-9264
2.	Alvina's Canoe and Boat Rental	Interlochen	Betsie	616-276-9514
3.	Arrowhead Canoe Trips	Indian River	Sturgeon	616-238-8701
4.	Baldwin Canoe Rental	Baldwin	Pine Pere Marquette Little Manistee	616-745-4669
5.	Borcher's Au Sable Canoe Livery	Grayling	Au Sable	517-348-4921
6.	Campbell's Canoes	Roscommon	Au Sable	517-275-5810
7.	Carlisle Canoes	Grayling	Au Sable	517-348-2301
8.	Carl's Canoe Livery	Luther	Pine	616-797-5156 616-862-3402
9.	Carr's Pioneer Canoe Livery	Grayling	Au Sable Manistee	517-348-5851
10.	Cedar Springs Campground	Sterling	Rifle	517-654-3195
11.	Crystal Harbor Marina	Glen Arbor	Crystal	616-334-3033
12.	Double R Ranch Resort	Smyrna	Flat	616-794-0520
13.	Famous Jarolim Canoes	Wellston	Pine	616-862-3475
14.	Float Trips Inc	Croton Dam	Muskegon	616-652-6037
15.	Gleason's Landing	Saugatuck	Kalamazoo	616-857-4729
16.	Grand Rogue Campground	Belmont	Grand, Rogue	616-361-1053
17.	Greenwood Campground	Alger	Rifle	517-345-2778
18.	Happy Mohawk Canoe Livery	Montague	White	616-894-4209
19.	Hiawatha Canoe Livery	Roscommon	Au Sable	517-275-5213

APPENDIX 2
Canoe Liveries

20.	Hinchman Acres Canoe Rental	Mio	Au Sable	517-826-3267
21.	Horina Canoe Rental	Wellston	Pine	616-862-3470
22.	Hunt's Canoes	Oscoda	Au Sable	517-739-4408
23.	Ivan's Canoe Rental	Baldwin	Pere Marquette	616-745-3361
24.	Jim's Canoe Livery	Grayling	Au Sable	517-348-3203
25.	John's Canoe Livery	Sheperd	Chippewa	517-835-5657
26.	Jolly Redskin Canoe Livery	Grayling	Au Sable	517-348-5611
27.	Kellogg Canoe Livery	Hesperia	White	616-854-1415
28.	Long's Canoe Livery	Grayling	Manistee	517-348-7224
29.	Manistee River Canoe Livery	Grayling	Manistee	517-348-9555
30.	Marrik's Pine River Canoe Service	Cadillac	Pine	616-862-3471
31.	Mead's Canoe Livery	Roscommon	Au Sable	517-275-5696
32.	Michigan Canoe Outfitters	Cadillac	Manistee Pine Pere Marquette Rifle Au Sable Betsie Boardman Sturgeon	616-775-4744
33.	Misty Valley Canoe Livery	Lowell	Flat, Grand	616-897-9105 616-458-9595
34.	Nature Outfitters	Bellaire	Jordan, Betsie	616-533-8764
35.	North Branch Boat & Canoe Livery	Muskegon	Muskegon	616-744-1119
36.	Northland Outfitters	Germfask	Manistique, Fox Grand Island Isle Royale	906-586-9801
37.	The Old Log	Marion	Muskegon	616-743-2775
38.	Paddle Brave Canoe Livery	Roscommon	Au Sable	517-275-5273
39.	Parks Canoe Livery	Battle Creek	Kalamazoo	616-963-5014
40.	Paw Paw River	Watervliet	Paw Paw St Joseph	616-463-3344
41.	Penrods	Grayling	Au Sable	517-348-2910
42.	Pines Canoe Rental	Baldwin	Pere Marquette	616-745-4138 616-745-7648

APPENDIX 2
Canoe Liveries

43.	Pioneer Canoe Livery	Benzonia		616-882-7783
44.	Port O'Call Canoe Rental	Indian River	Sturgeon, Pigeon	616-238-8181
45.	Quiet Waters Canoe Livery	Rives Junction	Grand	517-569-2508
46.	Ray's Au Sable & Manistee Canoeing	Grayling	Au Sable Manistee	517-348-5844 517-348-7108
47.	River's Edge Campground	Midland	White	616-821-2735
48.	Riverside Canoe Trips	Honor	Platte, Betsie	616-325-5622
49.	Russell Canoes	Omer	Rifle	517-653-2644
50.	Rustic Run Outfitters	Mesick	Manistee	616-885-1099
51.	Sawyer Canoe Company	Oscoda	Au Sable	517-739-9181
52.	Skip's Huron River	Ann Arbor	Huron	313-769-8686
53.	Sportsmans Port Canoe Camp	Wellston	Pine	616-862-3571
54.	Swiss Hideaway	Mancelona	Jordan	616-536-2341
55.	Sylvania Outfitters	Watersmeet	Sylvania Ontonagon	906-358-4766
56.	Tall Pines Campsites	Morley	Little Muskegon	616-856-4556 616-856-7826
57.	Tomahawk Trails Canoe Livery	Indian River	Sturgeon, Pigeon	616-238-8703
58.	The Trading Post	Honor	Platte	616-325-2981
59.	Twin Pines Campground	Hanover	Kalamazoo	517-524-6298
60.	U-Rent-Em Canoe Livery	Hastings	Thornapple	616-945-3191
61.	Vacation Trailer Park	Benzonia	Betsie	616-882-5101
62.	Vic's Canoes, Tubes, Camping	Grant	Muskegon	616-834-5494 616-776-0129
63.	Wacousta Canoes	Wacousta	Looking Glass	517-626-6873
64.	Walnut Hills Camp and Canoe	Durand	Shiawassee	517-634-9782
65.	White's Canoe Livery	Sterling	Rifle	517-654-2654
66.	Wolynski Canoe Rental	Milford	Huron	313-685-1851
67.	Yates Canoe Rental	Rochester Hills	Clinton	313-651-1012